CULTIVATING A
HOLY
HEART

Clemens Russell

WestBow
PRESS®
A DIVISION OF THOMAS NELSON
& ZONDERVAN

WestBow Press books may be ordered through booksellers or by contacting:

WestBow Press
A Division of Thomas Nelson & Zondervan
1663 Liberty Drive
Bloomington, IN 47403
www.westbowpress.com
1 (866) 928-1240

ISBN: 978-1-9736-4886-4 (sc)
ISBN: 978-1-9736-4888-8 (hc)
ISBN: 978-1-9736-4887-1 (e)

Library of Congress Control Number: 2018914804

Print information available on the last page.

WestBow Press rev. date: 07/18/2019

DEDICATION

This book is dedicated to my wife Sharon. She has always inspired and challenged me to pursue true holiness.

INTRODUCTION

As the writing of these devotionals came over the span of several years, this introduction is actually the last part of this book that I am writing. It is also proving to be the most difficult. I never started out to write a book. The contents are the compilations of personal notes written in the course of my own Bible reading and private time with God. But trying to convey the purpose of this devotional to those who may choose to read it is indeed challenging. Perhaps a different direction is necessary.

My personal spiritual development was nurtured in the evangelical tradition. But I presently view myself as a Biblical Christian while still connected to the roots of historical evangelicalism. This is the foundation of these devotionals. With the modern church in the midst of social and spiritual upheaval, many sincere believers are becoming fearful, confused and even paralyzed. Reactions run the gamut of self-centered emotionalism to defiant isolationism. The world continues to plummet into spiritual famine and moral wickedness. More and more, good is being called evil and evil is being called good. Meanwhile, the church aimlessly scurries around hoping that they can keep up with this technologically rich but morally bankrupt world. Bleak though it may seem, that is my take on today's society.

Fortunately I am not a fatalist. God is still in control. What we are seeing is the obvious fulfillment of biblical prophecy and the nearing of the return of our Lord. We as believers need to get back to our true spiritual roots. Perhaps the self-centered and emotionally driven 'God will bless me if I....' theology has still left you empty. You want to be open and accepting but the items on the menu of what is and is not acceptable are becoming harder to swallow. Or maybe you are feeling tired and defeated. For years you have been faithful to God and your church. But the changes that are being hurled toward you have left you isolated and discouraged. You just want to give up. Or you may be feeling defiant and angry. Railing against the evils of society and those who promote them may give you some temporary satisfaction. But lingering deep inside is the undeniable claims of Christ to love Him, your neighbor, other believers and even your enemies. How can we love the sinner and hate the sin in a realistic and practical way?

There are two things that stand out to me about what it means to be a true believer in these turbulent times. The first is that we are to live every moment in the totality of love. The greatest commandment is to love God with all of your heart, strength, soul and mind. This implies that you have a deep and personal relationship with the God of the universe through Jesus Christ. The flip side of this greatest commandment is that we love our neighbor as ourselves. We are also called to love other believers and to even love our enemies. But do not make the mistake of allowing the world to define the parameters of this love. The Bible gives very clear instructions as to the characteristics and practical applications of Godly love. The second thing is that we are to be salt and light. We should have an impact in the lives of others that can only come from a life truly committed to Christ. This is our ultimate purpose in this life and the reason God still has us here on this planet. Obviously these two things are closely intertwined. You cannot be salt and light without a close connection with God and a heart overflowing with divine love. Neither can you claim to have all the aspects of His love and not have a desire to be the salt and light He calls us to be. I believe that Christians need to strive to excel in these two areas. Our worship, service, fellowship and daily walk should all contribute to these goals.

It is also of great importance to remain faithful to God's word. The Bible is not a buffet where we can pick and choose what we like and agree with, but then reject those passages and teachings that are difficult or speak against what is socially acceptable today. The Bible is God's revealed truth. His word still stands in its totality and reveals His will and purpose for all mankind. Therefore it is vital that we read the Bible in a consistent manner. How you choose to read the Bible is completely personal and there are many effective methods and resources available to help you get the most from God's word. You can find one method in the back of this book. It is my hope that these devotionals will give you additional guidance and inspiration in your relationship with God and help fuel your desire to walk in holiness and love.

THE AWESOMENESS OF GOD

Genesis1:1 "In the beginning God created the heavens and the earth."

There was no fanfare or pomp. There was only this simple statement at the very beginning of our Bible. God did it. Everything else that comes is overshadowed by the fact that God is the Creator. All of the stories in the Bible and all of history: the wars, triumphs, tragedies, explorations, discoveries and everything else that has ever transpired in humanity is secondary to the creative power of God. We cannot even begin to fathom His greatness. In our highest aspirations, in our greatest moments of faith and awe and worship, we do not even touch the outskirts of God's majesty and glory. Yet, for all this, the creator and sustainer of the universe loves us. And, when we fell and turned our backs on the source of it all; when we, in our self-centered pride and arrogance, replaced the awesomeness of the Creator with the puniness of our own existence, the giver of life gave His own life to restore us to Himself. God, in all of His unfathomable greatness, actually cares for us. Inconceivable but true!

DRIVING OFF THE BUZZARDS

Genesis 15:11 "Then birds of prey came down on the carcasses, but Abram drove them away."

We don't offer the animal sacrifices of the Old Testament today. The sacrifices we offer are of a more spiritual sort; such as praise, time, money and talents. Probably the most important sacrifice we offer is ourselves. The Apostle Paul called it a 'living sacrifice'. Yet, even though the nature of our sacrifices has changed, there are still 'birds of prey' that try to interfere. They may appear as people, who would dissuade us from giving our all to God. They may be temptations, which try to remove God from the throne of our hearts. Many times they appear as doubts, fears and questions in our own minds. Even our positive circumstances can rob us of our total devotion to God. Whenever we recognize these 'birds of prey', trying to sully and steal our sacrifice, we need to drive them away as Abram did. Yes, it is work. We have to, constantly, be on our guard. These buzzards like to come down, when we least expect them. But our faithfulness and vigilance will be rewarded, as our walk with God strengthens and grows.

SIMPLIFY

Genesis 18:18 "You, and these people who come to you, will only wear yourselves out. The work is too heavy for you; you cannot handle it alone."

Sometimes, in the course of our lives, just like the attic or the junk drawer in the kitchen, things become too cluttered and cramped. It's not that we have intentionally allowed our lives to become overgrown, it just happens. Maybe today would be a good day to take a few moments and simplify our lives. Let's sort through and discard those things that, even though they are not wrong in themselves, are interfering with our ability to live effectively. Let's remove the things that are cluttering up our lives and keeping us from spending time daily with the Lord. Let's reestablish our priorities and start allowing others to share those burdens God never intended us to carry alone. Then, we can focus on those things that God wants us to see as really important. We will be amazed how refreshed and revived we will feel when the 'junk drawer' has been cleaned and reorganized!

OUR EXAMPLE

Genesis 21:9 "But Sarah saw that the son whom Hagar the Egyptian had borne to Abraham was mocking,"

About 14 years old. That was the age of this mocking son of Abraham. No one knows all of the intrigue that went on between Sarah and Hagar. But this teenager was probably just acting out what he had learned from his mother. After all, she had despised Sarah when Ishmael was conceived. And, although she submitted to Sarah, this jealousy and animosity still remained and now expressed itself through her son. We, as parents, have a strong influence on our children- but not by what we say and teach. Our actions are the greatest instructor of our kids. We cannot expect our children to steer clear of drugs when we have alcohol and nicotine habits. We cannot expect our children to be kind and courteous when we tear others down in the privacy of our homes. We cannot expect our children to have healthy marriages when we continually berate and belittle our spouses. And we cannot expect our children to have a strong walk with God when our own walk is characterized by shallowness, self-centeredness and hypocrisy. The adage, 'What you do is so loud that I can't hear what you say.' is more applicable in the family than anywhere else.

GUIDANCE

Genesis 22:2 "Then God said, 'Take your son, your only son Isaac, whom you love, and go to the region of Moriah. Sacrifice him there as a burnt offering on one of the mountains I will tell you about'"

How often do you hear the voice of God? Today God seldom speaks in an audible voice. He has filled us with His Spirit and we have guidance, from Him, inside our hearts. Yet, we still struggle to discern God's guidance from our own desires. For Abraham to hear the voice of God and obey was amazing. And the fact that he knew it was God's voice, even though the command was contrary to what Abraham believed about God, is even more incredible. One of the reasons Abraham recognized God's voice was because he cultivated a relationship with God. He knew God's voice because he had heard and obeyed God before. The same is true for us today. We grow in our relationship with God when we study and obey His word and when we follow His leading on a consistent basis. Then we are able to clearly hear Him when He speaks to our hearts in the more difficult and confusing times of our lives.

PARENTING

Genesis 25:28 "Isaac, who had a taste for wild game, loved Esau, but Rebecca loved Jacob."

Parents have been playing favorites with their children for centuries. And nothing good comes from it. Jacob and Esau were as opposite twins as you could find. Jacob was a home-body mama's boy who enjoyed domestic endeavors like cooking, while Esau was a he-man good-ol'-boy who wore his masculinity like a badge. We are permitted to choose friends that exhibit the traits and characteristics we appreciate but as parents we do not have that luxury. All of us, who have kids, have heard, either teasingly or in a more serious vein, that so-and-so is your favorite. And, the truth is, we may like one child differently because their personality clicks with ours and they exhibit those traits and characteristics that we would seek out in a friend. But we should always affirm our love and support for all of our children no matter how different they may be. And there is nothing wrong with expanding our own interests beyond our present sphere to include some of the hobbies and activities of all our children.

RESPECTING GOD'S WORD

Genesis 31:49 "It was also called Mizpah because he said, "May the Lord keep watch between you and me when we are away from each other.""

It is interesting how some Bible verses have evolved over time. This verse is commonly used as an encouraging statement when friends are parting. But, in the original context, it served as a caution for both Laban and Jacob who were in conflict with each other, to respect each other's interests and not pass where they had placed their pillar to harm one another. How this verse changed from being a negative warning to a positive encouragement is unclear. But it is a good illustration of the care and respect we must use as we utilize God's word in our lives. There is always a danger of trying to mold the word to fit our particular situation when the actual context implies something else. God does individualize His word to us but not for the purpose of satisfying our own self-centered wants and needs. When the Bible speaks to our particular circumstances it is giving us the divine perspective within the context of God's over-arching involvement in the crucible of human experience.

GOD, THE GOD OF _____

Genesis 33:20 "There he set up an altar and called it 'El-Elohe Israel".

All of his life, up to this point, Jacob had referred to God as 'the God of my fathers'. Basically, Jacob tried to use God, just as he used others, for his own personal benefit. Jacob even bargained with God by promising God that he would serve Him if God would bless him. But all of Jacob's schemes became futile when he heard Esau was coming with 400 men. For all Jacob knew, this was the end. The impending crisis with his brother precipitated a crisis in his faith. Jacob was forced to accept God's terms and in the process he received the name Israel. The significance of this altar is that, not only does Jacob accept his new name, but now God is no longer just the God of his fathers. Jacob has embraced the Lord as his God. El-Elohe Israel- God, the God of Israel as well as Abraham and Isaac. God wants to bring every believer to that point of total commitment where they embrace God, not for who they want Him to be, but for who He is. God, the God of _____. We need to be able to fill in the blank with our own name.

RESISTING TEMPTATION

Genesis 39:10 "And though she spoke to Joseph day after day, he refused to go to bed with her or even be with her."

'The devil made me do it'. 'The temptation is too strong'. 'I was caught at a weak moment'. The list of excuses why Christians sin goes on and on. It seems like so many believers are continuously perched on the precipice of failure, unable to keep from obeying God. But, if anyone had an excuse to falter, it was Joseph. Not only was he assailed on a daily basis by Potiphar's wife, but, he was trapped. As a slave, he had to remain in this trying situation. Yet, his moral integrity stayed intact because he avoided her as much as possible. But, more importantly, he did not want to sin against God. It was Joseph's strong relationship with his Heavenly Father that was his main source of strength and moral courage. And, even when his righteousness seemed to be rewarded by hardship, betrayal and imprisonment, he still remained faithful to God. When our only motivation for living holy and pure lives is fear of retribution, the chance of 'getting caught' or losing the blessings of God, we will more than likely fall. But, by developing and maintaining a strong and loving relationship with our Lord, we will discover a continuous supply of strength, power and courage to resist every snare and temptation we meet, regardless of our emotions or situation. Loving God supremely inspires us to choose not to sin.

GOD IS IN CONTROL

Genesis 50:20 "You intended to harm me, but God intended it for good to accomplish what is now being done, the saving of many lives."

It's amazing how much God is really in control. God's plans are above all we can imagine. Even though we live in a sinful and depraved world and are continually subject, not only to its evil but also to our own shortcomings, God is still calling the shots and working out His will. When bad things happen and tribulations overwhelm us, God sees, knows, understands and desires that we trust in Him. He can take the most hopeless and heartbreaking situation, whether it is the betrayal of Joseph by his brothers or the sudden death of a loved one or the execution of His own Son, and work miracles. Our part is to stay focused on Him, to continually trust Him and to stay faithful to His will and word. God allowed Joseph to be sold into slavery by his own brothers, to be tempted and then falsely accused by his master's wife and to be thrown into prison and forgotten by Pharaoh's cupbearer. All this happened before Joseph had any notion of God's plan to save his family. His example of faithfulness and integrity, in the midst of great trials, is one we should all follow.

THE CHALLENGE OF DOING GOD'S WILL

Exodus 5:23 "Ever since I went to Pharaoh to speak in Your name, he has brought trouble upon this people, and You have not rescued Your people at all."

It seems to be inevitable that the moment we determine to follow God and obey His will our circumstances take a turn for the worse. Moses, the reluctant leader, probably had the mistaken notion that just because he was doing God's work everything should happen smoothly and easily. He didn't reckon with Pharaoh's opposition to God's plan. We lose sight of the fact that there is a power at work in this world that is antagonistic to God and is working hard to thwart God's plans. Some of Satan's best weapons are discouragement, disillusionment and self-pity. Many times he uses these to manipulate our worldly circumstances. We can defend ourselves from these attacks by staying focused on God's will and making sure that we are not too dependent on our feelings and circumstances to bring us satisfaction. We must not get too comfortable in our worldly situation by drawing joy and contentment from the things of this world. For then, when we launch out to obey God in some great endeavor, our adversary has an easy opening to dissuade us and to keep us sidetracked from persevering in God's plan and will.

OVERCOMING LIFE'S SETBACKS

Exodus 6:9 "Moses reported this to the Israelites but they did not listen to him because of their discouragement and cruel bondage."

Moses had a wonderful message to deliver to his people. The previous verses of this chapter are filled with statements of encouragement and promises of deliverance. But something happened between the reception of the message and its deliverance. The Israelite's discouragement and cruel bondage got in the way. The reality of life choked God's marvelous words of hope. Let's face it- it's challenging to listen to God and walk victoriously in the light when life's circumstances are causing us hardship and grief. The challenges and tribulations of this life can put a stranglehold on the things of God and asphyxiate our life in the Spirit. It is important to remember that we must not become so dependent upon and involved in the things of this world that God's voice is muffled. We need to also consider our brother's misery when we offer spiritual insights or guidance. We must first reach out to soothe their hurts in compassionate and practical ways. Finally it is vital to remember that God's promises are true regardless of how we think or feel. There is no situation that is even remotely capable of nullifying God's purposes or will.

CLEMENS RUSSELL

CIRCUMSTANTIAL SETBACKS

Exodus 6:12 "But Moses said to the Lord, 'If the Israelites will not listen to me, why would Pharaoh listen to me, since I speak with faltering lips?"

Sometimes our circumstances can overwhelm us to the point that we miss God's will and the higher road. The discouragement and cruel bondage that the Israelites felt polluted the message of incredible hope that Moses had for them. It also influenced them negatively toward Moses and discouraged Moses himself. The Israelites had become so accustomed to the burdens of day-to-day existence that they were blinded to the greater reality of their position as the chosen people. They forgot God's desire to bless and deliver them. Even Moses became frustrated and began to doubt God's ability to keep His promises. We can also make that same error in our walk with God. We have the burdens of our daily lives. We have our own discouragements, trials and tribulations while trying to survive in a wicked world. There is also the frustration of living in the Spirit while our flesh is being assailed on every side. And these can all rob us of God's higher calling...IF WE LET THEM! We must truly commit ourselves to Him and determine to live controlled by the Spirit and not the flesh. Then we can not only survive but triumphantly overcome all that this world throws our way.

KNOWING GOD'S WILL -I

Exodus 13:21 "By day the Lord went ahead of them in a pillar of cloud to guide them on their way and by night a pillar of fire to give them light, so that they could travel by day or night."

Wouldn't it be nice if we could have simple, clear guidance like this from God today? It would be nice if we could say 'There's the pillar. I have to do this or go there!' But even with the pillar of cloud and fire it seems that the Israelites eventually got used to them, took them for granted, and continually refused to follow God's guidance. Still, God does give us clear ways to know His will today. Proverbs 3:5 & 6 tells us that by trusting Him with all our hearts, not leaning on our own understanding and acknowledging Him in all we do, He will give us direction. And Romans 12:1 & 2 informs us that we can prove His will if we will give ourselves completely to Him and not be conformed to this world but allow God to transform us in our minds. This method of knowing His will is much more personal and dynamic than a pillar of cloud or fire. When our hearts and minds are focused on God and our desire is to do His will, He is then able to give our lives clear and simple guidance.

UNCONDITIONAL LOYALTY

Exodus 14:31 "And when the Israelites saw the great power the Lord displayed against the Egyptians, the people feared the Lord and put their trust in Him and in Moses His servant."

On the surface this seems like a positive verse of hope and encouragement. Finally, the people are starting to believe in the right way. But then we remember that the Lord had already displayed His great power earlier when He sent the ten plagues on Egypt. And, after this great deliverance from the army of Pharaoh, the Israelites found more reasons to grumble and complain. The problem the Israelites faced was twofold. First, they seemed to be too dependent on the supernatural for their faith. When God manifested His power it was easy and prudent for them to believe. But, in the day to day challenges, the chosen people would falter and fail. Second, their trust in God was based on their circumstances. Things going good = strong faith in God. Things going not so good = fear, doubt and backsliding. If these scenarios sound familiar it's because many people today are just like the children of Israel. Their faith is focused on their circumstances and manifestations of what they consider as supernatural. Take either or both away and they soon falter and fail. This is another reminder that it's not about us, it's about God. He deserves our loyalty no matter what our situation.

SACRIFICIAL LOVE

Exodus 32:32 "But now, please forgive their sin- but if not, then blot me out of the book You have written."

How much do we love others? Moses cared about the Israelites to the extent that he was willing to have his own name blotted out of 'the book' if God would not forgive their sin of worshipping a golden calf. This was compassion, not for a good and holy people, but for a people who had quickly turned their back on God. Perhaps we think Moses was just being dramatic or simply trying to persuade God. Then we are reminded of Jesus' command to us that we should love one another as He loved us. He also said that there is no greater love than that a man should lay down his life for his friends. It was while we were yet sinners sacrificing to our own golden calves that Christ died for us. Most of us are willing to help others as long as it doesn't interfere with our own plans or inconvenience us too much. When others needs or problems break in on our personal lives and comfort and we respond with resentment, frustration or indignation instead of pure compassion and love, the true nature of our concern for others is revealed. Jesus went all the way to the tomb for us. How far are we gladly willing to go for others so they may enjoy the same benefits of Christ that we enjoy?

TIME ALONE ON THE MOUNTAIN

Exodus 35:29 "When Moses came down from Mt. Sinai with the two tablets of the testimony in his hands, he was not aware that his face was radiant because he had spoken with the Lord."

Spending time alone with God on the mountain is important. We need it to recharge our spiritual walk and to grow in our faith and knowledge. Time alone on the mountain is part of the key. Five minutes amid the turmoil of life may help us refocus and stay in tune, but it is vital that we also take a decent amount of time to be alone with God in a place that is protected from the clamor and distractions of everyday life. The quick five minutes is the passing shower whereas the devoted fifteen minutes or longer is the soaking rain. A consistent and deliberate devotional life will bear amazing fruit in our lives. We will begin to live in holiness in a more effortless and natural way. Our initial reaction to troubles and tribulations will be based in the spirit instead of in the flesh. We will wear godliness like a comfortable shirt instead of a new suit. God will become a close, respectable friend instead of a distant, impersonal deity. And without any effort on our part our lives will radiate to others that we dwell continually in the presence of God. We will truly become mirrors who reflect the glory, grace and image of God.

THANKSGIVING

Leviticus 7:15 "The meat of his fellowship offering of thanksgiving must be eaten on the day it is offered; he must leave none of it till morning."

How discouraging this verse could be! After all, what is the best part of Thanksgiving dinner if not the leftover turkey for the next few days? Seldom does anyone consume the entire turkey on Thanksgiving Day. Of course we know that these are two entirely different events- the Jewish fellowship offering and the American tradition of a Thanksgiving feast. Or are they? Both celebrate thankfulness to God for His blessings. But unlike the Jewish offering we have the freedom in Christ to express our thankfulness whenever we want without having to bring an animal to the altar. With so much to be thankful for, and the freedom to express that thankfulness whenever and wherever we want, thanksgiving should be a daily celebration in our lives!

DEVOTION MADE SIMPLE

Leviticus 8:36 "So Aaron and his sons did everything the Lord commanded through Moses."

When you read this whole chapter you realize how much was involved in just preparing Aaron and his sons to fulfill their duty as priests to the Lord for the Israelites. There were all the regulations for the different sacrifices and for clean and unclean. On top of this were rules for keeping the Sabbath and a host of other laws. Trying to live holy in a way to please God through our own efforts is virtually impossible! We cannot help but be grateful that the requirements of the law were perfectly fulfilled through Christ. He has also made it much easier and simpler for us to be cleansed and to come into the presence of our Heavenly Father. Grace and mercy have replaced works as the way to reconciliation, restoration and fellowship with God. Yet with such a great gift comes a great motivation for us to live lives of inward righteousness and heart purity. When we truly receive the redemption and renewal provided by the cross our obedience and devotion to God should become second nature. They should flow out of hearts that have been changed and desires that are focused on pleasing God.

INCREDIBLE CLEANSING

Leviticus 14:32 "These are the regulations for anyone who has an infectious skin disease and who cannot afford the regular offerings for his cleansing."

What were these regulations? If a person who had a skin disease wanted to be ceremonially clean, they had to offer a guilt, sin and burnt offering. There were even offerings for sins a person didn't even know they had committed. This is not God being picky- it's an indication of His awesome holiness. God cannot even tolerate unintentional or ignorant sins. Anything less than 100% purity in body, mind and spirit disqualifies us from His presence. No one is good enough! This places a much brighter light on the sacrifice Jesus made for us and how great the power of His grace, mercy and forgiveness is. What a wonderful thought that Jesus' blood can and does cleanse us from all sins- intentional (once they are confessed!), ignorant and unknown- day after day- as we continually walk in His light!

THE MOTIVATION FOR HOLINESS

Leviticus 20:26 "You are to be holy to Me because I, the Lord, am holy, and I have set you apart from the nations to be My own."

When God called the Israelites to be His people He gave them many rules and regulations about how they were supposed to live. They had to eat only certain foods, behave in certain ways and sacrifice to God only in the prescribed manner. These were not arbitrary laws God created to burden His people. They were required to honor and preserve His holiness. But the fact that no one could perfectly keep God's commands exposed man's inability to outwardly be holy by his own efforts. One of the great aspects of what Jesus did was that He provided the opportunity for us to have our hearts cleansed and made holy. He alluded to this when He spoke of the importance of having the inside of the cup cleansed which would lead to the outside also being clean. True holiness does not begin with what we do. True holiness begins when the center of our life is cleansed and filled with the Holy Spirit and God creates in us a clean heart. Only when our efforts to keep His commands and live according to His will become motivated by both a clean heart and a pure desire to please Him will we be able to live in the power and purity of divine holiness.

WHY LIVE HOLY LIVES

Leviticus 22:32 "Do not profane my holy name. I must be acknowledged as holy by the Israelites. I am the Lord who makes you holy."

We must be very careful in this age of grace to continually maintain a proper awe and reverence for God. The tendency is to become relaxed and get careless in how we live. After all, we reason, 'everyone makes mistakes' and 'God's forgiveness is unlimited'. So we plod along in our Christian walk living primarily to please and serve ourselves. We stumble and falter along the way and even tolerate outright sin and disobedience in our lives because we have allowed the focus to fall on ourselves. But even though we are no longer required to keep the rules and regulations of the Levitical law we are still required to live holy lives. We must remember that our salvation, our sanctification and our admonitions to live holy lives are not about us. The whole redemptive and restorative work of God is for His honor and glory. Just as our inability to live holy lives in our own strength reveals the true aspect of our fallen nature, so our ability to live holy lives in the strength and power of the Spirit gives honor and glory to God. God's grace and mercy should be our means and inspiration to live lives that continually and consistently honor and glorify Him.

OUR TRUE POSSESSION

Leviticus 25:23 "The land must not be sold permanently, because the land is Mine and you are but aliens and tenants."

If God considered the Israelites, who were His chosen people, as aliens and tenants in the land He promised them, then how does He consider us? As we well know, the land of Israel was a sacred possession for the Jews. It was their land of promise and the cornerstone of their relationship with God. Yet, from the start, God did not intend the Promised Land to be the focal point for His people. He Himself was to be their focus and priority. As they loved, honored and glorified God in their daily lives, He in turn would bless and keep them in the land He had assigned to be their possession. The problem the Israelites encountered was that they began to look at their country as their right and privilege. They used it to satisfy their own desires and will instead of honoring God. Christians fall into the same error when they equate material and physical prosperity with God's blessing. All good things do come from God. But the rewards we reap for living holy and obedient lives lie predominantly in the spiritual realm, thereby drawing us closer to God and enabling us to serve Him more effectively. These blessings help to keep the source of our joy and contentment on Him instead of on this world.

OBEDIENCE IS IMPORTANT-II

Leviticus 26:3 "If you follow My decrees and are careful to obey My commands,"

God has never altered His promises or changed His conditions for mankind. He created us, loves us and desires for us to be restored to fellowship with Him. But this road is not a 'free ride'. God still requires our obedience. He wants us to follow His decrees- which means a daily, consistent and devoted determination to live a holy life. He also wants us to be careful to obey His commands. Obedience is not a haphazard, emotionally fed whim where our feelings and mood determine our submission to His will. We must make a dedicated effort to keep His commands. Recognizing all of this, we must also remember what His commands entail. Too many times we focus on the 'do's and don'ts' or the rules and regulations of our particular doctrine. Christ's commands were simple and clear. First, we are to love the Lord our God with all our heart, soul, strength and mind. Second, we are to love our neighbor as our self. And third, we are to love other believers as He loves us. All that we do as Christians should have these commands as our prime motivation and our main objective.

KNOWING GOD'S WILL-II

Numbers 9:17 "Whenever the cloud lifted from above the Tent, the Israelites set out; whenever the cloud settled, the Israelites encamped."

Many today wish that God's guidance could be this easy. They throw out their fleeces, play the 'if this happens then I'll do that' game and practice other methods of making the discernment of God's will easy. 'Why doesn't God just tell me what He wants me to do, people lament. The truth is that, although knowing God's will is not always easy, it is simple. It starts with having a committed relationship with Him. Total surrender to God is one of the keys to knowing His 'good, pleasing and perfect will'. Why should God share His will with us if we are not totally dedicated to doing His will? We must also continually read and study God's word. Much of what God would have us learn is to be discovered in the Bible. God's leading will always dovetail perfectly with His written revelation. And many times God uses other Christians to guide us. Having a group of believers whom we trust and are willing to be accountable to plays a vital role in knowing His will. When we are walking in the light and living in obedience to our Lord we discover that He desires to reveal His will to us- to hearts that are fully determined to do His will.

WE CAN CERTAINLY DO IT

Numbers 13:30 "Then Caleb silenced the people before Moses and said, 'We should go up and take possession of the land, for we can certainly do it'"

What was the difference between Caleb and the other Israelite spies who were giving a bad report? Simply put, Caleb believed. It didn't matter the circumstances. It didn't matter the situation or the appearance of overwhelming odds. God promised to give the Israelites the land. He promised to go before them and give them victory. And that was good enough for Caleb. God still promises the same thing today. And, although the land for us is a spiritual victory and not a physical place, we can be continually victorious if we will simply believe. We can be holy. We can return good for evil. We can turn the other cheek. We can love our neighbor as ourselves. We can love our enemies. We can resist temptation. We can be like Jesus. In any place, under any pressures, through all circumstances, in the face of every challenge, we can be what God wants us to be. The level of victory we dwell in is a mirror of the depth of our faith. There is absolutely no doubt that we can live in daily victory. God is more than strong enough to do it. The question becomes; do we believe we too can 'certainly do it'?

GETTING RID OF EGYPT

Numbers 14:4 "And they said to each other, 'We should choose a leader and go back to Egypt'."

When we received Christ as our Savior and were delivered from our sins it was a pivotal moment. It was similar to the initial deliverance of the Israelites from Egypt. The sea closing in on their enemies was pivotal in their deliverance from the Egyptians. But as we grow and mature in our walk with God we begin to discover that His ways are higher than our ways. We find that He would have us walk in the light by the Spirit instead of walking in darkness by the flesh - just as the Israelites were challenged to believe God and keep His commands instead of yearning for the physical security and fleshly satisfaction they had in Egypt. And during this process of development perhaps we have considered during our most trying times to give up and return to our old ways- just like the Israelites who grumbled and complained and wanted to return to Egypt every time they faced a significant challenge. There is something about human nature that desires those things we did when our lives were about fulfilling the lust of the flesh, the lust of the eyes and the pride of life. And therein lays the key to victory. We must crucify the flesh and its lusts. We must be filled with a new Spirit and a new desire to follow Christ. We have gotten out of Egypt via our salvation- now we must get Egypt out of us!

MEDIOCRITY

Numbers 14:19 "In accordance with Your great love, forgive the sin of these people, just as You have pardoned them from the time they left Egypt until now."

It is both wonderful and comforting to know that God will always forgive us. His grace and mercy are unlimited. Because of this we can live our lives free of fear, guilt and condemnation. But, sadly, many use this liberty to never grow and to continue to live lives of shallowness, immaturity and failure. They are in continual emotional and spiritual upheaval as they ricochet between defeat and victory. Becoming mired in the muck of their instability and mediocrity they end up living lives of self-centeredness. They wander around in a desert of spiritual dryness and emptiness. They bear little or no fruit and are never able to reach their full potential. They continually fall short of the promised land of spiritual victory, consistency, maturity and stability. They will never experience the milk and honey of abundant fruitfulness. Not only does sinful disobedience place a barrier between us and God, it also limits God's ability to bless us and lead us to higher ground. Don't be misled. God will forgive. But continually playing with this religious yo-yo will keep us on shallow ground. Our lives will be filled with missed opportunities, continual failure, and constant defeat.

A DIFFERENT SPIRIT

Numbers 14:24 "But because my servant Caleb has a different spirit and follows Me wholeheartedly, I will bring him into the land he went to, and his descendants will inherit it."

Have you ever wondered why some Christians seem to be head and shoulders above everyone else when it comes to spiritual matters? This verse gives us a key as to why. Caleb was willing to go against the tide of popular opinion and stand firm on the promises and faithfulness of God. He had a different spirit- one that saw the true importance of God in relation to everything else. And he also followed God wholeheartedly. His was not a commitment that fluctuated whenever circumstances became challenging or emotions became out of whack. Caleb was totally dedicated to serving God because it was the right thing to do. In our efforts to rightly emphasize grace we have sometimes wrongly deemphasized our responsibility to be men and women of a different spirit who follow God wholeheartedly.

NO EXCUSES

Numbers 20:12 "But the Lord said to Moses and Aaron, 'Because you did not trust in Me enough to honor Me as holy in the sight of the Israelites, you will not bring this community into the land I give them.'"

It seems like such a small indiscretion on Moses' part. Instead of speaking to the rock as God commanded he strikes the rock twice with his staff. And, when you consider the extenuating circumstances, you begin to have sympathy for Moses' plight. His sister, Miriam, had recently died. He had experienced continual frustration by the whining of the Israelites. Aaron, his right hand man, was also frustrated. And the last time Moses brought water from the rock he had struck the rock with his staff. So it seems on the surface that Moses can hardly be blamed for his small act of disobedience. But despite all of Moses' negative circumstances God still expected him to obey. God's holiness demands it! Trust and obey, for there's no other way. We must be very cautious because we may use the same sympathy and justification we give Moses to excuse indiscretions and disobedience in our own lives. There is never any reason or excuse for sin. The same blood that purged us from our iniquities is also available, through the Holy Spirit, to empower us to live holy lives regardless of our circumstances.

BALAAM'S ERROR

Numbers 22:29 "Balaam answered the donkey, 'you have made a fool of me! If I had a sword in my hand, I would kill you right now,'"

In this sadly humorous story one has to wonder what is more foolish, a talking donkey or someone answering a talking donkey. God uses a simple beast of burden in a most unusual way to get His message across to a stubborn and self-willed prophet. Balaam knew he was wrong but obstinately pressed forward in rebellion and disobedience. Whether it was the lure of reward or his own personal disdain for the Israelites that caused him to thrust God's will aside is irrelevant. Balaam was being disobedient and he knew it! Most of us have been there as well. God speaks to us clearly on an issue or brings about a strong conviction on our hearts that is unmistakable. But our fleshly desires or pressure from our peers tempt us to set aside God's clear direction for us and to look for an 'out'. We try to find a way we can justify compromising His will- knowing all along, deep in our hearts, that we are wrong. We slide into the foolish error of Balaam; blinding ourselves to God's will and spiritually shooting ourselves in the foot. When we begin to pile up excuses as to why we can compromise 'just this once' we can be assured that we are heading down a foolish path that we will soon regret. Uncompromising integrity is the only path with no regrets.

DISCOURAGER OR ENCOURAGER?

Numbers 32:9 "After they went up to the valley of Eshcol and viewed the land, they discouraged the Israelites from entering the land the Lord had given them."

Have you ever thought about the word 'discourage'? It means 'no courage' or 'not encouraged'. That's what negative people do to others- they focus on the bad circumstances or harmful possibilities and rob others of the courage they need to attempt something challenging. What's even worse is that these negativity spreaders can keep individuals, and even whole churches, from following God's will. Whether it's stating the obstacles to living a holy life, whining about the reasons a church cannot grow, or constantly nitpicking and condemning anything new or different, these self-centered nay-sayers are doing more than just 'expressing my opinion'. What they are doing is wrong and sinful! What matters is not 'our opinion'- the word 'our' betrays its self-centered origin. What matters is the will of God. Work now to make sure your influence in the kingdom of God is one built on encouragement, a positive attitude, and spiritual strength.

REMOVING THE BARBS AND THORNS

Numbers 33:55 "But if you do not drive out the inhabitants of the land, those you allow to remain will become barbs in your eyes and thorns in you side. They will give you trouble in the land where you will live."

God made it clear what would happen to the Israelites if they did not drive out all the inhabitants of the land. And they didn't drive them all out. And sure enough these people tempted the Israelites to sin and gave them trouble. Today we have no promised land in this world but we do have the frontiers of our souls. God's desire is that we drive out every single thing that does not belong in our lives and that will hinder us from loving our heavenly Father with a pure heart. As we daily walk with Him He will place His finger on those things that may become barbs in our eyes and thorns in our sides. It's not enough to just acknowledge our flaws and shortcomings. We must drive them out. This implies that it will most likely take some effort and persistence because many of the things God wants removed are firmly entrenched in our lives. They are also buffered by our own excuses and justifications. Still, they must go if there is to be complete obedience, heart holiness and room made for the blessings of God. As we willingly eliminate the things in our lives that compete with God we will find our hearts drawing ever closer to Him.

MISSED OPPORTUNITIES

Deuteronomy 1:42 "But the Lord said to me, 'Tell them, do not go up and fight, because I will not be with you. You will be defeated by your enemies.'"

In much of Christendom today there is such an obsession with grace that the prevalent attitude is, 'So what if we sin? We will always be forgiven!' And it is certainly true that when we sincerely seek forgiveness we will always find it. But we forget that when we disobey God time and again we litter our lives with missed opportunities to grow or to be used by our Lord. God forgives our sins not just for our benefit but also so that He may use us in His work. The Israelites blew their opportunity to possess the Promised Land. And, although they found forgiveness, they never received a second chance and suffered through forty years of wandering in the wilderness as a result of their disobedience. God works the wonder of His grace and mercy in our lives with a much higher purpose in mind- to cast us into the image of His Son. We must be careful that, just because God's forgiveness is unlimited, we don't live our lives as an attempt to prove how inexhaustible His grace and mercy are. If God loathed sin in our lives to the extent that He willingly sacrificed Himself then we should also loathe sin in our lives to the extent that we are willing to sacrifice ourselves to live holy lives.

MATURE HOLINESS

Deuteronomy 3:25-26 "Let me go over and see the good land beyond the hill country and Lebanon. But because of you the Lord was angry with me and would not listen to me. 'That is enough,' the Lord said. 'Do not speak to me anymore about this matter.'"

Some might want to say that God was too stern and hard on Moses. After all, Moses has been faithful up to this point. He's had to put up with the continual grumbling and complaining of the Israelites. He's interceded numerous times on their behalf and even rejected an opportunity for his own success. He even put his standing with God on the line for his people. And all he did wrong was strike the rock instead of speaking to the rock to give the people water. But this incident is not an indictment on God's sternness. It is a revelation of the true grandeur and awesomeness of God's holiness. Not only did Moses disobey, but he also gave himself the glory and credit for supplying water from the rock. And because of Moses' maturity level and his standing with God, he should have been able to rise above the emotion of the moment. Sadly, many Christians today are too quick to make excuses for their failures and depend too much on their emotional strength to maintain their walk with God. His holiness demands a deeper loyalty, a stronger determination and a sterner mindset. We must have complete trust in God's strength and ability to enable us to live holy lives.

THE PRIVILEDGE OF FELLOWSHIP

Deuteronomy 4:7 "What other nation is so great as to have their gods near them the way the Lord our God is near whenever we pray to Him?"

For the Israelites, keeping God's laws and commandments afforded them the wonderful privilege of having God near them whenever they prayed. By sending His Son to die on the cross God is now able to draw near to all who have repented of their sins and received Christ as their Savior. The blood of Jesus cleanses us from all sin and enables us to be in the presence of an awesome and holy God. Whether we pray in our closets, in our cars or on the go, whenever and wherever, God is able to draw near to us because of Jesus. This is the essence of divine fellowship and the overarching purpose of Calvary- to restore us to a right relationship with our Creator and Father. Each time we whisper a prayer or our thoughts turn heavenward God is able to meet with us in fellowship and sweet communion because of the cross. When we realize that God desires to be near us and that He truly loves us, that He wants to be the central part of our lives and yearns for fellowship with us, our hearts should be overwhelmed with amazement, awe, joy and gratitude. This is what God has made possible through the sacrifice of His Son.

RETURN TO HIM

Deuteronomy 4:29- "But if from there you seek the Lord your God, you will find Him if you look for Him with all your heart and with all your soul."

One of the key phrases in this verse is 'if from there'. This promise is to those who have wandered off and become distracted by the world or have rebelled against God and returned to a life of sin and disobedience. It is in this backslidden state of separation from God that He gives this wonderful promise of restoration. And God states the conditions of restoration in very simple and clear terms- you must seek for Him with all of your heart and soul. Sometimes we can become so enamored by God's love, forgiveness and mercy that we lose track of the fact that He is also holy and pure. He demands nothing less than 100% commitment from us. Half-hearted, conditional or incomplete seeking will not suffice. In fact, that very type of lukewarm dedication is more than likely the reason someone finds themselves in a backslidden state. God wants you back but it must be on His terms, which are absolute repentance and submission to Him. He requires all or nothing with no excuses! If we 'lose our lives' for His sake then we will find real life in Him.

THE ESSENCE OF OUR RELATIONSHIP

Deuteronomy 6:5 "Love the Lord your God with all your heart and with all your soul and with all your strength."

God's desire for the Israelites was that they would love Him completely. Then, as a result of that love, they would gladly keep His commandments and serve Him. Their love for God would be the motivation for having a relationship with Him. This relationship was fleshed out by their faithfulness to His laws and decrees. After a few thousand years God's desire for His people to love Him and have a relationship with Him has not changed. But now He has made it much easier for us by replacing the written code with the sacrifice of His Son. God receives us through the merits of Christ and extends to all mankind grace and mercy. God is now able to write His law on our transformed hearts by the power of the Holy Spirit. God's desire for the Israelites was foiled by their own self-centeredness. Instead of God being someone they could love and have a relationship with, He became a tool to gratify their own desires. And when things didn't go their way they were quick to turn to other gods. Let's stay focused on the true essence of our Christianity. It is the ability to have a loving relationship with God through the work of His Son that will last for all eternity!

A NEW HEART

Deuteronomy 6:6 "These commandments that I give you today are to be upon your hearts."

Herein lays one of our greatest disparities. On the one side God desires us to have His commandments on our hearts. He calls us to love Him with all of our hearts. He wants our hearts to be circumcised. His desire is for us to serve Him wholeheartedly and keep our hearts steadfast and fixed on Him. Yet, on the other side, God states that the inclinations of our hearts are evil from childhood and that they can easily become hardened and uncircumcised. He tells us that our hearts can become proud, conceited and self-centered and we are prone to turn away from Him. For anyone who is battling this spiritual contradiction the situation can be exasperating and exhausting. It can even create a sense of hopelessness about ever being able to live a consistently holy life. Fortunately God recognizes the scope of this struggle and has offered the solution. Nothing short of a complete heart transplant will suffice. God wants to remove our stubborn, selfish and corrupt heart of stone and replace it with a soft and moldable heart of flesh. He wants to give us a heart that desires, above all else, to please and to serve Him. This was one of the achievements of Calvary. It was accomplished through the blood of Christ and brought to reality by the power of the Holy Spirit. Ezekiel tells of a new heart. Paul speaks of a new life, a new way, a renewed mind, a new batch, a new covenant, a new man and a new creation. God wants to give us that new heart!

RIGHTEOUS WORKS

Deuteronomy 6:25 "And if we are careful to obey all this law before the Lord our God, as He has commanded us, that will be our righteousness."

The key to self-righteousness is keeping all of God's laws and commandments. If someone were to desire perfection in God's sight then they would need to perfectly keep all of God's rules, regulations and admonitions. And as we all know, and as history has continually confirmed, this is impossible. The Israelites were constantly struggling with idolatry, greed and hypocrisy. They served God and worshipped graven images. The Pharisees of Jesus' time were condemned because their hearts did not reflect their actions. Their show of holiness and dedication to God was exactly that- a show. Yet the scriptures are full of stories of men and women who, in the midst of all the idolatry, double-mindedness and hypocrisy, sought to serve God to the best of their ability. These folks had within themselves a sincere love for God and a desire to be faithful and true. Today our righteousness is embodied in Christ Jesus. But multitudes are still ensnared by the self-driven desire to let their works and lifestyle be their righteousness. They have deceptively allowed themselves to become the focus instead of Christ. Our works become righteous only when they are reflections of hearts renewed and empowered by the Holy Spirit. When our actions are motivated by our love and loyalty to Jesus Christ they become acceptable in Hus sight.

DISCIPLINE

Deuteronomy 8:5 "Know then in your heart that as a man disciplines his son, so the Lord your God disciplines you."

Now there is a word that nobody really likes- discipline. But if we consider the dynamics of discipline maybe our thoughts about it can become more encouraging. The most severe discipline follows willful disobedience. When we allow thoughts and actions into our lives that we know are wrong we should expect our Father to do whatever is necessary to humble us and bring us back into the center of His will. This correction is usually accomplished through our circumstances, church family and the absence of peace and joy in our lives. Many times the fruits we reap because of our disobedience can be a form of discipline in and of themselves. Yet, for most Christians, discipline involves teaching more than correction. God desires for us to become Christ like and to avoid the pitfalls of this world. He wants us to live in joy, peace and contentment. He does not want our lives to be a rollercoaster of spiritual successes and failures but instead, a stable and consistent maturing into Christ likeness. He uses our prayer and devotional life, as well as other Christians and circumstantial opportunities, to exercise our faithfulness so that we may grow into strong and victorious Christians. For the child of God who has finally surrendered their disobedient will to Him, this type of discipline becomes an exciting adventure!

SERVING GOD FROM THE HEART

Deuteronomy 10:12 "And now, O Israel, what does the LORD your God ask of you but to fear the LORD your God, to walk in all his ways, to love him, to serve the LORD your God with all your heart and with all your soul"

We have all heard phrases like 'you've gotta have heart' or 'his heart's not in it'. They indicate the generally accepted truth that dedication and commitment come from deep within. It's not enough to give intellectual or mental assent. Even sheer determination will fall short without the inward burning. Serving God from the heart is an important key to consistent spiritual victory. Just like our love for our spouses and children keeps us faithful and hard-working even when temptation strikes, so our love for God keeps us faithful and loyal to Him even when our circumstances entice us to falter or fail. The prize of eternal life is a great encouragement for us as we journey through this life. But, without a relationship between us and our Lord, heaven itself becomes a hollow and self-serving ambition. Who wants to spend eternity with a God whom they don't love with all their heart, soul, strength and mind? Our prime motivation to live holy lives should not be to avoid punishment or solidify our eternal destiny. We should strive to be holy because we truly love God with all of our heart and desire from deep within to live a life pleasing to Him.

STRENGTH FROM OBEDIENCE

Deuteronomy 11:8 "Observe therefore all the commands I am giving you today, so that you may have the strength to go in and take over the land that you are crossing the Jordan to possess."

Obedience is one of the most important aspects of living a victorious life. It gives evidence to our faith and allows God to bless us in much more abundant ways. Our obedience keeps us in God's light and will. We find strength and encouragement through the harder paths when our lives are lived in harmony with God's commands. Many struggles and trials are a result of disobedience in our lives. We follow our own desires and get into hot water. Then we expect God to bail us out without having to suffer the consequences of our foolishness. The truth is that, even though we can always find forgiveness for our sins, part of God's discipline process is allowing us to reap what we sow. So many people treat God like some great enabler who will immediately deliver them out of every mess their self-will gets them into. They falsely believe God should protect them from all the fruits of their own sinful behavior. But God deserves, and even requires, our obedience. He is ready to bless, strengthen, and encourage those who live daily in holiness and submission to Him.

KEEPING FOCUS

Deuteronomy 12:32 "See that you do all I command you; do not add to it or take away from it."

When you read all of the laws and regulations God had for the Israelites, you begin to realize how overwhelming it was for them to fully keep God's commands. How tempting and easy it must have been to "add to it or take away from it". Fortunately for Christians today, Jesus has simplified things. We are to love God with all of our heart, soul, strength, and mind. We are also to love our neighbor as ourselves and love one another, i.e. fellow Christians, as Christ loved us. The challenges we face rise, not from understanding what God wants us to do, but from the practical application and daily practice of obedience. The hundreds of different denominations and thousands of independent churches testify to the difficulty we face in reaching unity as to what being a Christian entails. One thing that will greatly reduce friction and help clarify God's will for our lives is remembering what the true battle for every believer is. That battle is the struggle between the Spirit and the flesh. We must discern between God's will and our own will masquerading as Christian devotion. We should be promoting God's kingdom instead of our own agenda, Are we glorifying God or just trying to make ourselves look good? Keeping our focus on God will greatly increase unity and enable us to keep Christ's commands in a naturally flowing way.

UNCONDITIONAL BLESSINGS

Deuteronomy 15:5 "if only you fully obey the Lord your God and are careful to follow all these commands I am giving you today."

God's love and forgiveness for us are unconditional. There is nothing we can do to earn these gifts – we already have them. We also receive daily blessings of life that are based on His favor and not on our efforts. This is what grace is all about. But the Bible is also clear about the blessings that God has for those who live obediently to His word and will. So many people trudge through life wondering why God seems to bless others and not them. They need only to look at their own hearts to see why. They hope for financial relief yet do not joyfully and faithfully give. They want a good marriage but are selfish towards their spouse. They desire peace, fulfillment, and contentment while harboring secret sin and living with areas of disobedience in their lives. They want to serve God yet also hang on to the things of this world. Living holy and obedient lives does not guarantee that we will be healthy, wealthy, and wise. Life is much more complex than that. But when we fully obey God and His word we remove many barriers and hindrances that prevent God from blessing us with His peace and provision.

TITHE TO SERVE, NOT TO GAIN

Deuteronomy 15:10 "Give generously to Him and do so without a grudging heart; then because of this the Lord your God will bless you in all your work and in everything you put your hand to."

There are several misconceptions today about giving and receiving. One of the more prevalent is that if you give to God He will give back to you even more. People then end up using God like an investment banker – paying their tithe or giving an offering with the expectation that they will be receiving much more in return. The motivation for giving becomes self-centered and only focuses on God's material blessings. God has promised to provide all of our needs. But what He truly desires is for us to hold Him, and not the things of this world, as supreme in our life. When our hearts are totally committed to the Lord we discover that we are less enamored by the stuff of this world. Our motivation for giving evolves from the shallowness of "if I give, God will give back" or the fearfulness of "if I don't pay my tithe, God won't bless me" to the joyful simplicity of being obedient to God. Our giving becomes a compassionate response to hurting and needy people. Our focus is no longer on "what's in it for me". Instead, we view our giving as another opportunity to serve the Lord, to glorify God and to love our neighbor as our self.

JESUS: BLAMELESS LIVING MADE EASIER

Deuteronomy 18:13 "You must be blameless before the Lord your God."

Therein lays the dilemma of all mankind. We must be blameless. But most of us have trouble just being consistently good. In order to show the Israelites what He meant God gave them a book of laws, rules and regulations to follow. Still it was impossible to live daily in this world and not fall short. Yet throughout the Old Testament we find stories of men and women whom God took pride and pleasure in. It wasn't that they kept the law blamelessly – nobody could. It wasn't that they never made a mistake – we all do. It was that they set their minds and hearts on God and determined to love and serve Him with steadfast devotion. These people rise as pillars of inspiration and encourage us to follow in their footsteps. Today we have a much greater advantage than the Old Testament saints. We have complete forgiveness through the blood of Jesus. We have the power of the Holy Spirit to purify our hearts and give us strength to live faithfully for God. And we have been made a new creation – set apart to live blameless lives. If Abraham, Noah, Joseph, Moses, David, Daniel, and the rest could do it back then, without our advantages, we should be able to do it today!

OVERCOMING NEGATIVITY

Deuteronomy 20:8 "Then the officer shall add, 'Is any man afraid or fainthearted? Let him go home so that his brothers will not become disheartened too.'"

Everyone is familiar with sayings like 'One bad apple spoils the bunch, or 'A chain is only as strong as its weakest link'. It is amazing how strong an influence that one fearful or negative person can have. We see it on our jobs, in our churches and even in our families. Find a group of excited and encouraged people- add one gloom and doom sour puss- and the whole tenor of the meeting will change. Unless... The best protection against the fearful negativity spreaders is competent, confident and positive leadership. And in this respect we all carry influence. When we are insecure about our walk with God and unsure of what He wants us to do we can be easily swayed by someone who is fearful, self-centered and negative. It is only when we are strong and fearless in the Lord and fully confident in the direction He wants us to go that we have the power to silence the nay-sayers. And, at the same time, we will be an encouragement to the others on our team. The truth is that most people would much rather follow a shining star than succumb to the muck and mire of depressing negativity.

THE CALL TO TOTAL COMMITMENT

Deuteronomy26:17 "You have declared this day that the Lord is your God and that you will walk in His ways, that you will keep His decrees, commands and laws, and that you will obey Him."

The Israelites, after forty years of wandering, had come to a decision. They would follow the Lord. It is important to realize that this commitment to obedience did not occur in an atmosphere of ignorance. They had been learning what God's ways, decrees, commands and laws were for forty years under the training and leadership of Moses and Aaron. They knew what was expected of them and were fully aware of God's requirements. You could say that this was an intelligent and thought-out commitment. Every Christian today needs to come to a personal decision similar to the corporate decision made by the Israelites. Most people initially become Christians to find relief from guilt, forgiveness and cleansing from sin, and a home in heaven. They are fulfilling a basic desire to follow God and serve Jesus Christ. As we grow in our faith we learn what it means to fully serve God, to die out to self, and to have our lives hid with Christ. We need to reach that place where we totally surrender and submit to the Lord. We need to present ourselves as living sacrifices and to be crucified with Christ. We must come to the place where it's no longer I that lives but Christ who lives in me. This is God's call and will for all who have received Christ as their Savior.

SERVING OTHER GODS

Deuteronomy 28:14 "Do not turn aside from any of the commands I give you today, to the right or to the left, following other gods and serving them."

It's interesting how we as Christians focus so eagerly on the blessings of God. Love, mercy and grace are a vital part of our daily pilgrimage- as well they should be. And God has promised blessings to those who are His. But we seldom mention the opposite truth that God has also promised curses to those who do not follow Him and keep His commands but turn aside from their first love. The Israelites never completely abandoned God. They followed the Lord and worshipped other gods. They sacrificed to both Jehovah and idols. That is the danger we face today. God demands our complete loyalty and we are to follow Him wholeheartedly. Yet many Christians try to serve God while also serving their own selves. God is part of their life when it is easy or convenient. But loyalty to Him is quickly set aside when a self-serving or flesh pleasing opportunity arises. Many have replaced the idols of wood, stone and gold with the more sinister and deceitful idol of self-centeredness. They are serving the creature comforts instead of the creator.

LOVE FOR GOD

Deuteronomy 30:6 "The Lord your God will circumcise your hearts and the hearts of your descendants so that you may love Him with all your heart and with all your soul and live,"

There are two aspects of our love for God that, although vitally important, go virtually unacknowledged. The first is that our ability to love God is a result of His working in our hearts and not our own meager efforts to manufacture some sort of affection for the divine. We love Him because He first loved us. He has done a miraculous work in our hearts by removing our sin and self-centeredness. And then He has replaced it with the desire and ability to wholeheartedly love Him. We do not 'fall in love' with God, so to speak. Our love for Him is not a result of our own will or emotional connection. It is a result of His Spirit drawing us unto Himself.

The second is the unique fact that we are commanded to love God. This removes the impetus of our love for God out of our emotional realm and places it within our will. We love God because we choose to, not because we feel like it. When we can raise our love for God out of our emotional instability and into the higher level of our surrendered will we can begin to experience a wonderful maturity and steadfastness in our relationship with Him.

THE DOOR TO HOLINESS

Deuteronomy 30:11 "Now what I am commanding you today is not too difficult for you or beyond your reach."

What was true for the Israelites back then is still true for us in the 21st century. God's commands are not too difficult. We can live lives of obedience. We can live above willful sin. We can love God supremely. We can love our neighbor as ourselves. The door to holy and victorious living swings on three hinges. The first is that we love God with our entire being- heart, soul, mind and strength. He must always have first place in our lives. The second is that we die to self-will. We need to continually pray as Jesus prayed, 'Not my will, but Yours be done'. If we travel the road of self-indulgence we will quickly meet with spiritual failure. The third hinge is that we must live in the present. Focusing on what God wants for us today is not only wise, it is commanded by Christ. God gives us strength and courage for the task at hand, not for what we may worry about or fear tomorrow. It is not the planning and preparation that God forbids. It is the worrying and fretting. And remember that the Holy Spirit is the oil that keeps the hinges working smoothly and effectively on this door to personal spiritual victory and holy living.

BEING STRONG WHILE FEELING WEAK

Joshua 1:7 "Be strong and very courageous. Be careful to obey all the law my servant Moses gave you; do not turn from it to the right or to the left, that you may be successful wherever you go."

Four times in this first chapter Joshua is challenged to be strong and courageous. Sometimes we view strength and courage as traits we must wait around for, that God will mystically give us without us having to lift a finger. But in order to fully benefit from God's help we need to be living daily lives of faithfulness and obedience. Strength, courage, fearlessness, compassion and even love are all commanded of us. God expects compliance regardless of our feelings or emotions. Too many times we wait around for our feelings to line up with what we know to be right before we act. We must step out in faith and do what we know is right. We need to be strong and courageous in the midst of trying circumstances. We should follow God's will and word regardless of the surrounding clamor to give in to worldly ways. And to do all of this while feelings and emotions seek to push us in the opposite direction is the hallmark of true faithfulness, commitment and maturity.

PRAYER AND ACTION-I

Joshua 7:10 "The Lord said to Joshua, "Stand up! What are you doing down on your face?"

Sometimes prayer can be a waste of time. Many use prayer to put off being obedient to God or taking necessary action. There are many things in the Bible that simply need to be done. In Joshua's situation there was sin in the camp and it needed immediate attention. Just praying would not remove the problem-action was required. Tithing, forgiving someone, ending an illicit affair, divorce and totally surrendering one's heart to God are just a few samples of areas where God's will is clear and action takes precedence over prayer. Praying for the strength and courage to do the right thing and to obey God's will is fine- if it is immediately followed by correct behavior. Strength and courage come not just during our time of prayer. They become a reality when we rise from our knees, put our hand to the plow and obey God's clear will. Anything less is simply our feeble attempt to continue indulging our flesh and asserting our will over His. When we use prayer to postpone obedience or to offer excuses or complaints to God for our own reluctance, then prayer itself can become a form of disobedience.

INQUIRING OF THE LORD

Joshua 9:14 "The men of Israel sampled their provisions but did not inquire of the Lord."

Sometimes circumstances force us to make certain decisions, especially when they offer us only one option. But for the most part circumstances alone are not dependable for seeking guidance. We need to get into the habit of inquiring of the Lord. Too many times we forge blindly ahead, letting situations and chance guide our choices. Then when the important decisions confront us, we are unable to discern God's will and usually end up blundering and fumbling our way through. God desires to guide our steps every day. As we cultivate a closer walk with Him we will begin to filter all of life's choices through His Holy Spirit. We cannot obey God's will unless we first know God's will. When we commit our lives to live according to His will, and to follow Him wherever and whenever He leads, we develop a 'sixth sense'. It is that small inner voice that is the gentle and persistent leadership of the Holy Spirit. Eventually, seeking God's will for all aspects of our lives will become as natural as breathing.

WE NEVER SIN ALONE

Joshua 22:20 "When Achan, son of Zerah, acted unfaithfully regarding the devoted things, did not wrath come upon the whole community of Israel? He was not the only one who died for his sin."

It wasn't much- just a robe and a little silver and gold. Nobody saw and nobody knew. But God's command was clear. All of the silver and gold from Jericho was to go into the Lord's treasury and everything else was to be totally destroyed. Achan may have thought that no one saw or knew, but God did. And Achan may have felt that his disobedience would not matter but it did. Thirty six Israelites lost their lives in the next battle and the whole community was demoralized. Achan's sin was selfish and greedy and ultimately cost him his own life and the lives of his children as well. Most people believe that if their moral indiscretions do not directly and immediately 'hurt' someone then they are somehow either excused or justified in their sin. Even Christians will tolerate 'minor' acts of disobedience in their lives as long as no one knows or seems negatively affected by them. But God's commands and standards are clear. Sin destroys not only the life of the sinner but also has devastating repercussions on others that we cannot begin to fathom. Whether it is a fatherless child, an abused wife, a disgraced pastor, a ruined witness, or any number of other fruits of private sin, what we do is always known and will always produce a ripple effect of negative consequences whether we see them or not.

GOD'S PROMISES ARE CONDITIONAL

Joshua 23:14 "You know with all your heart and soul that not one of all the good promises the Lord your God gave you has failed. Every promise has been fulfilled; not one has failed."

God's grace and mercy are unearned and undeserved. He loves equally all whom He has created. On the other hand most of God's promises are conditional. His guarantees of protection, strength and blessing are based on our faithfulness and obedience. When we walk in the light and follow God daily then we become the recipients of His favor. Although He watches over everyone and causes His sun to shine on the good and the wicked, living a holy life of obedience brings us into His shadow and under His wings. But when we insist on doing our own thing and going our own way then we remove ourselves from allowing Him to work in our lives and use us for His glory. Jesus said about Jerusalem "how often I have longed to gather your children together, as a hen gathers her chicks under her wings, BUT YOU WERE NOT WILLING!" God's promises of peace, contentment and love cannot be fulfilled in the lives of those who choose the path of disobedience and self-centeredness. It is only when we daily stay true and faithful and are willing to be "gathered together" that we realize how 'every promise has been fulfilled'.

OUR TRUE SOURCE OF STRENGTH

Judges 16:20 "Then she called, 'Samson, the Philistines are upon you!'. He awoke from his sleep and thought, 'I'll go out as before and shake myself free'. But he didn't know that the Lord had left him."

Ask just about anyone where Samson's strength came from and they will probably say 'his hair', sighting the fact that he lost his strength when his head was shaved. But the truth is that his strength came from the Lord. His long hair was only a sign of the Nazarite vow that committed him to God. Sadly, Samson began to believe his strength was in himself. When he dishonored God by breaking the vow he lost not only his strength, but the Lord Himself. We need to be cautious as we grow and mature as Christians that our confidence does not subtly change from God to ourselves. Our works, faithfulness, church involvement, Biblical knowledge, wisdom, and everything else that develops as we grow and mature, can deceptively replace the Lord as our source of confidence and strength. No matter where we are in our spiritual journey, what we are as far as being holy is solely a result of God's work in our lives. He must always remain our only and exclusive source of strength.

THE VICTORY IS GOD'S

I Samuel 17:40 "Then he took his staff in hand, choose five smooth stones from the stream, put them in the pouch of his shepherd's bag and, with his sling in his hand, approached the Philistine."

It's interesting to note that David had any weapon of war at his disposal- even king Saul's. But instead of trying to do battle with weapons he was unfamiliar with, David chooses his own staff and sling. The result…a great victory! As we follow the Lord we continuously add to our personal storehouse of faith, experience, talents and tools which serve us well on a daily basis. Yet for some reason, when we face our own Goliaths, we yearn for someone else's gifts and abilities or feel that what we possess is inadequate for the task we are facing. But God knows what He is doing and He is more than able to use our own existing gifts and talents to accomplish the tasks He has for us to do. The truth is that, while David was more comfortable with his own staff and sling, he knew that it was the Lord who would give him the ultimate victory. We need to appreciate and have confidence in what God has given us, knowing that we can defeat our Goliaths, not because of our skills and talents, but because it is God who works within us and through us to accomplish His good purpose.

TRUE SATISFACTION

I Kings 4:20 "The people of Judah and Israel were as numerous as the sand on the seashore; they ate, they drank, and they were happy."

It's about the best the world can hope for- to eat, to drink, and to be happy. In verse 25 the Bible also describes that the Israelites 'lived in safety, each man under his own vine and fig tree'. Solomon himself had the world at his fingertips. He had wisdom, power and wealth and indulged his every whim. Yet he was still dissatisfied. The book of Ecclesiastes reveals that even in a nation and culture that experienced God's blessing in a predominantly material way there was still discontent and even emptiness. Those who go to sleep having indulged their every physical desire and pleasure always wake up empty and spiritually famished. The truth is that we were created to live in fellowship and communion with God and will only find contentment and fulfillment when we are spiritually whole. That is why someone who has everything this world can offer and is able to satisfy every fleshly desire despairs of life, while someone who has lost everything, or who has virtually nothing to begin with, can still radiate peace and contentment. We will only be truly happy when God is the center and desire of our hearts, and our ultimate purpose for living.

CLEMENS RUSSELL

THE AFTERMATH OF SIN

I Kings 15:5 "For David had done what was right in the eyes of the Lord and had not failed to keep any of the Lord's commands all the days of his life- except in the case of Uriah the Hittite."

We can look at this verse from a couple of different perspectives. One is that David lived an exemplary life and only had one major indiscretion. He was able to live an almost perfect life. Another is that David's sin haunted him all of his life. His devotion to God would always be marred by his affair with Bathsheba and the murder of Uriah the Hittite. It is interesting that, although David's disobedience did stain his reputation and cause him family grief, his repentance and continued relationship with God inspired God to bless David's descendants for many generations. This blessing culminated with Christ Himself David's victory over failure, coupled with the depth of his walk with God, has been an encouragement and inspiration to millions. The consequences of willful disobedience can be tragic and may overwhelm us with sorrow and grief. Yet God is more than willing to cleanse and forgive. He also desires to renew our relationship with Himself. But even better, God is able to keep us from falling in the first place by giving us strength and courage not to willfully disobey. He can truly guide us into daily victorious living.

WHO ARE YOU FOLLOWING?

I Kings 18:21 "Elijah went before the people and said, 'How long will you waiver between two opinions? If the Lord is God, follow Him; But is Baal is God, follow him.' But the people said nothing."

Every day we are challenged to live our lives in a way that validates the lordship of Jesus Christ. There should be finality to our faith that inspires us and enables us to dwell in a state of continual victory. But for many, the wavering between two opinions is a way of life. They may state that they believe in God but their actions prove otherwise. The Lord they vacillate between is Jesus Christ and themselves. They follow God when things go well or they experience an emotional surge. But when they are called upon to trust and believe in God when circumstances become less than optimal, they succumb to selfish desires and temptations. And any challenges to realize their double mindedness and change fall on deaf ears. They refuse to make a definite choice and devote themselves completely to God. Many people would rather do nothing and continue to live in spiritual obscurity than sell out to God, take a stand and proclaim the lordship of Jesus Christ. Consistent spiritual victory should be our way of life not just in a church service or prayer meeting, but in our homes, our schools, our jobs- in every aspect and at every moment of our lives.

ONE OF THE 7,000

I Kings 19:18 "Yet I reserve seven thousand in Israel- all whose knees have not bowed down to Baal and all whose mouths have not kissed him."

This world continues to go downhill at an increasingly alarming rate! Combine the abandonment of Biblical morals with the pervasive acceptance of blatant wickedness. Add the escalation of violent crime and the polytheistic inclinations of the majority of 'enlightened' humanity. The picture seems to be pretty bleak. Usually the church has risen above the stench and stagnation of social decay as a pillar of moral truth and spiritual stability. But in today's environment even the church is beset with conflicting ideologies. It is racked with compromising morals, a self-centered theology and a lukewarm commitment to the Lord Jesus Christ. For those who embrace God's word and strive to faithfully follow in the footsteps of Jesus these can indeed be challenging and frustrating times. We may occasionally feel like Elijah- alone and discouraged. But be assured that there are still many- much more than seven thousand- who have not become ensnared by the lure of this world. They are steadfastly holding on to their confidence that God is still in control. As we remain true to our Savior and endure the filth of this world, as we suffer through the widespread hypocrisy in the church and continue to hold fast to our Biblical faith, we join with the 'seven thousand' in encouraging others to stand strong as well!

LIMITED FORGIVENESS

II Kings 24:4 "For he had filled Jerusalem with innocent blood and the Lord was not willing to forgive."

If this verse strikes you in an odd way it is probably because of the statement that the Lord was not willing to forgive. We are taught that God is a forgiving God who will always forgive us no matter what we do or how many times we do it. Yet the Bible does indicate that there are those instances where God will not forgive or is unwilling to forgive. Jesus plainly taught that God would refuse to forgive us our sins if we do not forgive others from our hearts. And in this passage the Israelites, under Manasseh the king, had corrupted themselves to the point that, even though Manasseh himself sought and found forgiveness, the people's hearts had completely turned away from God. The truth is that our ability to repent and come to God is not initiated by our own sense of need. It is God who draws us to Himself. But when we only half-heartedly repent as we seek forgiveness for the same acts of disobedience time and time again we tread on dangerous ground. When our surrender to Jesus Christ is based on conditions and God is seen as simply another tool to bring us comfort, security and happiness in this world, we actually end up removing ourselves further away from Him and trampling the Son of God under foot. Yet for those who sincerely repent and desire to keep God first by walking daily in His light, God will always be ready and willing to forgive.

THE ROAD TO RESTORATION

I Chronicles 21:24 "But David replied to Araunah, 'No, I insist on paying the full price. I will not take for the Lord what is yours, or sacrifice a burnt offering that costs me nothing'."

David had sinned when he took a census of his soldiers and now the Angel of the Lord was dealing out God's judgment by destroying the Israelites. Quite a bit of stress had fallen on David but now the punishment was about to end. Araunah had freely given everything David needed to offer a sacrifice. It seemed like everything was falling in to place to bring an end to this sullied event in David's life. But, although David was distressed and grieved over what his disobedience had visited upon his people, he did not allow his senses or judgment to be clouded by the extremity of the moment. David accepted full responsibility for his failure and he was going to resolve his predicament the correct and honorable way. He refused to take the cheap and easy way out. Sometimes we allow our distress, discomfort or dismay to make us look for the least painful and easiest way out of our own indiscretions. We think, 'Anything to get me out of this mess!' But we need to be cautious so that we neither compromise God's standards nor shortcut the necessary road to restoration God has mapped out before us. A truly repentant and humble heart will take full responsibility for disobedience. They will show heartfelt compassion toward those who are hurt and will offer whatever sacrifice is necessary to make full restitution and achieve complete restoration.

PRACTICE WHAT WE PREACH
TO OUR CHILDREN

I Chronicles 28:9 "And you, my son Solomon, acknowledge the God of your father, and serve Him with whole hearted devotion and with a willing mind, for the Lord searches every heart and understands every motive behind the thoughts. If you seek Him, He will be found by you; but if you forsake Him, He will reject you forever,"

It is the desire of every parent to have their children succeed and be happy. We want them to be well educated, meet the right person, have a good job, be responsible and enjoy overall goodness. But David shows us what should be our most important desire for our children. Many of us faithfully take our children to church, try to have family altars and surround them with spiritual influences. Most of our children respond, at least on the surface, in a positive way to this environment. But when crunch time comes and they are forced to stand and act on their own many of them stumble and even desert the spiritual heritage they were given. David gives us the key to giving our children an enduring spiritual legacy. They must serve God with wholehearted devotion and a willing mind. They must see the Lord as their Lord and not just their parents' Lord. In all of our teaching and training, we parents must make certain that we ourselves are serving God with wholehearted devotion and a willing mind. Not only can God see and understand any false motives or duplicity, our children can also detect whether He is real in our lives and will respond accordingly.

ACKNOWLEDGE HIM

I Chronicles 28:9 "And you, my son Solomon, acknowledge the God of your father, and serve Him with whole hearted devotion and with a willing mind, for the Lord searches every heart and understands every motive behind the thoughts. If you seek Him, He will be found by you; but if you forsake Him, He will reject you forever,"

As simple as it seems, one of the basic keys to having a healthy walk with God is to acknowledge Him. Yet two things can make this a challenging issue. First, David commands Solomon to acknowledge the 'God of your father'. God has not changed. But in today's world many people have allowed society to change their concept of God. We need to once again acknowledge and embrace the God of our fathers; the God of the Bible. He is still as valid today as He was 50 or 100 years ago! Second, we need to acknowledge God in all our ways. Not just at church or when we are in a 'spiritual' situation but also in our homes and backyards, on the job, at school or the local Wal-Mart or driving down the highway. Acknowledging a holy God in our everyday life will keep us close to Him and help us to stay unpolluted by the wickedness of this world.

WHOLEHEARTEDLY SEEKING THE LORD

II Chronicles 12:14 "He did evil because he had not set his heart on seeking the Lord."

This is a pretty simple and straightforward summation as to why Christians sin. Most of us came into our relationship with Christ primarily through self-centered motives. We were weary of our life of sin and desired release from the heavy weight of guilt. We also wanted the wonderful reward of eternal life and to experience the blessings of God. These motivations are not surprising because God could not reach out spiritually to those who are spiritually dead. He could only awaken that spark of the divine by calling us to a higher level of living in this world and bringing us to a point where we could be born again- that is, experience a spiritual resurrection. As we then began to grow in grace and in the knowledge of our Lord Jesus Christ, we encountered the continuous battlefield between the Spirit and the flesh. It is in this constant ebb and flow between pleasing our carnal nature and pleasing God that most of our willful disobedience occurs. It is because we have not surrendered our will to God and put to death what belongs to our earthly nature that we struggle in this unstable tide. This state of being opens the door wide for willful sin. We are unable to completely set our heart on seeking the Lord until we have crucified the sinful man. We can have decisive and lasting victory over sin when we make this complete surrender to Christ and set our minds to wholeheartedly seek the Lord.

A WONDERFUL AND ENCOURAGING PROMISE

II Chronicles 16:9 "For the eyes of the Lord range throughout the earth to strengthen those whose hearts are fully committed to Him."

What a wonderful and encouraging promise- God is actually seeking men and women whose hearts are fully committed to Him in order to strengthen them. The question arises, though, 'How can we know our hearts are fully committed?". The true measure of our commitment to God doesn't come in the church service where we are surrounded by other worshipping believers or when our lives are blessed and it is easy to be faithful to Christ. It comes when we are in the world and are tempted to lower our guard. It comes when we are emotionally down and temptation threatens to destroy our lives and witness. It happens when troubles beset us and tragedy strikes and we desire to succumb to our circumstances. It comes when the unholy nature of this world places its evil hand upon our lives and smothers us with grief and sorrow. It comes when we feel that we are abandoned and alone in our spiritual walk and cannot bear to go on. For it is then that our heart's commitment is tested and we need divine power, not for our tribulations to end, but for our spiritual fiber and resolve to be strengthened. It is then when our hearts need to be reinforced with the will to endure and overcome. What a wonderful and encouraging promise!

WHAT IS YOUR IMPACT?

II Chronicles 21:20 "Jehoram was thirty-two years old when he became king and he reigned in Jerusalem eight years. He passed away to no ones regret..."

Imagine living your life in such a way that when you die no one mourns for you. Most of us have heard stories of small or unattended funerals. What does a person have to do to come to such an end? We could make a list of Jehorams' sins or a laundry list of other things that could make a person unlovable or scornful. But it can probably be summed up in the phrase 'They lived only for themselves'. All of us battle self-centeredness in our lives. But, for those who continually give in to whatever their fleshly heart desires, this downward spiral can easily lead them to the place where king Jehoram ended and they too pass away to no ones regret. Accept the challenge from God to live a life devoted to His will and not to your own selfish desires. If you live by the Spirit you will not fulfill the desires of the flesh- and you will make an impact in life that will help you avoid the same dismal end as king Jehoram.

SOMETIMES THE TIME IS NOW

II Chronicles 29:36 "Hezekiah and all the people rejoiced at what God had brought about for His people, because it was done so quickly."

Sometimes God works slow by our standards and we must show patience and wait on Him. This can be especially true when we are seeking guidance or going through tribulation. It is vitally important that we wait for God's timing. But God can also work quickly. For instance, He does not want us to wait one more second to be saved. And God desires to sanctify us right now. It's human nature to procrastinate. Yet God desires for us to quit bad habits or to spend more time with Him daily or to pray more faithfully or to quit sinning right now. He may work slowly when it comes to His timing and will for us and for His church- even His return. But, in areas of personal salvation and holy living today is the day. When we take the immediate steps needed to deal with issues of sin or compromise in our lives we can be assured of God's immediate forgiveness and strength.

HEARTBROKEN OVER SIN

Ezra 9:3 "When I heard this I tore my tunic and cloak, pulled hair from my head and beard, and sat down appalled."

In today's society Ezra probably would have been forced to seek counseling for self-mutilation and the psychological issues behind it. But what we have here is not a mental problem needing therapy. It is the expression of total humility, conviction and repentance. Although this type of physical self-abuse would not be required or recommended today, the heart and spirit behind Ezra's abasement is still valid and needed. There is such an abundance of wickedness in the world that many Christians have become calloused and insensitive. Couples are living together outside of marriage. Sexual promiscuity is rampant among our youth. We murder over 7,000 unborn children every day. Homosexuality is becoming an acceptable alternative lifestyle in our society. And we know many who consider themselves Christians who live in a worldly and compromising way. Sin in their lives is not defeated, but instead is accepted on a daily, hourly and even moment to moment basis. If Ezra were alive today his heart would break at the conditions in society in general and the church in particular. And our hearts should be broken as well.

ZEALOUS LIVING

Nehemiah 3:20 "Next to him, Baruch, son of Zabbai, zealously repaired another section from the angle to the entrance of the house of Eliashib the high priest."

In the midst of this third chapter of Nehemiah, which consists of a long list of the names of people involved with the rebuilding of Jerusalem's walls, is this man Baruch. The list includes goldsmiths, perfumers, priests, merchants, rulers and others who all joined together on this important project. But Baruch is the only person who is said to have zealously repaired his section. Whether it was because of fear of the surrounding enemies or because it was an endeavor for God we don't know. Nevertheless, it should impress us that Baruch did his work in such a way that the writer felt impressed to use the word 'zealous' to describe his efforts. As we go about our routines we always have an opportunity to put a descriptive tag on our work. It's easy to allow the monotony of daily living to lull us into giving less than our best effort. Then, when an opportunity for doing God's work appears, our laziness carries over into our efforts for Him. The truth is that we should see everything we do as doing 'God's work' for we are commanded to do everything as 'unto the Lord'. Remember that people are always watching! Give everything your best!

PRAYER AND ACTION-II

Nehemiah 4:9 "But we prayed to our God and posted a guard day and night to meet this threat."

Here is another verse that shows the important relationship between prayer and action. When the Jews were attempting to rebuild the walls of Jerusalem after their return from captivity they were faced with a very real threat of violence from enemies opposed to their efforts. Obviously prayer is of vital importance when we are faced with troubles and tribulations. Through prayer we find strength and encouragement and we receive divine guidance. Yet many will simply pray but neglect the necessity of taking action as well. There are definitely times to pray and wait for the Lord- especially when one of the aspects of our prayer is seeking what course of action to take. And there are also many times when the action needed is clear. But instead of coupling definite action with our prayers for strength, wisdom and courage we tend to use prayer to bury our heads in the sand. We end up putting off a course of action that we know we should pursue because we are too paralyzed by fear and doubt to move forward. Examples could be witnessing to someone about Christ or seeking reconciliation with someone we have wronged or surrendering a bad habit or sin to God. We resort to just 'praying about it' in order to postpone something we know we need to do. Yet these are all situations that require prayer and action combined,

VICTORY OVER THE SEE-SAW

Nehemiah 9:28 "But as soon as they were at rest, they again did what was evil in Your sight. Then You abandoned them to the hand of their enemies so that they ruled over them. And when they cried out to You again, You heard from heaven and in Your compassion You delivered them time after time."

It's a rough way to live, this see-saw, roller coaster, hot and cold lifestyle. When things are good God takes the back seat but when troubles come we cry out to Him. Then He faithfully and lovingly delivers us or comforts us. Then when we get through the crisis God is again relegated to the back seat. And so the cycle continues. God will deliver us 'time after time' but this lifestyle will eventually lead to arrogance, stubbornness and stiff-necked refusal to listen to Him. Why does this seem to be the condition of so many? One of the main reasons is because their relationship with God is based primarily on His blessings in this life. Faith then becomes rooted in what our circumstances are instead of in the Lordship of Jesus Christ. When problems or trials come we get frustrated or angry and the flesh takes over and down we go. We need to build our faith on Christ and grow our relationship with Him, instead of focusing on what He does for us and the material blessings He gives. Then we will find strength, stability and steadfastness in our daily walk.

GIVING PROPER RESPECT

Esther 2:20 "But Esther had kept secret her family background and nationality just as Mordecai had told her to do, for she continued to follow Mordecai's instructions as she had done when he was bringing her up."

Eighteen is an arbitrary number. Yet that is the age our society has chosen to determine that a child is now an adult. But we have all met eighteen year olds who had the maturity of someone thirty and thirty year olds who acted like they were seventeen. Along with arbitrary adulthood we also launch our young people into the world with the attitude that they have reached that magical age where they are all grown up. The truth is we never stop growing. And even if we have been properly raised as children no arbitrary age is going to transform us into responsible and mature adults. Esther had the benefit of a proper upbringing. This is confirmed not only by the way she lived her life but also by the wisdom she exhibited when, even as queen, she continued to respect and honor her guardian Mordecai. And he was only her cousin! There is a wealth of wisdom, experience, guidance and direction to be found in those who have been faithful and consistent in their walk with God. Whether they are parents, grandparents, aunts or uncles, or others whose faithfulness to God has been steadfast and continuous year after year, we would do well to consider their counsel and advice.

TO BE USED OF GOD

Esther 4:14 "For if you remain silent at this time, relief and deliverance for the Jews will arise from another place, but you and your father's family will perish. And who knows but that you have come to royal position for such a time as this?"

The dynamic between God's will and our own will is sometimes hard to comprehend. Up to this point you can see so many events in the story of Esther that show God's hand and providence. Yet Esther still had to make the decision to put her life at risk to save her people. The Bible has many stories where the fulfillment of God's will succeeded or failed on the choices of His creation. For some unfathomable reason God has given us the right to choose whether or not we want to be a part of His plan. He is constantly working to find ways to fulfill His will. Fortunately He can work around our disobedience- deliverance can arise from another place. But then we must suffer the consequences of our unwillingness to lay aside our fears and self-centeredness. To be used of God for such a time as this requires that we live daily in humble submission and obedience to His will. The life God desires to use is the life that has been totally consecrated and committed to Him.

FEAR INSPIRES HOLY LIVING

Job 28:28 "And He said to man, 'The fear of the Lord- that is wisdom, and to shun evil is understanding.'"

He is God. Sometimes people lose track of that fact. We talk about Him being our 'daddy' or friend- and this is certainly true. But we must never lose sight of the importance of His majesty. The fear of the Lord is not cringing terror, but it does have to do with honor, respect and awe. We don't like to think about being afraid of God. Yet the Bible is clear that God hates sin and will punish the sinner. He will also discipline His children who step out of line and allow compromise into their lives. As we grow and mature in our relationship with God, our motivation to live holy lives shifts from fear to love. This is right and good. Yet as we do mature, God expects us to not become entangled in the baser sins. He desires us to live in continual victory- not live as spiritual children who are controlled by our emotions instead of by the Holy Spirit. Those who have a stronger and deeper walk with God also have a higher accountability to live in daily, consistent obedience. We will never reach a point of mutual respect with God. That is arrogance and pride. He will always be the Potter; we will always be the clay.

BECOMING BETTER AND BETTER

Job 39:17-18 "for God did not endow her with wisdom or give her a share of good sense. Yet when she spreads her feathers to run, she laughs at horse and rider."

The ostrich is a comical bird. Not just to look at, but also because of her lack of good sense. Yet she can run like the wind! God has a purpose and a plan for everything and everyone. And we all have weaknesses and strengths in the proportion that God intended. But, unlike the ostrich, we have opportunity to improve. We can grow and learn to better ourselves. We can work to make our negative traits more insignificant while developing new positive traits. We don't have to accept ourselves the way we are and stay mired in our mediocrity. We can replace the excuses of 'This is how God made me' with the vision of 'This is how God is making me'. We can use our one talent and be faithful in those few things so that God is able to give us more. One of the greatest miracles of salvation is that no matter who we are, we can become like Christ! We can indeed do all things through Christ who strengthens us. We can be better today than we were yesterday with the confidence and assurance that, with God's help and guidance, we will be even better tomorrow.

INCREASING KNOWLEDGE INCREASES AWE

Psalm 8:4 "What is man that You are mindful of him, the son of man that You care for him?"

As David considers the awesomeness of the celestial sky, he is struck with the seeming insignificance of man. Today we can relate to this comparison as we discover more and more of the immensity of space. But David did not have this knowledge. The sun, moon and stars were simply lights hung in the heavens which gave him warmth, light, comfort and inspiration. He was unaware that the sun was 93 million miles away or that it was hundreds of times larger than the earth. He simply had a firsthand experience with the majesty and beauty of the night sky, unsullied by city lights or pollution, as he kept watch over his flocks. And the fact that he had virtually no scientific understanding of outer space did not dim his respect and appreciation of God's work. We have a tendency as our understanding of creation increases to no longer be as inspired by the vastness, glory and mystery of it all. It's as if God's hand becomes somewhat tempered by our ability to figure things out. We suffer from the very arrogance David attempted to dispel. As we continue trying to figure out how the watch works and discover more and more of its complexities and intricacies we should be increasingly amazed at the skill and wisdom of the Watchmaker!

SOME GLAD MORNING...

Psalm 10:17 "You hear, O Lord, the desire of the afflicted; You encourage them and You listen to their cry."

The psalmist has just spent most of the previous verses describing how the wicked seem to prosper with no negative consequences. And this seems true today as well. Not only does evil abound more and more but those who live for themselves seem to suffer little or no retribution for their wickedness. It's not surprising seeing as this is a fallen world. But we who have embraced Christ must remember that we are not seeking our success and satisfaction in this life. God's blessings in our lives are manifest primarily to enable us to live holy and Godly lives while we eagerly await a new heaven and earth. There we will be rewarded for our faithfulness. And there also, those who indulge in the wickedness of this world will be eternally banned. God does bless us in this world and faithfully provides our basic needs. But our focus must remain on Him. Our contentment, peace and joy must not be grounded in our worldly situation and circumstances. It must be grounded in the reality of our faith that a better world is coming and that we will one day be rewarded for our faithfulness.

HOLY HATRED

Psalm 11:5 "The Lord examines the righteous, but the wicked and those who love violence His soul hates."

God hates. Yet God is love. How can these two opposites co-exist? And God's hate seems to go beyond a person's actions to the people themselves. What we need to realize is that God's hatred is not controlled by His emotions. He continues to grant life and care for the most wicked person. He is always ready and willing to forgive and restore. When you consider that there is no middle ground between love and hate then God's love-hate relationship with humanity can be more clearly understood. His perfection and holiness cannot allow Him to even consider tolerating or approving of either sin or those whom sin has corrupted. The only alternative is hate- a perfect hate directed at the devastation of sin. We on the other hand have no right or cause to hate anyone for we have all sinned and come short of God's holiness. We should hate the deeds of the flesh- the actions of wickedness- but those who commit them are no different from us apart from the grace of God. When we direct our hatred toward those who sin we are being hypocritical and acting out of the flesh. God's hatred is a perfect hatred required by His absolute holiness.

LIVING TO PLEASE GOD

Psalm 18:20 "The Lord has dealt with me according to my righteousness; according to the cleanness of my hands He has rewarded me."

Wait a minute. Isn't our righteousness as filthy rags? Actually the statement about 'filthy rags', from Isaiah 64:6, is preceded by 'You come to the help of those who gladly do right' in verse 5. Some clarification is necessary between these two seemingly conflicting verses. When we go our own way and reduce or reject God in our lives then even the good we do reeks of the stench of selfishness. Our righteousness only nourishes our prideful and arrogant belief that we can live good enough lives apart from God or that somehow we can make ourselves acceptable to God through our own efforts. This is 'filthy rags' righteousness. On the other hand there is great blessing and reward to those who live holy lives motivated by love, reverence and devotion to God. After the blood of Jesus has swept away our sins, we can gladly and successfully live a life pleasing to Him. There are scores of admonitions in His word to live righteously. When our hearts are cleansed and our motivation is purified what we do has a positive impact on our walk with God and actually pleases Him!

MEASURED MIGHT

Psalm 21:13 "Be exalted, O Lord, in Your strength; we will sing and praise Your might."

One of the evidences of God's greatness is that He at times actually holds back His power. The miracles we have, recorded in Scripture, although awesome in our reckoning, are minor interventions from God's perspective. The One who flooded the earth and rained down burning sulfur on Sodom and Gomorrah simply spoke the universe into existence. The One who walked on water, healed the sick, and fed five thousand also willingly surrendered His life and shed His blood. This was an act which was powerful enough to reconcile all humanity to God. As much as God hates wickedness He still holds back His wrath and judgment. And as much as God loves us He does not compel or coerce us to acknowledge Him. He allows us to freely make a choice to serve Him. These are all significant displays of His measured might. Sometimes greatness is manifest more in what one chooses not to do instead of what one does. Grace and mercy are two of the most powerful evidences of God's omnipotence. And our ability to extend that grace and mercy to others is confirmation of God's presence and power at work in us.

OPTOMISTIC ENDURANCE

Psalm 27:14 "Wait for the Lord; be strong and take heart and wait for the Lord."

Most of us at one time or another have probably asked God, 'How much more?' or 'How much longer?' in the midst of tribulation- only to have our situation seem to get worse instead of better! The false notion that, just because we are Christians nothing negative should happen to us, crashes upon the rocks and reefs of real life experience. David's own situation while he was in the midst of it only worsened over time. The difference between a child of God and a child of this world when faced with trials lies in our response. For us there is always hope because our hearts and eyes are focused on the Lord. We can be patient because we know He holds us in the palm of His hand. But David takes our response to troubles a step further. Our waiting is not supposed to be sluggish, discouraged and depressed submission to our circumstances. Instead we are to 'be strong and take heart'. When our hope is truly in the Lord and we firmly believe that He is in control, and when we are faithfully submitting our lives to Him in obedience to His will, then we can confidently wait for Him. We know without a doubt that He will victoriously see us through!

BE STRONG AND TAKE HEART

Psalm 31:24 "Be strong and take heart, all of you who hope in the Lord."

Let's face it. Trying circumstances have gotten to us all. It could be the pressures of life or the loss of a loved one. Maybe it is the tragedy of terminal illness, the heartbreak of someone dear to us shipwrecking their faith or the anguish of being the wrongful target of someone's hatred and anger. The list could go on and on. Just because we have put God first and have committed our lives completely to Him does not mean that we will be spared tribulation. David speaks of his hope and anguish almost simultaneously in this 31ˢᵗ Psalm ending with these wonderful words of admonition. Our hope is in the Lord! When we face the troubles that inevitably come from living in a fallen world we can be assured that God is there. He will either give us deliverance from the hard times we are experiencing or He will give us the strength we need. And this strength is not just to endure but to victoriously overcome anything the world may send our way. We can be more than conquerors! And permeating it all is the confidence that someday we will be with Him for all eternity- the one thing that this world cannot take away from us. We have good reason to be strong and take heart!

GOD IS STILL IN CONTROL

Psalm 33:11 "But the plans of the Lord stand firm forever, the purposes of His heart through all generations."

It's a particularly evil and corrupt world we are living in. Wars, famine and oppression are still abundant and the specter of terrorism hangs like an ominous shadow. Sin abounds and wickedness consumes the hearts and lives of our youth. The idolization of self grows and society is continuing to squeeze God into a meaningless, self-centered and convenient ideology. Those who embrace the Bible and hold true to the teachings of Jesus Christ and the necessity for conviction, repentance, salvation and regeneration are being classified as narrow-minded, societal misfits. The world is hurtling down the fast lane of secularism, recklessly accelerating toward the total rejection of true Christianity and the deification of humanity. The unacknowledged goal seems to be a world of spiritual and physical self-indulgence with no regard for a Holy God and the inherent evil of a fallen mankind. In the midst of all this it is still comforting to know, and to be continually reminded, that God is in control and that His plans still stand firm. The course of this world was mapped out long ago- just revisit Matthew 24, Romans 2 and the book of Revelation. Stay encouraged, be strong, lift up your heads for our redemption is indeed nearer then when we first believed!

TOTAL HOLINESS

Psalm 36:2 "For in his own eyes he flatters himself too much to detect or hate his sin."

Few people want to think of themselves as being wicked. This is especially true of believers. After all, we have repented of our sins, received forgiveness and now are living our lives to please God. We will go to great ends to preserve our righteousness. When we stumble, fall short, relapse, make a mistake, slip into the shadows, (our language seems to be full of terms to soften or minimize sin), we often respond with a myriad of excuses and self-justifications. We lust and say 'It's ok to look as long as you don't touch.' We lie and comment 'I don't want to hurt someone's feelings.' We cheat and respond 'They won't miss it.' We break the speed limit because 'Everyone else is doing it.' We compromise our integrity and convictions and reason 'Nobody's perfect- everyone sins every day.' We actively do wrong and state 'That's why there is grace and mercy.' Only when we acknowledge all the 'shortcomings' and 'mistakes' in our lives as sin and only when we actually reach the point where we hate that sin will we find the power for victory over sin. We are holy, not because we think we are, but, because we have allowed God to deal with ALL of the sin in our lives and are empowered by the Spirit to live truly holy, and honestly pure, lives.

PERSEVERING THROUGH EMOTIONAL LOWS

Psalm 42:11 "Why are you downcast, O my soul? Why so disturbed within me? Put your hope in God; for I will yet praise Him, my Savior and my God."

The fact that David was a man after God's heart has led some to believe that he must have been a 'super saint'. But one only needs to read the Psalms to see that David experienced tremendous highs and lows in his emotional life- to the extent that some have called him bi-polar! But it is plain to see that, despite David's emotional ups and downs, he maintained a steadfast and consistent trust and confidence in God. As far as scripture records, David was never condemned for feeling blue. It was only when he disobeyed that he experienced God's heavy hand of judgment and correction. This 42nd psalm is a great example of this. David speaks of thirsting for God and of happier days gone by. He tells of being downcast, overwhelmed, forgotten and oppressed. But, in spite of the seemingly morbid hopelessness of his condition, he confesses continued faith and confidence in God's presence, power and deliverance. No matter how deep his valley, David knew he would once again praise God on the mountain top. When negative moods and circumstances beset us, as a result of disobedience, then we need to repent. We are reaping what we have sown. But for those times common to all, when we are suffering tribulation from living in a wicked world with earthly bodies, it is comforting to know that God is with us and that we will soon praise Him on the mountain!

BAD THINGS HAPPEN TO GOOD PEOPLE

Psalm 44:17-18 "All this happened to us, though we had not forgotten You or been false to Your covenant. Our hearts had not turned back; our feet had not strayed from Your path."

Let's face it again. Bad things happen to those who are following God faithfully. Loved ones die, accidents occur, disease appears and a host of other tribulations as well. Somewhere along the way many have acquired this false notion that if you faithfully follow God you will not experience anything negative. This idea goes hand in hand with the equally erroneous assumption that if something negative does happen you must be doing something wrong or have unconfessed sin in your life. There are times when people receive God's judgment for sin in their life. The Lord will also send discipline upon His children to turn them back to Himself or to keep them from wandering. There is also persecution that comes from the world as a result of living holy lives and being citizens of God's kingdom. When we are redeemed and regenerated we no longer fit in this world. But much of the tribulation we face is simply a result of living in a sinful world. Our physical bodies remain susceptible to all the imperfections in this life. God is always in control yet He continues to allow negative things to happen. This is where our faith comes to the forefront by believing God will work in our worst circumstances. We must trust that He will give us the strength to persevere and that He will someday deliver us from the burdens and weaknesses of this earthly life and body.

THIRSTING FOR GOD

Psalm 42:1 "As the deer pants for streams of water, so my soul pants for You, O God."

This is a well-known and popular verse today. We even sing a worship chorus about this desire for God. But the true impact of this verse has been blurred. Most of us sing the refrain with uplifted hands as our spirits soar. We feel the presence of God and want even more of Him. This is a good, proper and wonderful aspiration. Yet, in the context of this Psalm, the writer states his yearning in the midst of spiritual drought, not abundance. It is easy for us to seek more of God when we are feeling His Spirit and He seems especially near. The challenge is to seek Him when we are experiencing a time of dryness or when our soul is downcast. When others question our faith and we feel forgotten or when we are disturbed within, this increased sense of emptiness should cause us to turn to God with added fervor and persistence. The deer pants after water when he is the most dry and needful. Our tendency is to turn away from God and allow our dryness and need to drive a wedge between ourselves and Him. We then become sulky and self-focused which plunges us deeper into despair. Seek Him with all of your heart and put your hope in God when you are facing those dry times. He will come to you, He will deliver you, and He will quench your thirsty soul.

TRUSTING GOD WHEN IT
REALLY COUNTS

Psalm 55:17 "Evening, morning and noon I cry out in distress, and He hears my voice."

Most know David as someone who had a close and vibrant relationship with God. Yet he experienced many trials in his life. Some were brought about by his adulterous affair with Bathsheba. And even though David found forgiveness and his relationship with God was restored, he still reaped the negative consequences of his sin for the rest of his life. He continually faced family discord and strife, but David also had to struggle with troubles unrelated to his disobedience. He speaks of his thoughts troubling him, being distraught, his heart being in anguish and fear and trembling besetting him. At the same time he claims that the Lord saves him, that He hears, that He will sustain, and that He will never let the righteous fall. David states unequivocally that he will continue to trust in God. Many think that trusting in God and being emotionally distraught are incompatible. Yet that is the very situation in which trusting God actually means something and faith is truly exercised. It is when we are able to rise above our emotional state and negative circumstances and put our unconditional confidence in Him that He is then able to strengthen us, sustain us and deliver us from our anguish and doubts.

OUR SPIRITUAL STRONG TOWER

Psalm 61:3 "For You have been my refuge, a strong tower against the foe."

For King David this verse obviously speaks toward all the battles he fought against the enemies of Israel. His foes were actual human foes that he defeated with the help of God. As you read the account of David you discover that he was a mighty leader and warrior who continually routed his enemies. Today, however, most of us don't have the same kind of challenges. We may have people who don't like us or who are antagonistic toward our Christian faith. But very few of us have actual physical enemies who are bent on destroying us. What we do have, though, is a spiritual adversary who seeks to devour our souls and destroy our spiritual lives. For believers this is the real battle. Though they are a gift from God to be respected and cared for, our physical lives fade in comparison to the importance of our spiritual existence. If God was willing to guard and protect David's physical life, how much more is our Lord willing to provide a haven and deliverance from those things that would threaten our relationship with Him.

MY SOUL IS SATISFIED

Psalm 63:5 "My soul will be satisfied with the richest of foods."

Do you remember the last time you had a great meal? Not one that left you feeling bloated and stuffed, or a good meal that left you still a little hungry, but one that truly satisfied your physical need for food- that 'hit the spot'. That is the satisfaction David anticipated for his soul. God desires to satisfy our souls completely so there is no longer any craving or spiritual hunger. That will be just a part of the wonder of heaven!

REALIZING THE GOOD

Psalm 65:9 "You care for the land and water it; You enrich it abundantly. The streams of God are filled with water to provide the people with grain, for so You have ordained it."

Sometimes it's easy to forget all the good things God does. They go unnoticed for the most part. We think of catastrophic events such as hurricanes, tornadoes, earthquakes and tidal waves and are overwhelmed at their destructive power- even calling them 'acts of God'. Yet God's power is even more evident in the gentle rains, flowing streams and growing crops. His will and desire is to bless mankind and do us good. But humanity keeps interrupting that part of God's plan through continued greed, sin and disobedience. We live in a chaotic world that ebbs and flows between God's blessings and the negative consequences of the wickedness of mankind. Though we as a race have brought torment upon this world because of sin, the truth is that God's blessings still far outweigh the evil that seems to abound. This world is fraught with sickness, tragedies, heartache and death. But love, joy, life, health and fruitfulness also abound. Our duty as believers is to faithfully endure the negative while rejoicing and being thankful for the positive. We need to share with others, as we look forward to it ourselves, the hope of a new heaven and earth where all evil is banished for eternity. There God will give us unlimited and unrestricted blessings as we enjoy perfect unity and fellowship with the Father and with our Lord Jesus Christ!

WHY GOD BLESSES

Psalm 67:1 "May God be gracious to us and bless us and make His face shine upon us."

There are many today who latch on to a verse such as this as proof that God desires to bless us. And in truth, God does love us and shows us His grace. But in today's self-focused society we can quickly fall into the error of believing that it's all about us. We need to read verse two of this Psalm to get a more accurate picture of the purpose of God's blessings, "that Your ways may be known on earth, Your salvation among all nations." God's blessings in our lives are meant to be tools for us to use for His glory and purposes. It may be material blessings to bring comfort to our lives or financial blessings that remove the burdens of monetary cares. Perhaps it is health blessings that enable us to be more active and energized or emotional and personality blessings that make us likable and stable in our relationships with others. God may shower us with spiritual blessings that give us a clearer understanding of the gospel and the things of God. However God has blessed us we must remember that their ultimate purpose is to enable us to be better workers for Him. Our purpose on this earth is not to live in as much comfort and ease as possible until we get to heaven. God wants us to use His blessings in our lives to make His ways known through holy and righteous living. We must daily proclaim His salvation and the gospel of our Lord Jesus Christ to the whole world.'

WHY BE STRONG?

Psalm 69:6 "May those who hope in You not be disgraced because of me."

People are watching you- especially if they know you are a Christian. What do they see when you face hard times and the 'waters have come up to my neck'? (Psalm 69:1) Our lives are not lived in a box where we can falter without consequences. When we stumble it affects not only our relationship with God but also the lives of others, Christians and non-believers alike. Christians can become disheartened when we fail. Non- believers who have been seeking the truth that will set them free may become disillusioned once again by our lack of consistency and steadfastness. Being strong in the valleys of life is not only vital in preserving our own walk with God but is also an important part of our encouragement of one another and our witness to a lost world.

THE RIGHT PERSPECTIVE TO PERSEVERE

Psalm 73:2-3 "But as for me, my feet had almost slipped; I had nearly lost my foothold. For I envied the arrogant when I saw the prosperity of the wicked."

As the psalmist gazed on the wicked and saw that their lot in life was no worse, and in some ways seemingly better, than his own he got discouraged. But if we look to God to only make our lives on this earth more comfortable we will be disappointed. It wasn't until the psalmist "entered the sanctuary of God" that he understood. Although God has promised to meet our needs, His plan to reward us for being faithful involves a place called heaven. Remember that the holy lives we are living today will ultimately be rewarded after we leave this life. We are storing up our treasures in heaven. Dwelling in God's presence here in the midst of trials, tribulations and temptations helps us to keep the right perspective. This encourages us to be faithful in living pure and holy lives so that we will eventually dwell in God's presence for eternity- free from all those trials, tribulations and temptations.

NO ROOM FOR COMPROMISE

Psalm 73:13 "Surely in vain have I kept my heart pure; in vain have I washed my hands in innocence."

Let's face it. Sometimes living a holy life can be a struggle, especially when we look around and see the continued success and prosperity of the wicked. Even more frustrating is when we see church people living compromising lives. Yet they seem to prosper and suffer no ill effects from their lukewarmness and indiscretions. There are also times in our own lives when it seems that the harder we try to live in holiness and do the right things, the more struggles confront us. The temptation may even come to just give up and give in by lowering our standards and indulging ourselves, to 'take a break' from holy living. But we must remember that it is NEVER worth it. God is in control and He will reward those who are diligent and faithful to Him. Our hope and encouragement are not to be found in this world. The greatest reward for our steadfastness and faithfulness is an unbroken and deepening relationship with the Lord we love. We will also experience the joy and privilege of always being ready to be used by God in the work of His kingdom. And we will have peace, contentment and assurance abiding with us continually as we walk in the light and live in the center of His will.

WHAT ANGERS GOD

Psalm 76:7 "You alone are to be feared. Who can stand before You when You are angry?"

There seems to be a dearth of healthy fear of God in Christianity today. We are all more than willing to embrace His love, grace and mercy. We are quick to call Him 'Abba' Father and boast of our familiarity with God. Some even falsely believe that they can continue living in willful sin and that God will automatically turn a blind eye to their wickedness. But God does get angry and this willful disobedience and nonchalant attitude toward sin angers Him as much as anything. It was Israel's stubborn refusal to keep God's law and commands that eventually brought about His wrath and judgment. We need to not lose sight of the fact that God commands us to live holy lives. Just because we can find inexhaustible grace and unlimited forgiveness from God is no reason to continue to sin and constantly stumble. The person who rides this up and down rollercoaster is obviously putting the flesh and their own will and desires ahead of their love and devotion to God. They profess Jesus as their Savior and Friend but refuse to live in daily submission to Him. They have not surrendered to the Lordship of Christ. This pseudo-Christianity is what angers God and will place those who live in this hypocritical manner under His anger, wrath and judgment.

THROUGH THE VALLEYS

Psalm 77:10 "Then I thought, 'To this I will appeal: the years of the right hand of the Most High.'"

Life is full of hills and valleys. We can all look back and see times when we felt the presence and power of God in a very real way or when God miraculously blessed or delivered us. We also remember times of spiritual drought when God seemed distant and the trials and tribulations of this world overwhelmed us. It is a cycle common to almost everyone. There is considerable victory that can be gained in the valleys though. First we need to remember all the times God delivered us in the past- the years of the 'right hand of the Most High'. He has never failed us. Second, we need to continue to grow and mature spiritually. When the source of our contentment and joy shifts from our circumstances and worldly condition and becomes grounded in our spiritual life and our daily walk with God, then the trials and tribulations we face will not be so apt to push us to the point of despair and defeat. To know and truly believe that our relationship with God is the most important priority we have and that there is absolutely nothing, apart from ourselves, that can interfere with our walk with Him is a great source of comfort and strength when the road of life leads us through those inevitable valleys.

CHURCH

Psalm 84:10 "Better is one day in your courts than a thousand elsewhere; I would rather be a doorkeeper in the house of my God than dwell in the tents of the wicked."

How important is church to you? Not the building but the assembly of other believers? For many Christians church can become a burden or drudgery- 'Come on, it's time to go to church. Aw...do we have to?' Part of the reason is that many churches have wandered from being places of mutual praise, worship, encouragement and accountability and are only religious social clubs where people go to pay their dues and fulfill their spiritual obligations. Another reason is because many have grown so comfortable in this world and have dulled their spiritual senses so much that they are actually uncomfortable in church and find little joy or encouragement in attending. And then there are those who have rebelled against God, are living once again in disobedience, and to whom church bring a pang of guilt to their conscience. When our walk with God is where it should be then the highlights of our week should be those opportunities we have to fellowship and worship with other believers. After all, this is exactly what is in store for us in eternity!

ALL SPIRITUAL BLESSINGS

Psalm 91:9-10 "If you make the Most High your dwelling...then no harm will befall you."

Why do Christians suffer today? Is this promise no longer true? What we sometimes fail to realize is the difference between Old Testament and New Testament faith. In the Old Testament God promised material rewards to those who kept the law and did the right things. In the New Testament God promises spiritual blessings to those who accept Christ as their Savior and then commit themselves to living by the Spirit and not by the flesh. We just get caught up in living in this world so much that we mistakenly look for God's blessings in this life as validation of His care for us. The truth is that the spiritual life we have received and all that it entails is far greater than any temporal material blessing. What is greater than new life in Christ with the resultant peace, joy, contentment and satisfaction? And what is more encouraging than the sure hope of eternal life free from all the cares, suffering and tribulations of this world?

RESISTING TEMPTATION

Psalm 94:18-19 "When I said, 'My foot is slipping,' Your love, O Lord, supported me. When anxiety was great within me, Your consolation brought joy to my soul."

When the psalmist speaks of his foot slipping- that is, succumbing to the temptation to do evil- he proclaims that it is God's love that supports him. How can God's love give us practical support when we are tempted to sin? Actually God's love is our most powerful ally in the war against the flesh. The implication is that there is a strong relationship between the psalmist and God. Resisting temptation becomes motivated by more than just fear of negative consequences. Developing a loving relationship with God will put within our hearts a desire to please Him and live victorious holy lives on a daily basis. We say 'no' to wrongdoing and the flesh because we want to, not because we have to. And with God's love comes His consolation to comfort our anxious souls and to replace that anxiety with joy. Our faith, holiness, strength, courage, power and ability to resist evil and walk daily in the light will increase in direct proportion to the growth of our personal relationship with God. This is accomplished through prayer, Bible study, Christian fellowship and walking in His light in continual obedience.

OUR 'MONDAY THROUGH SATURDAY' LIVES

Psalm 99:3 "Let them praise Your great and awesome name- He is Holy."

It is easy in the hustle and bustle of daily life to lose track of the true nature and greatness of God. When we gather together in church and feel the presence of His Spirit we are filled with awe and wonder. As hearts are filled to overflowing and hands are lifted in praise and worship we experience a glimpse of the wonder and glory of the spiritual abandonment we will revel in through all eternity. But we need to take that spiritual power with us into our ordinary lives and allow His greatness, awesomeness and holiness to permeate our real-world existence. If we leave the wonder and glory within the walls of the church building and try to rationalize that these experiences are great on Sunday but can't impact the reality of our Monday through Saturday lives then we are neglecting a great source of strength and power to live daily victorious lives. We end up delegating God to a degrading, feel-good role which serves about the same purpose as a day off or a party- giving us a temporary respite from the drudgery of our lives but having little practical value. We need to allow God's majesty and holiness to infect the routine of our 'Monday through Saturday lives'. Then we will start to experience continual and consistent power, peace, joy, contentment and victory.

LIVING IN HOLY VICTORY

Psalm 101:2 "I will be careful to lead a blameless life- when will You come to me? I will walk in my house with blameless heart."

Most of us would like to live lives pleasing to God. For Christians there is a God given desire to be holy. But sadly, the reality is that many believers struggle almost daily to "lead a blameless life". David gives us two important keys to what it takes to be holy. First, he states that he will be careful to lead a blameless life. Holy living just doesn't happen. It takes commitment and dedication on our part. We must not only desire to live blamelessly. We must also 'give heed' (NASB) or 'behave myself wisely' (KJV) or 'be careful' (NIV) in our daily walk. The will and desire to be holy only comes naturally to those who are walking in the Spirit. Staying continually connected to Him is our best empowerment for living a holy life. Second, David states 'I will walk in my house with a blameless heart'. Just like charity, holiness begins at home. If those who know us most intimately cannot testify to consistent holiness in our lives all else is deceit. Our thoughts and actions in our most private moments are one of the best indicators of the blamelessness of our hearts. The Christian who lives in holy victory in their house, i.e. their personal lives, will most always live in holy victory everywhere else.

HOLY FELLOWSHIP

Psalm 101:6 "My eyes will be on the faithful in the land that they may dwell with me; he whose walk is blameless will minister to me."

It does matter the company we keep. David's success as a king and a man after God's own heart was impacted by those around him, as is true of each one of us. We are social creatures by nature and it is when we fellowship with others who are committed to the Lord that we find strength, encouragement, council and wisdom to live victorious holy lives. Many have stumbled and fallen away because of the negative influence of spiritually shallow or antagonistic friends and family. There truly is no fellowship between light and darkness. And while it is a fact that we dwell in a fallen world and cannot escape the influence of wicked humanity, we do have a choice when it comes to selecting those whom we allow into our circle of friends and sphere of influence. Jesus and Paul were both holy and positive influences in a sinful world and interacted with ungodly people on a daily basis. But when it came to their personal need for fellowship and comradeship they relied on other believers. Those closest to them in the world were those who shared their beliefs, convictions and faith in God. This is an important aspect of what it means to be in the world but not of the world.

UNLIMITED GRACE

Psalm 103:10 "He does not treat us as our sins deserve or repay us according to our iniquities."

Have you ever thought about how the world classifies people as good or bad? They say things like, 'She is so kind.' or 'He will give you the shirt off his back.' or 'I never hurt anyone.' Yet simple math tells us how wicked we all truly are. If you allow a person ten sins a day, and that's being pretty generous, at the end of a seventy year life span they have committed 255,500 sins! Against God! The truth is that there is none righteous. Thank God for His wonderful grace! We only need someone to sin against us a few times before we are ready to write them off. Yet God's love for us is so great that He continues to bless us in the midst of our sinfulness. He continues to love us in spite of our rebellion. He is willing to forgive us time and time and time again. And He was willing to give His all in Jesus Christ while we were yet sinners. Praise the Lord- He certainly deserves it!!

GOD'S LOVE- AND GOD'S HATE

Psalm 103:11 "For as high as the heavens are above the earth, so great is His love for those who fear Him."

Doesn't God love everybody? Isn't His compassion all-encompassing to include the whole world? Yes, God does love all mankind. Yet He also hates sin and those who are wicked. Although this seems a contradiction to us, God in His perfection is capable of both. His love gives all humanity life, breath and hope. He does not treat people as their sins deserve. (vs.10) He is more than willing to forgive and have compassion on all His creation. He came to this earth to suffer and die so that 'whosoever will may come'. But scripture is also clear on the fact that He hates sin and that He will judge those who turn their hearts away from Him and follow their own evil passions and lusts. When we live self-centered lives that revolve around our will and seek to fulfill the 'lust of the flesh' we become the target of God's wrath and judgment. But when we honor God and seek to live lives that are pleasing to Him and when we desire to dwell in the center of His will we will see greater benefits of God's love unhindered by our disobedience and self-will. Only when we turn to God in repentance and commit our lives to Him can we begin to receive all the benefits of His love, compassion and care.

OUR FATHER KNOWS

Psalm 103:13 "As a father has compassion on his children, so the Lord has compassion on those who fear Him."

The picture of a stern, harsh God who is constantly displeased with us and is just waiting to send us punishment at the least little failure on our part is common among many of His children. The truth is that we are created, loved and cared for by a loving and compassionate Father. God's desire for us is peace and contentment. He favors us as parents favor a new born baby. He takes pleasure in us and desires for us to be restored to fellowship with Him and for us to take pleasure in Him. What breaks His heart is that, having met all of our needs through the sacrifice of His only Son, we would still prefer to wander around in the darkness of sin and self-centeredness. As our Creator and Lord God knows us better than we know ourselves. He truly has our best interests in mind when He implores us to turn from our lives of self-seeking sin and embrace Him and the complete salvation He offers through the blood of Christ. Trust Him enough to believe He not only knows what is best, but that He wants the best for you!

THE PURPOSE OF GOD'S BLESSINGS

Psalm 105:45 "that they might keep His precepts and observe His laws. Praise the Lord."

The interesting thing about this verse is that the previous 44 verses speak about how God blessed the Israelites. There is a purpose to God's material blessing- so that we may glorify Him by living a holy life and by using His blessings to touch others. He provides all our needs and many of our wants, but He also expects us to live faithfully for Him and to praise His name. So does this imply that the lack of material blessings indicates God's displeasure? That is a possibility. We may not be materially blessed because we have not been faithful with what He has already given us or consistent in living for His glory instead of our own. God will not increase our store of talents until we are faithfully using what He has already given us. But lack of material blessings is not always an indicator of God's judgment. There are many who have very little material things, yet are not only in the center of God's will, but are also completely at ease with their situation in life. More than likely, someone who does not have peace, joy and contentment in the midst of their overall situation is either chaffing at where God has them or has some area of resistance or rebellion in their life.

SINGING FROM STRENGTH

Psalm 108:1 "My heart is steadfast, O God; I will sing and make music with all my soul."

Most people love music and love to sing, or at least try. And one reason is because we are glad and joyful. When our spirits are soaring and we are feeling at the top of the world it is hard not to burst forth in jubilant song- or at least hum a happy tune. David was one such person. We know he was a skilled musician and singer. He is also credited with writing many of the Psalms. David celebrated with all his soul as evidenced when the Ark of the Covenant was brought into Jerusalem. But this verse gives us a little extra insight into David's celebratory nature. Although these were very emotional experiences, there is also no doubt that David's rejoicing, singing, and praising were rooted in a steadfast heart. His loyalty and faithfulness to God were the foundation upon which he sang and made music with all his soul. Sometimes we allow music to mask our hurts and ills. We use music to give us an emotional lift when we have allowed ourselves to slip or compromise. We need to address the real issues of unfaithfulness or disobedience which need to be confessed and not sung to. Music should reflect our devotion to God and not act as a panacea for hearts that have not been steadfast. When our hearts are pure then we can truly sing and make music with all our souls!

SELF LOVE OR LOVE OF SELF

Psalm 116:1-2 "I love the Lord, for He heard my voice; He heard my cry for mercy. Because He turned His ear to me I will call on Him as long as I live."

Without a doubt God deserves our love, our praise, our worship and our constant devotion simply for who He is. He is God. Yet in our human state He has also created within us a need to be cherished, loved and cared for. This form of self-love is a necessary part of our makeup and is the standard by which we are able to love our neighbors. It is also what triggers and fuels our love and praise for God. How we love ourselves impacts our ability to enjoy all of the good things God has blessed us with and to appreciate His practical love and care for us. To respond with heartfelt praise and adoration for His presence in our lives and the fellowship we have with Him are all predicated by a healthy self-love which He has placed within each of us. It is only when self-love denigrates to love of self and when desire is replaced by lust that we lose our focus. When God's goodness to us becomes and end in itself instead of a means to an end we expose ourselves to the dangers of I-dolatry. Certainly we must thank and praise God for all of the good things He bestows upon us. But, when these 'things' become the sum and substance of our relationship with Him we have unwittingly allowed a corrupt love of self to usurp a healthy self-love.

DESIRING STEDFASTNESS

Psalm 119:5-6 "Oh, that my ways were steadfast in obeying Your decrees! Then I would not be put to shame when I consider all Your commands."

The wonder of grace and mercy that brings about conviction, repentance and restoration, is truly amazing. To have our guilt exposed and then washed away is an incredible experience. God not only forgives us but He also cleanses us from the burden of guilt so that we inwardly feel like new born babies in our souls. But for some reason, many who are initially delivered from sin and its guilt quickly fall back into disobedience. The guilt that post-salvation sin brings is somewhat different because now we know better. And through Jesus Christ we do have the power and ability to resist temptation and live holy lives. This frustrating dilemma affects every Christian as we wage battle between our flesh, which seeks pleasure and fulfillment through this world, and our spirit, which seeks to please God. We cry out with David, praying that our ways would be steadfast in obeying God. Fortunately there is a path which will lead us to this great victory. It begins with the total and absolute surrender of our will to God. When we empty ourselves of self will, God is able to remove from our lives any hindrances to total obedience. He does this by filling us completely with His Spirit and empowering us to live holy lives so that living to please Him becomes the very heartbeat of our lives.

CLEMENS RUSSELL

STRENGTH TO TRIUMPH

Psalm 119:56 "This has been my practice: I obey Your precepts."

Many of us find comfort and encouragement from the Psalms. The 23rd Psalm is probably the best know passage in the entire Bible. So many times, when sudden tragedy or tribulation strikes us, we cry out to God and look to Him for help and deliverance. Yet many fail to find the help they are looking for or miss the comfort God sends. A significant part of the problem is that we fail to realize that much of what David prayed for and received was possible because of his close walk with God. He made it his practice to pray, to daily look to God, and to live a life of obedience. Living his life this way enabled him to grow strong in his faith so that when severe tribulation came he was steadfast and strong. Sadly, many today live their lives with God as simply a footnote or a good luck charm. They follow their own path, do their own thing and seldom bring God into the realm of their daily lives. They struggle to even spend ten minutes a day with the Lord. Then when trouble comes and they cry out to God they discover that their reservoir of faith is all but dried up. Fortunately, God in His mercy is always there. But we will miss out on so much fear, heartache and defeat when we face the crisis of our lives from a foundation of steadfastness, faithfulness, obedience, and living moment to moment in His presence.

LIVING HOLY LIVES TO GLORIFY GOD

Psalm 119:74 "May those who fear You rejoice when they see me, for I have put my hope in Your word."

It seems that many Christians fall into two categories. Either they desire the spotlight and want people to notice them or they wish to live their Christian lives in spiritual obscurity hoping that no one is scrutinizing them. Both categories are wrong because they are rooted in the self- 'Look at ME!' or 'Leave ME alone!' David gives us a glimpse of the correct attitude we should have. He recognizes that the life he lives as a result of putting his hope in God's word will be an encouragement to others who fear and honor God. One of the results of living our lives for God's glory is that people will notice. In fact, that's exactly why God has left us here. He wants us to be His witnesses to a lost world and to be a source of mutual strength and encouragement to one another as we walk this Christian journey together. We are supposed to be the 'salt of the earth' and 'to let our light shine' and to let people see our good works and glorify our Father in heaven. If God's sole intention of saving us was to get us to heaven, we'd be there right now. He has left us here for a reason!

THOROUGHLY TESTED

Psalm 119:140 "Your promises have been thoroughly tested and Your servant loves them."

Today there are so many voices calling for us to go this way or follow that path. It seems that even in Christendom the way has become a blur as new ministries and books inundate us with better ways to live or a sure-fire road to success and spiritual victory. Christianity has seen its fair share of fads in the last few years. And many have found help or encouragement from some of them. But, periodically, it is important to reestablish the influence of God's word in our lives. The books and fads will come and go. Those who have been walking with the Lord for some time can probably remember several different ones that have appeared with a bang and then faded away. But, as you read the next book or attend the next seminar and find encouragement or guidance from them, make sure you continually keep yourself established in the thoroughly tested promises and teachings of the word of God. The Bible is our best source of guidance and our only source of absolute truth.

A HIGHER VICTORY

Psalm 121:7 "The Lord will keep you from all harm- He will watch over your life."

As we walk with God and live in obedience to His word God will protect us two ways. One, by living in the center of His will, we will not stumble or be harmed by the consequences of deliberate sin in our lives. Holy living protects us from sins personal destruction. Two, we are also protected from Satan's direct assaults on our lives. Only when we step out of the light do we make ourselves vulnerable to the enemy's personal attacks. Yet we still live in a fallen world in earthly bodies. So we must still face the bumps and bruises of pain, sickness, tragedy, hard times and death that are common to all mankind. In these circumstances, as we rely on His grace and strength, we can do more than just get through. We can be victorious in ways unreachable by the world. Those who live in the flesh allow these things to discourage and defeat them. But those who live by the Spirit will not allow the uncontrollable circumstance of life to dissuade them. They acknowledge God is at work even in the toughest of times. Their faith carries them through as they trust that God knows best. Their hearts remain steadfast and set on Christ!

CLEMENS RUSSELL

THE GOOD SIDE OF SLAVERY

Psalm 123:2 "As the eyes of slaves look to the hand of their master, as the eyes of a maid look to the hand of her mistress, so our eyes look to the Lord our God, till He shows us His mercy."

The abolition of slavery was great- no man should own another; although there are other types of slavery still in existence. Today this verse is a little difficult to understand. The truth is we are made to serve. Whether we serve God or the flesh is our choice. But once we sell out to God we become enslaved to Him. Just as a slave was totally dependent upon their master for everything, so we must be totally dependent on God. Just as a slave's life was devoted to serving their master, so we must be devoted to serving God. Just as a slave looked to their master for kindness and mercy, so our eyes look to the Lord our God till He shows us His Mercy. As the apostle Paul says, we are not our own, we are bought with a price. God made us, saved us and owns us! God is a far greater master than the flesh, this world or our selves. It is a great mystery that we will never know true freedom until we become enslaved to Christ, until we know the Truth and until we sell out completely to God. We were created to be slaves- slaves of Jesus Christ!

GOD'S INSPIRATIONAL GREATNESS

Psalm 124:8 "Our help is in the name of the Lord, the Maker of heaven and earth."

What an awesomely encouraging thought! We spend so much of our time on this globe going through our daily routines. We try to balance our jobs, family obligations, recreation and entertainment with our walk with God. And in the melting pot of everyday living most of us do acknowledge God's presence and care. Even when troubles beset us we, for the most part, are quick to turn to Him for help and encouragement. Yet there is the subtle and almost imperceptible tendency to allow our view of God to drift away from being a concrete reality to a 'Someone up there who may or may not help but who will at least, more than likely, give me enough strength to struggle through and survive by the skin of my teeth. But as long as I hang on and have heaven to look forward to I will somehow make it through…'- you get the idea by now. It is spiritually rewarding to renew the realization that the Maker of heaven and earth is our help. It is our level of faith and our scope of the true greatness of God that determines whether we trudge in defeat through the tribulations of life or we march through in triumph and victory. Our hope is in the living God who says that we are more than conquerors through Jesus Christ. Remembering who God truly is inspires unconquerable hope!

THE DAWN ALWAYS COMES

Psalm 130:6 "My soul waits for the Lord more than watchmen wait for the morning, more than watchmen wait for the morning."

Have you ever been in complete darkness with only the stars to cast their miniscule light? For watchmen in Biblical times there were no streetlights, flashlights, headlights, city lights; nothing but the stars. So their anticipation of the coming light of dawn was very great. Not only did the morning sun dispel the darkness but it also chased away the terrors of the night. Mankind, as a whole, has always been afraid of the dark. So the watchmen waited- anxious for the dawn and certain of its arrival even when it seemed that the night would last forever. David's anticipation of the Lord's faithfulness and his certainty that He would come was even greater. His was not a feeble, faithless, dwindling hope that the Lord might just this once appear to help and encourage him. His hope was a strong, confident assurance that, just as the sun always rises, so the Lord would come and dispel his own darkness. This hope should be ours as well. For even though it is always darkest before the dawn, the dawn always comes.

SIMPLE TRUST IN A COMPLEX GOD

Psalm 131:1b-2a "I do not concern myself with great matters or things too wonderful for me. But I have stilled and quieted my soul;"

Remember the philosophical question of, 'If God can do anything, can He make a rock so big that not even He can lift it?' If questions like this concern you and challenge your faith then Psalm 131 is for you. Pride is an enemy of faith. We will NEVER understand, comprehend or even begin to fathom the greatness and mystery of God. We don't need to. Sometimes it is best to lay aside our questions, doubts and fears. There are times that we should just enjoy the presence of God and marvel at the truth that He loves us and cares for us in the midst of His unimaginable greatness. A child doesn't try to analyze the complexities of a mother's care and compassion or concern themselves with the mysteries of a mother's love. They just joyfully receive it. This simple trust and contentment should be a foundational characteristic of our relationship with God. Being able to still and quiet our soul in the midst of the hustle and bustle of life should come as naturally to us as breathing.

LETTING OUR WORDS REFLECT OUR HEARTS

Psalm 142:1-2- "I cry aloud to the Lord; I lift up my voice to the Lord for mercy. I pour out my complaint before Him; before Him I tell my trouble."

Have you ever had someone unload their built up emotions on you as they poured out their heart? This is what David did as he cried out, lifted up, poured out and told God his trouble. And this is one of the reasons he was a man after God's own heart. Too many times in our prayer life we tiptoe around our true feelings and emotions as we formulate what would constitute a proper prayer. But if we would think about it for just a moment we would realize how foolish we are to try to be 'proper' in our prayers. God is not only listening to our word, He is also listening to our hearts. Expressing our heart's cry with words is for our benefit, not God's. When we couch our prayers in nice sounding phraseology and resist pouring out our heart to God we are not fooling Him. We are only cheating ourselves. What David did is the practical application of casting our cares upon Him. Begin to let your heart speak out with words in your prayer life and experience new life and excitement in your time spent with God.

WAGING WAR

Psalm 144:1 "Praise be to the Lord my Rock, who trains my hands for war, my fingers for battle."

In David's day this was praise for the ability to handle weapons of war. Today there are still battles to be fought. But the weapons of our warfare are not worldly. They are spiritual, for we wage spiritual warfare against the powers that want to defeat Christianity and keep the world bound by sin. We can continually win this spiritual battle against us by studying the Bible, praying without ceasing, remaining in fellowship and accountability with each other and denying ourselves daily. By walking in the light we will be given the strength and power to win every battle. Then, only as we keep ourselves ready, can we take the offensive and go into the world to be used by God to seek the lost and lead them to salvation through Jesus Christ. In today's church there seems to be tremendous attention on personal victory but very little emphasis on why we need personal victory- not just to get through this life and make it to heaven but to be tools in God's hands to win the lost. We should be taking the battle to the gates of hell!

HE'S GOT THE WHOLE
WORLD IN HIS HANDS

Psalm 145:9 "The Lord is good to all; He has compassion on all He has made."

The arms of God are wide enough to embrace the whole world. He created it all, sustains it all and died for it all. Sometimes we become careless in our walk with God concerning those outside of the fold. As we draw closer to God and live more and more according to His will we can be easily assaulted by spiritual pride. This pride looks down on those who are still entangled in the sinful muck and mire of this world. We may also begin to harbor a judgmental or critical spirit toward those who, in their quest for spiritual fulfillment or as a result of their cultural environment, have stumbled into a false religion or cultic deception. And, even though it is true that they are responding to their situation in worldly, self-centered and even wicked ways, we must constantly remind ourselves that the only thing separating us from them is the grace of God. We are wrong to suppose that we would never do this wicked thing or commit that particular sin because we have no idea what direction our path would have taken us apart from God's grace and mercy. Letting our light shine before men involves both showing them and telling them what God can do. We should be giving God the glory for the new life we enjoy. We should also be extending hands of grace, mercy, hope and compassion to those whom God loves just as much as He loves us.

A LIFESTYLE OF PRAISE

Psalm 146:2 "I will praise the Lord all my life; I will sing praise to my God as long as I live."

This is it. This Christian thing is not an experiment or a hobby. It's not like a job that you can change or a phase of life. It's not something you do like going out to eat or taking a vacation. When we surrender our lives to Christ and make the decision to follow Him our lives are totally revolutionized. God does the miraculous when He forgives all of our sins, frees us from guilt, cleanses our hearts and then sets up residence in our lives. Being born again is a life changing experience because it changes the rest of our life. Most of us entered into a relationship with Jesus on the basis of our immediate needs- forgiveness, deliverance from a destructive lifestyle and the desire for contentment, satisfaction and meaning in our lives. But in the maturing process we begin to realize the full scope of what it means to be a Christian. God saved us so that He could once again have a relationship with us. He most certainly is worthy and deserving of our praise, not only for as long as we live on this earth, but for all of our eternity of living! When this truth becomes the natural outcry of our hearts instead of just a mental acknowledgement of Christian teaching we will have reached a significant milestone in our walk with God.

ONLY PRAISE

Psalm 147:1 "Praise the Lord. How good it is to sing praises to our God, how pleasant and fitting to praise Him."

For many Christians their daily walk is composed of devotions, (if we remember or have time) and snippets of thoughts, prayers and requests throughout the day. Sunday is our big day of praise, worship and focusing on God. Yet we could serve ourselves and our Lord better by beginning to practice praise every day. After all, it's a good thing to praise Him. Every time we praise Him we are doing something right, especially in the midst of the tribulations of the day. And it is pleasant to praise Him. Praising God is a source of pleasure for us- it brings us gladness, comfort and joy. It is also fitting to praise the Lord. Think about it! Praise will be the focal point of our relationship with God throughout eternity. There will be no pleadings, no requests, no crying out for strength or comfort or mercy. There will be no spiritual warfare or the need to pray for the lost or the sick. There will only be the wonder and joy of praise! So why not get into practice now on a daily basis what we will be doing for all eternity?

RECYCLING THE OLD FAVORITES

Proverbs 3:5 "Trust in the Lord with all your heart and lean not on your own understanding."

Among Christians this is a very well-known verse. Many have committed it to memory and this is good. Yet we must be cautioned on one of the dangers of memorizing scripture and that is the tendency to take it for granted. Usually a verse is remembered because of its impact upon us at a certain time in our lives. Yet the dynamics of God's word allows that same verse to impact us in a different way according to our present circumstance. In this short verse we find truths about trusting, the importance of trusting with all your heart, the part our heart plays in trust, what we should not lean on or trust in and how we should trust in the Lord even when our own understanding is contrary or unclear. Maybe today's truth can be found in the fact that this verse is a command, taking it outside the realm of emotional consent and placing trust in the realm of willful obedience. Always look for ways that old favorite verses might speak to you in new and significant ways.

THE FOLLY OF SPIRITUAL
SELF-SUFFICIENCY

Proverbs 5:12-13 "You will say, 'How I hated discipline! How my heart spurned correction. I would not obey my teachers or listen to my instructors.'"

Whether 8, 18 or 80 we should all be learners. We all need people that love and care for us enough to teach us and correct us. It may be a spouse, parent, teacher, pastor, elder or boss. We all should have someone to whom we are accountable. But pride and arrogance can easily interfere with a humble and teachable spirit. And when pride and arrogance are evident then the lusts of the flesh are more easily indulged. Some may say 'I have the Lord and that's all I need.' Yet scripture teaches that God uses the love and correction of others more than any other method to encourage, teach, admonish and discipline us. When we get to a place where we believe we are smarter and wiser that everyone else we come dangerously close to failure. Yet the very nature of the sin of pride and arrogance prevents us from listening to, and heeding the council of, those who can view our situation objectively and give us sound guidance. When you think that you do not need accountability and advice then you most certainly do. Do not let pride and arrogance keep you from remaining humble enough to receive God's wisdom from others.

DON'T EVEN LOOK

Proverbs 6:25-26 "Do not lust in your heart after her beauty or let her captivate you with her eyes, for the prostitute reduces you to a loaf of bread and the adulteress preys upon your very life."

In today's society sex outside of marriage is so prevalent that it has become the norm. Adultery and premarital sex have even become common in the church. From Playboy to the Sports Illustrated swimsuit issue, sex is blared from all forms of media. The very root of the family is being attacked. Part of the problem is the acceptance of the philosophy 'look, but don't touch' or 'it's OK to window shop as long as you don't sample the merchandise'. But sexual sin begins in the heart- it is only consummated in the act. For many, when human beauty and sensuality are observed, the lust gear can kick in almost immediately. And if a man or woman is caught up in the habitual look of lust, pornography, or sexual fantasizing, then when an opportunity surprises them to commit the act their defenses have already been severely weakened and failure is almost certain. There are two keys to staying pure. First, when our eyes are assaulted by sensuality, we need to simply look away before captivation and lust causes us to stumble and fall without ever even having to act it out. Second, we must be vigilant in keeping our hearts and our thought life holy as well.

INTEGRITY OR DUPLICITY

Proverbs 11:3 "The integrity of the upright guides them, but the unfaithful are destroyed by their duplicity."

Integrity seems to be a lost quality in today's world. The ability to firmly stick to Godly beliefs and not compromise simply because of our situation is becoming increasingly rare. Many Christians know what they believe and may even be very passionate about their beliefs. Yet in this time of self-centered thinking and self-gratification, which has even invaded the church, we are losing the integrity necessary to remain true to our convictions. Duplicity of thought and action is creating an atmosphere of unfaithfulness in the Christian realm. Not only does this negatively affect the individual but it also does great harm to the church. James reinforces this danger when he tells us that a double minded man is unstable in all of his ways. It is not enough just to believe the right way if we do not possess the integrity to act on that belief in tangible ways on a daily, and even moment by moment, basis. Are you being guided by your integrity or destroyed by your duplicity?

TRULY BEING GENEROUS

Proverbs 11:25 "A generous man will prosper; he who refreshes others will himself be refreshed."

Most of us know the importance of being generous, giving freely from our hearts, and not loving money or the self-indulgences it can buy. Mature Christians have usually settled the issue of tithing and are fairly generous when special needs arise or extra offerings are necessary. But there seems to be another area of our lives where we are becoming increasingly stingy. That is in the realm of our time. The business of our lives and jobs that enables us to give more financially has robbed us of the ability to give more of ourselves. For many of us our lives consist of week nights collapsed in exhaustion in front of the T.V. and weekends filled with doing all the things we couldn't get done during the week. And if we can squeeze a few moments in for God then we feel we are OK and the cycle continues. But when we take the time to make a phone call or send a card, to visit someone in need or to do something else that forces us to pause in our hectic schedules, we are being generous with our time and we will find our souls being truly refreshed in ways that simply giving money cannot provide.

THE VIRTUE OF WORK

Proverbs 12:11 "He who works his land will have abundant food, but he who chases fantasies lacks judgment."

Hard work and daily, consistent commitment are an important part of our philosophy of life. The virtues of faithfulness in our work are extolled throughout scripture- even so far as to encourage us to consider the diligent labor of the ant. Yet today there are multitudes who look to the 'get rich quick' schemes or waste their resources on the chance to win millions in lotteries or sweepstakes for material rewards. Meanwhile they just tolerate, or even resent, their present lot in life and loathe the necessity of hard work. Instead of seeking contentment by working diligently and faithfully in the circumstances in which providence has placed them they live a life of dissatisfaction and discouragement- hoping for that inheritance, lawsuit, or winning ticket that will bring them their dream of true success and contentment. You truly are living a life of fantasy if you believe that the key to your happiness is more money, possessions or prestige. True contentment is found by those who treat life as a means to an end and not an end in itself. Faithfulness and hard work is more than just a pathway to success in this life. It is an act of obedience to God.

HUMBLING MEASURES

Proverbs 13:10 "Pride only breeds quarrels, but wisdom is found in those who take advice."

Why is it that we find it difficult to receive advice or take constructive criticism? Even when we know the person speaking to us has a strong walk with God, sincerely cares about us, and wants what is best; we will still fume and fidget when they express their concerns. Our pride kicks in and we become defensive and even combative. God desires us to not only receive Him humbly but to also walk humbly with Him. An important facet of walking humbly is to realize that we are not completely perfect. We don't know everything and still make mistakes. We pray for God to guide us and show us His direction. But when God uses His primary instruments to give us that guidance and direction- other Christians- we become threatened, quarrelsome and resistant. This is especially true when we are already under conviction or the other person is somewhat less of a Christian, in our estimation, than we ourselves are. Our pride interferes with God's ability to work in our lives however He deems best. It may even be that God purposely uses an uncomfortable method or mechanism in order to remove our pride and humble our heart. We need to maintain a humble and meek spirit, allowing God to lead us as He deems best and to use whatever means He desires to grow us to spiritual maturity.

THE CANCER OF ENVY

Proverbs 14:30 "A heart at peace gives life to the body, but envy rots the bones."

The truth of this proverb is revealed every day in our society. We are bombarded with ads telling us how much happier we would be if we had this product or purchased that merchandise. There is an abundance of medications and there are many doctors to help us deal with the depression and anxiety caused by our discontentment with our station in life and our exhausting efforts to improve it. Sadly, this problem of envy is also seen in the ministry of our churches as people strive to serve on boards or committees and desire gifts and talents that others have. Many church boards, committees and ministries are manned by people based on their popularity and social standing instead of their spiritual maturity and gifts. And many who have little, whether material or spiritual, resent those who have more. Envy is a cancerous sin that goes deep into a person's heart and can ruin lives as well as churches. The opposite of envy is contentment. If you are in the center of God's will then accept your position in life and seek to improve your condition based on God's plan, not by coveting the lives, possessions and talents of others. God promises perfect peace to the person whose mind is set, not on those around them or their station or circumstance in life, but on Him!

NO ROOM FOR SIN

Proverbs 15:9 "The Lord detests the way of the wicked, but He loves those who pursue righteousness."

We have God's love which gave us the ultimate sacrifice of His Son. We have God's grace which He abundantly pours out upon us undeserving people. And we have His mercy which makes Him willing to forgive us again and again. But none of these should be reasons for us to continue to sin. God hates sin and detests the way of the wicked. How much more must He despise sin in those who have received the benefits of His love, grace and mercy yet continue to allow willful sin to have a place in their lives. We have all of the power in the universe at our fingertips to enable us to overcome sin and live in daily victory over willful disobedience. Maybe, when we truly realize how much God hates sin and how our continual flirting with disobedience is a direct challenge to the lordship of Jesus Christ, we will then become convicted and renew our commitment to holy living and trust once again in His ability to keep us pure. Our sin and disobedience breaks God's heart- it needs to break our hearts as well.

PRIDE

Proverbs 16:18 "Pride goes before destruction, a haughty spirit before a fall."

Pride is a subtle and dangerous enemy. Its very nature keeps us from recognizing and dealing with it. A prideful person would not see themselves as proud and haughty- they are 'discerning' or 'mature' or 'better informed'. They see themselves as having risen above the pitfalls and shortcomings of less enlightened folk and either surround themselves with people who will idolize and patronize them or stand aloof from others while believing that no one measures up to their spiritual level. The cure for pride and arrogance is usually very harsh and humiliating. God will eventually force the prideful person into circumstances that will hopefully humble their heart. But even then the sin of pride makes it difficult to repent. Though others see the reality of their situation, the prideful person continues to be blind to the truth of their plight. The best protection against pride is to always remember that we are dust- there is nothing good in us apart from God. One facet of pride is that it robs God of His glory and gives it to us. Make sure you have people in your life who are honest and straight forward and who are unafraid to boldly confront you when the sin of pride begins to manifest itself in your heart.

THE TESTING OF OUR HEARTS

Proverbs 17:3 "The crucible for silver and the furnace for gold, but the Lord tests the heart."

You could wonder why God, who knows everything, would test our hearts. He already knows every minute detail of our innermost being. The problem is that we do not know. The rich, young ruler thought he had a solid walk with God. But Jesus tested his heart by calling on him to sell all he had. He failed the test because his riches were more important to him than God. There are times when God will test our hearts to see if we have allowed jobs, family, friends or possessions to eclipse His lordship in our lives. Every negative event or circumstance in our life affords us the opportunity to prove our loyalty and trust in God. This does not mean that we are immune to sadness and discouragement or anesthetized to the pain and heartache that tribulation and loss can bring. But it does mean that we should never despair and can remain in the center of God's will no matter what our situation. When God is first in our hearts there is nothing that can cause us to turn our backs on Him. Just ask Job!

FOOLS

Proverbs 17:28 "Even a fool is thought wise if he keeps silent, and discerning if he holds his tongue."

We do not talk much today about someone being a fool. The term is not widely used. For most people the term 'fool' conjures up a harlequin character such as a court jester or a clown. The image is of someone who is simple or stupid. But the word 'fool' occurs over seventy times in the book of Proverbs so it would seem wise to have a good understanding of its meaning. Fools despise wisdom and discipline and hate knowledge. They are chatterers, slanderers, deceivers and opinionated. A fool is reckless, quick tempered, arrogant, and a hot head. They are quick to quarrel and their lips are perverse. In the original Hebrew language five different words are translated 'fool'. They refer to being perverse, silly, lazy, wicked and vile. But the primary idea seems to be someone who only cares about themselves and their own comfort and esteem and has little or no regard for God and His commands. Psalm 14 tells us that a fool says in his heart, 'There is no God'. Notice that it is in his heart that a fool denies God. Sadly there are many people, even in our churches, who profess to believe in God yet deny His existence by the way they daily live and speak. Isaiah speaks of those who honor God with their lips but whose hearts are far from Him. Simply put, a fool is one who lives only for himself and does not have God reigning in his heart, evidenced by his self-centered way of life

THE SIN OF DOING NOTHING

Proverbs 18:9 "One who is slack in his work is brother to one who destroys."

Most Christians judge their own goodness based on the evil that they do not commit. The logic is that 'I am a good Christian because I don't _____' and you can fill in the blank with any sins you would choose. Part of most churches doctrines include 'Rules of Conduct' which specify those things that Christians should avoid. And, although these lists may include some arguable activities, the desire of all of Christ's followers should be to live holy lives free of willful sin. Even then there are areas of sin in the church, such as gossip, slander, lying, unholy attitudes, self centeredness and lack of true compassion, that go either unrecognized or are glossed over in the name of Christian love and unity. But what is generally missed completely is the evil of what we should be doing- but aren't. The obvious things in this area include habits we should end, acts of obedience we should practice and letting our light shine brightly to a lost world. It is not good enough for us to refrain from sin. We must also be about our Lord's business and not be 'slack in our work'. We must 'give of our best', 'work with all our heart' and 'do our best'- all admonitions from scripture. Half hearted, slack and lazy efforts are sinful and unacceptable to our holy God.

LESSENING OUR TRIALS

Proverbs 19:3 "A man's own folly ruins his life, yet his heart rages against the Lord."

Hardship and tragedy strike everyone. This world dishes out a smorgasbord of trials and tribulation to all who reside on this orb. This was part of the curse of Adam and there is no escape except for death. Even death, while bringing final deliverance from the woes of this world to the one, adds additional grief to those left behind. Yet there is much heartache in this world that can be avoided if we would live by God's standards instead of our own selfish desires. The pain and suffering brought about by living in sin and disobedience or by foolishly looking to this world for hope and satisfaction is removed from the plate of those who choose to live according to God's will. To be able to discern first, between the challenges we endure because we live in a sin scarred world and, second, the hardships we face because we have disobeyed God and are living a sinful lifestyle, is vital to finding peace and encouragement. For the first we can expect God's grace and strength to carry us through. The second requires contrition, humility and repentance. Although we may continue to suffer the consequences of our own folly God will always forgive and once again restore our hearts to Himself.

AN HONEST SELF-EXAMINATION

Proverbs 21:2 "All a man's ways seem right to him, but the Lord weighs the heart."

We Christians have a way of getting around what is truly right. If we desire something, we can justify all kinds of ways to make it legitimate. We pledge to use the thing for God's glory or service. We imagine ways it will make us better Christians or help us manage our time so we can be more productive. If we don't like someone we do the same thing with them. We gossip in the name of prayer requests. We can be rude and abrupt and say we are just being honest. We pride ourselves on speaking our minds without any consideration of the blows and wounds we may be inflicting on others. We quote, 'Be angry and sin not' as justification for blowing up at someone while easing our conscience by believing that 'they had it coming'. We tantalize our flesh by disguising our lust with the pathetic excuse that God made the body beautiful and gave us eyes to enjoy that beauty. All of these self-centered indulgences give evidence to a divided heart. If we would be honest with ourselves and allow God to do a deep examination of our hearts we can truly be changed and escape the shallowness of this trap of hypocritical, self-centered living.

SLUGGARDS

Proverbs 22:13 "The sluggard says, 'There is a lion outside!' or 'I will be murdered in the streets.'"

Excuses, excuses! There are many who are just plain lazy. They refuse to take the time and effort to do the work necessary to provide for their basic needs. The Bible refers to them as sluggards or slothful- both references to very slow moving creatures. And not only are these people excessively lazy but they also continually take advantage of others to provide for their necessities and to constantly bail them out of hardship. But just try to admonish them and the excuses come flying out and you are labeled as having no compassion or not being Christ like. But even Paul said that if someone would not work they shall not eat and that such people need to settle down and earn the bread they eat. (II Thessalonians 2) The truly loving and compassionate thing to do with such people is not to keep bailing them out of trouble and enabling them. They need to be held accountable for their sinfulness. Yes, laziness is a sin! Obviously there are spiritual applications as well. Many Christians are spiritual sluggards by making excuses as to why they refuse to serve God by being a faithful witness. They allow sin to remain in their lives and abuse the body of Christ by constantly calling on other Christians to rescue them from their continual difficulties. The root of laziness- whether physical or spiritual- lies in the desire to satisfy the flesh. The cure is found when we repent of our laziness, put the flesh to death and determine to do everything as unto the Lord.

STEER CLEAR OF ENVY

Proverbs 23:17 "Do not let your heart envy sinners, but always be zealous for the fear of the Lord."

Most of us have probably done it. We see what we perceive to be the prosperity and outward contentedness of the wicked and wonder why, especially if at the time we ourselves are experiencing trials and tribulations. Or perhaps we have seen Christians who behave in a less that Christ like manner and yet there appears no retribution from God. Their lives just seem to continue to flourish and they suffer no ill effects from their disobedience. For many who faithfully follow Christ and persevere through much trouble and temptation this can be discouraging. But the writer of Proverbs gives us two great weapons to help us stay focused and to overcome. First is that we be zealous for the fear of the Lord. We must make sure that our hearts are set on our Lord instead of the things of this world that would appeal to our flesh- which is at the root of envy. When we allow ourselves to envy those who seem more prosperous and successful in the world we are letting self rear its ugly head and have unwittingly usurped Christ as Lord of our life. Second, we need to be reminded of what truly is important. In the next verse we are told that there is surely a future hope for us. We are striving for 'a crown of glory that will never fade away'. (I Peter 5:4) Let's keep our eye on the prize! Those who live for themselves are already receiving all the reward that they will get.

BEING STRONG IN THE LORD

Proverbs 24:10 "If you falter in times of trouble, how small is your strength!"

We all know them. We even have names for them like 'fair weather friend'. It seems like they are ready to surrender at the least little problem- and boy do they have problems! When the sun is shining and everything is well then they are pillars of spirituality ready to conquer the world for Christ. But let one little fly in the ointment and suddenly they become sullen, moody and ready to throw in the towel. It is sad how their strength seems to disappear and how quickly they are ready to jump ship. Why? The convenient answer is to say that they are trusting in their own strength and not God's. Although this is a proper observation we need to consider what it means to 'Be strong in the Lord'. The strength we find from God is a result of living daily in faith and obedience. One who can be strong in times of trouble has been consistently faithful. They believe God is in control and that He will give them strength and courage to endure. Holy living increases our confidence in the Lord and gives us a much clearer lens through which to view our trials. Obstacles can be overcome if we are sure of our path, living in obedience, and trusting God for victory.

ENJOYING LIFES PLEASURES

Proverbs 25:16 "If you find honey, eat just enough- too much of it and you will vomit."

There are many acceptable pleasures in life. God is constantly surprising us with gifts to be enjoyed. Whether chocolate, television, computers, recreational activities, video games- the list is indeed abundant. And for the most part these diversions are not wrong in and of themselves. They can be a source of joy in this life and we should thank God for them. It is only when these earthly pleasures become an end in themselves that they can be a snare. The battles we Christians fight are usually not over blatant sin and disobedience but in our overindulgences in acceptable hobbies, habits and activities. Too much ease, comfort and self-gratification is another more subtle and dangerous method of satisfying the flesh. The sin is not in the actions themselves but in our preoccupation with those actions to the neglect of our more important responsibilities. Jesus calls us to come and rest awhile in order to re-energize us for His continuing work. We must learn to enjoy the candy jar without emptying it in one sitting. God, not earthly pleasures, must continually be the focal point of our lives.

STAYING SHARP

Proverbs 27:17 "As iron sharpens iron, so one man sharpens another."

A dull knife is more dangerous than a sharp knife. For the knife to do what it was made for in the best and most efficient way it needs to be razor sharp. It also takes more effort to use a dull knife and the chances of it slipping and injuring the handler are much greater. This is also true of our lives. By staying sharp- that being committed, focused and pure- we are able to more easily and efficiently live the Christian life and be of service to God. But living in this world can definitely take the edge off our walk. When we lose that focus and commitment and begin to compromise then a spiritual dullness starts to set in. Our daily walk becomes ponderous and our service to God loses its joy and digresses into being a chore. That's why it is important to have friends who not only share your hobbies and interests but also love you enough to do what is necessary to keep you sharp. Another proverb says that wounds from a friend can be trusted. Our journey with God becomes much easier and more productive when we travel with others of like heart and mind, helping each other to stay sharp and to keep on the right road.

RIGHTEOUS ANGER

Proverbs 29:10 "A fool gives full vent to his anger, but a wise man keeps himself under control."

We call it 'righteous indignation' or we quote 'be angry and do not sin'. Some of us even ignorantly justify ourselves by trying to point out that Jesus got angry too. These are all lame and pitiful attempts to justify sinful anger in our lives. There is actually a fairly simple way to tell when anger is acceptable and when it is wrong. When this world's injustice and cruelty causes suffering and pain it should make us angry. When God is mocked and disrespected by those who should be giving Him praise and glory we should be angry. When thousands die every day and are lost for all eternity we should be angry. The anger prompted by these scenarios will then prompt us to positive, Godly actions. Anger gives us incentive to constructive actions. It is when we feel we are being personally wronged or attacked and lash out with spiteful speech, unholy attitudes or violent actions that anger becomes destructive and sinful. Fuming, uncontrolled outbursts, the cold, hard stare- the list goes on- are all by-products of sinful anger. The focus of our wrath and the actions that anger produces are what determines whether anger is righteous or sinful.

MORE THAN JUST 'ME AND GOD'

Ecclesiastes 4:12 "Though one may be overpowered, two can defend themselves. A cord of three strands is not quickly broken."

There are those in Christendom who try to stand alone. These are the ones who say they don't need to go to church to be a Christian. They claim the great outdoors is their church and they prefer to worship God in a cathedral of trees. Besides, the church is full of hypocrites anyway. Their walk with God is nobody else's business and what they do is between them and God. The problem lies in that, although there is an element of truth in these statements, they are heavily one-sided. We were never meant to stand alone. You cannot be a Christian and ostracize yourself from the rest of God's people. Worship needs to be both private and corporate. There are also hypocrites on the job, in our families and among our friends but we do not desert any of them. And we have an obligation to exhort, admonish and encourage one another because our successes and failures do affect others. We also need to be using our spiritual gifts for the benefit of other believers. Those who set themselves apart from others in their walk with God are usually just afraid of accountability and responsibility. Their brand of Christianity ends up being weak and shallow. We will not be alone with God in heaven and neither should we focus on just being alone with God in this world.

BUILDING FOR OUR DREAMS

Ecclesiastes 5:7 "Much dreaming and many words are meaningless. Therefore stand in awe of God."

Dream big dreams, people say. Expect great things. Make tomorrow better than today. Yet is it meaningless to hope, dream and expect great things? This admonition is not against having a vision, goals or big dreams. There are those whose lives are consumed with 'if onlys' and 'what ifs'. While their daily existence is filled with discouragement, disillusionment and defeat they continuously speak about how they are going to do this or that when such and such happens. Their hopes are dependent on winning the lottery, getting the inheritance, landing that dream job, finding that special someone or any number of other fantasies. But in their actual lives they are leaving a legacy of failures, missed opportunities and broken lives. It is important to have dreams and to set goals, but not in the vacuum of unproductive daily living. What we do faithfully today is the bedrock upon which our God-given dreams and hopes for tomorrow can be firmly anchored. By being faithful today we can fully realize God's plan and will for our lives. Living in faithful obedience and desiring God's will above all else must be at the core of all our dreams, visions and aspirations.

CLEMENS RUSSELL

REFOCUSING OUR APPETITE

Ecclesiastes 6:7 "All man's efforts are for his mouth, yet his appetite is never satisfied."

Let's face it. For most of us our time is consumed with putting food on the table, clothes on our backs and keeping a leak free roof over our heads. About half of our days are filled with activities to provide these necessary things and then we spend the other half of our 24 hours resting and recreating so we can do it all over again. But, when the only appetites we seek to fulfill are the physical appetites, then we will never be satisfied. It is when we develop a hunger and thirst for God and begin to do the things necessary to satisfy our spiritual appetite that we start to find purpose and meaning for our lives. And as our appetite for God increases we will discover that it takes less and less to satisfy our worldly appetites. We find that the food, clothes and shelter that our physical bodies need does not have to be the focus of our lives. The pendulum of our efforts begins to swing away from fulfilling our physical needs and towards meeting our spiritual desires. Caring for our bodies is no longer an end in itself but a means to a greater end- growing our relationship with God.

FUTILE PRAYERS

Isaiah 1:15 "When you spread out your hands in prayer, I will hide My eyes from you; even if you offer many prayers, I will not listen. Your hands are full of blood."

There is a misconception that God listens to everyone who prays. The idea is that God hears everybody no matter who they are or what they do. This causes many to mistake God's divine providence and care for answered prayer. God does hear and respond to every person who realizes their lost condition and out of remorse cries out to Him. But if prayer is coming into God's presence and bringing our requests and adoration before His throne then only those with clean hands and a pure heart will be given an audience. And only the blood of Jesus can cleanse us completely and enable us to stand in the Father's presence. God will never compromise His holiness. Fortunately, in His grace and mercy, He sees our condition and is constantly striving to bring us to, and keep us where, we need to be. For the true essence and power of prayer is not getting our laundry list of requests fulfilled. The foundation of prayer is having communion and fellowship with a loving and holy God. By knowing God in this way we gain tremendous power and effectiveness in our prayer life and in our daily walk with Him.

THE LORD ALONE

Isaiah 2:17 "The arrogance of man will be brought low and the pride of men humbled; the Lord alone will be exalted in that day."

When it comes right down to it, the arrogance and pride of man is at the root of rebellion against God. It may be exhibited in the ideas of secular humanism which exalts man and views this world through egocentric eyes. It can be evident in the stubborn refusal of someone to recognize their own sins, deficiencies and inadequacies which could lead them to repentance and cause them to turn their life over to God. Or it can be seen in the continual battles one fights between the flesh and the spirit because of their unwillingness to crucify the flesh and make a total and unconditional surrender to the authority and lordship of Jesus Christ. However the manifestation, self-centered arrogance and pride will always be found at the core of rebellion. Even our thoughts of heaven can become distorted when we only focus on what we will receive and how we will benefit and what's in it for us while the potential for continually praising and worshipping God and spending eternity in fellowship with Christ receives just an obligatory acknowledgement. 'The Lord alone will be exalted in that day' deserves more than passing recognition. His praise, worship and adoration should not only be the focal point of our life on this earth but also the reigning desire of our anticipation of eternity!

HOLD HIS STANDARDS HIGH

Isaiah 5:21 "Woe to those who call evil good and good evil, who put darkness for light and light for darkness, who put bitter for sweet and sweet for bitter."

You expect this type of thinking in the world. But in Isaiah's time, as well as our own, this mentality had swept over the people of God. In so many churches moral absolutes have been cast aside for moral relativism and redefinition of sin in the name of Christian love. Tolerance and acceptance are embraced for fear of being thought of as narrow minded and uncompassionate. Christianity has recalibrated her moral compass away from God's word and His will and towards the humanistic idealism of a carnal and self-centered world. Sadly, this has been mankind's legacy throughout the centuries. The danger of manipulating God's standards to accomplish our own agendas has always been a snare- whether it is the 'church' approving the slaying of thousands during the crusades and inquisitions or an individual justifying an adulterous affair. The moral and ethical standards of God and His word not only will never change, but they are just as valid and trustworthy today as ever. And even though the world will never embrace God's truth, we, as His children, must continue to hold high His most holy standards.

DO YOUR EYES SEE THE KING?

Isaiah 6:5 "'Woe to me!' I cried. 'I am ruined. For I am a man of unclean lips, and I live among a people of unclean lips, and my eyes have seen the King, the Lord Almighty'"

There is flippancy in much of Christendom concerning our attitude toward God. It seems as if many take for granted the fact that they can have an audience with the King of the universe at any time. Some even struggle with spending time in prayer and fellowship with God. We should continually remind ourselves of not only the privilege to commune with the Lord of Lords, but also the price that was paid to grant us this most holy honor. In our familiarity with God we should never lose those aspects of awe, reverence and fear that keep us humbled and inspired. Many of us will make fools of ourselves for worldly leaders and entertainers in hopes of catching a glimpse or receiving an autograph. We place our pastors and religious leaders on pedestals while we approach God as if we are doing Him a favor or fulfilling a tedious obligation. We need to ask God for a vision that will burn deep into our hearts the awesome truth of His holiness and glory, a vision that will inspire us to properly honor and revere Him each time we enter His presence.

EVERYONE DIES

Isaiah 25:7 "On this mountain He will destroy the shroud that enfolds all peoples, the sheet that covers all nations; He will swallow up death forever."

The curse of death is indeed universal. 100 years from now 99.9% of those alive today will be gone. Death is the one malady for which the world will never find a cure. Although our life spans have increased a few years it seems that the diseases of old age have multiplied as well. Billions of dollars are spent every year trying to reverse, retard or just mask the effects of aging. Yet eventually, everyone dies. We must remember however that death itself is the result of a larger problem- sin. God conquered death for us when He defeated sin through the perfect life and sacrifice of Jesus Christ. It is because of sin in our lives that death has a rightful claim upon our body, soul and spirit. But when we receive the cleansing Christ gives and our sins are washed away then deaths only claim is to our physical bodies which are made of the dust of this corrupted world. Our souls and spirits have been set free. And when this world is remade we will dwell here forever in an equally new and perfect physical body!

LIVING IN KING-SIZED COMFORT

Isaiah 28:20 "The bed is too short to stretch out on, the blanket too narrow to wrap around you."

A while back the bumper sticker 'God is my Co-Pilot' was popular- you can still see a few around today. Another bumper sticker more accurately depicts the truth, 'If God is your co-pilot, change seats'. There are many who want God to be a part of their life. The problem is that it's still 'their life'. God desires and deserves to be Lord. He wants nothing more or less than your all. Those who insist on having the final word, on doing their own thing, and on delegating to God a secondary place in their life, will never find true comfort or satisfaction. The bed will always be too short and the blanket too narrow. God is not a hobby to entertain us when we feel the urge or a lucky charm to protect us from our mistakes or 'bad luck'. He is King of Kings and Lord of Lords and He demands our absolute and total surrender, commitment, dedication, loyalty and obedience. Only then will we discover our king sized bed and our over-sized, down filled comforter- true and lasting contentment and satisfaction!

RIGHTEOUSNESS AT THE CORE

Isaiah 32:17 "The fruit of righteousness will be peace; the effect of righteousness will be quietness and confidence forever."

Sometimes we need to boil life down to our own personal relationship with God. It is wrong to become so inwardly focused that we ignore the needs and cries of the world or are indifferent to our brothers and sisters in Christ. After all, we are here to serve. But the peace, quietness and confidence in which we live are not dependent on our circumstances. The world may despise and abuse us. The church may disappoint and hurt us. But remember that we are not responsible for the results of our obedience. We are simply called to live consistent holy lives. Our righteousness does matter in that it keeps us in the center of God's will and under His watchful care. All we possess- even our health and life- can be taken away. But no one can touch the loyalty of our hearts. Our hearts stay pure and strong when we walk in love and in obedience to all of the will of God. When there is darkness all around we can keep our hearts right and abide in peace, quietness and confidence of soul by continuing to dwell in the glorious light of His will.

LONGING FOR HIM

Isaiah 33:2 "O Lord, be gracious to us; we long for You. Be our strength every morning, our salvation in time of distress."

All of us desire God's grace. We need God's grace. We could not be whole without it. And who would not want God's strength on a daily basis or His help in rough times? We would all relish this consistent closeness and intimacy with God. But easily overlooked is the simple phrase 'we long for You'. Usually our desire for God is for what He can do for us and not for God Himself. We despair and cry out to Him for whatever need we have at the moment. Our circumstances drive us to our knees and become the catalyst for our most urgent prayers. God does want to be our source of strength and help. Yet He also desires our fellowship, worship and adoration. When we only come to God if we need or want something and when our primary motivation for our petitions is self-focused then we are treating the Almighty like our personal Santa Claus. It is when we long for Him and when our desire is for His glory and presence that we can discover continual grace, strength and salvation in times of distress for our daily walk.

GOD IS GOD

Isaiah 40:25 "To whom will you compare Me? Or who is My equal" says the Holy One."

Every so often it is good for us to remember exactly who God is. The tendency is for us to gradually minimize God as we struggle with our day-to-day challenges and trials. He can slowly shrink to no more than someone to carry us through our next problem or to meet our needs or to provide for our wants- whether of the flesh or spirit. What degenerates within us is a God who exists mostly for our own desires and we end up living our lives in order to either curry His favor or avoid His wrath. The focus shifts from God to ourselves and we lose the freedom, spontaneity and intimacy of a relationship once based on His lordship and our servant hood. God is who He is and has the complete right to do whatever He pleases. The wonderful fact that it pleases Him to use us and bless us when we yield to His complete Lordship should inspire us to continually commit Him and reflect upon His greatness. Our lives find their greatest abundance and fulfillment when we maintain a right perspective of God and have a proper understanding of the true nature of our relationship with Him.

　　　CLEMENS RUSSELL

THE ONLY LORD

Isaiah 43:11 "I, even I, am the Lord, and apart from Me there is no Savior."

Many today cringe at the exclusiveness of our belief that there is only one God and Savior. The watch words are tolerance and acceptance. We are supposed to not just respect the religious beliefs of others but also to accept their validity as being true expressions of faith for those who embrace them. But for those who accept the authority of the Bible the message is crystal clear. There is only one God and one Savior, Jesus Christ. All other paths are dead ends leading to destruction and eternal separation from God. This may seem harsh and narrow minded to many but it is true just the same. When you consider that biblical Christianity focuses on God taking the initiative to reconcile man to Himself, while all other belief systems teach how we can reconcile ourselves to God through our own efforts, then the prideful and self-centered nature of these religions and cults becomes clear. For Christians God is the Lord, Christ is the Savior of the whole world and the Bible is His sole authority for us. Any additions or deviations from these truths will lead us into the quagmire of religious confusion and compromise.

WHO ARE THE WICKED?

Isaiah 48:22 "There is no peace', says the Lord, 'for the wicked."

To understand this verse we need to define two important words. First is peace. Peace is not the absence of war or the lack of troubles and trials. It is not dependent on outward conditions but transcends them. Peace is satisfaction and contentment based upon the presence of God in our lives and an active pursuit of a holy relationship with our Lord. Peace is dwelling in the center of His will. It is knowing by faith that no matter what may transpire in our lives we can trust God to bring us through and lead us to eternal life. The second needing definition is 'the wicked'. As humans we define wickedness by our actions and their consequences. We assume that the more vile and heinous the action, and the more devastating the consequences, then the greater the wickedness of the perpetrator. The problem is that, by adhering to this idea of wickedness, most of us can view ourselves as not being wicked because we haven't done any of 'those things'. But God defines the wicked as those who follow their own way instead of His. It is the act of our rebellion, not the result of our rebellion that classifies us as wicked. Peace is for those living in complete obedience to God's will, word and way.

THE SOURCE OF DOUBTS

Isaiah 51:7 "Hear me, you who know what is right, you people who have my law in your hearts: Do not fear the reproach of men or be terrified by their insults."

The Lord knows those who are His and we also know that we belong to Him. We know what is right and we know if our hearts are truly His. Our doubts have their roots in two areas. Our negative circumstances may have discouraged us and may cause us to question God's work in our lives. But we must remember that we have no control over our circumstances and that God's promises are true no matter what may be happening in our lives. We must keep our eyes on things above and not allow the negatives to take our hearts off our Lord and place them on the things of this world. Then there are those times when we fail in our walk, either by sinful acts or by sinful disobedience. Instead of simply confessing our sin and submitting to God's will we begin to make excuses or try to justify why we did this or why we can't do that. But deep inside we begin to feel a nagging sense that something is not right. That is when our doubts are truly justified. When circumstantial doubts assail us we need to have faith and commit ourselves to be strong and courageous. When we step out of line we need to confess our sin, rebellion and disobedience and recommit ourselves to putting God's will first in our lives.

GLADLY DOING RIGHT

Isaiah 64:5 "You come to the help of those who gladly do right, who remember Your ways."

How many times have we said things like 'I have to do the right thing' or 'Why is it so hard to be good?' Maybe we need to do an 'attitude check' on our holiness mentality. There is a joy in serving Jesus and living a righteous life. When our hearts are set on Him and our lives are continually devoted to doing His will then there is a joyful spontaneity in obeying Jesus. We should 'gladly do right' at every opportunity. Our dedication to Him should be reflected in our eagerness to do the right thing even when those around us would tempt us to compromise. Sometimes the flesh is allowed to gain an influence in our lives and then a conflict develops between the 'easy' way and the right way. For those devoted to Christ the easy way should always be the right way! The cost of indulging our sinful nature and the consequences of spiritual laziness should cause us to run to Him and joyfully embrace the right and holy path. Remember that Paul saw the need to 'die daily'. When we lose our spiritual edge and allow the flesh a foothold we begin to mistakenly focus on this life's joys. This results in our service to Christ digressing from a joy to a burden. There should always be a joy in doing right and in daily serving our Lord.

A GOD OF MERCY AND WRATH

Jeremiah 15:6 "You have rejected Me," declares the Lord. "You keep on backsliding. So I will lay hands on you and destroy you; I can no longer show you compassion."

The prevalent concept of God in today's world is that He is so full of love, mercy and compassion that, no matter what we do, He will always be good and kind and loving. God's love, mercy and compassion are indeed great but that is only one side of our Creator. He is also a God of wrath, justice, righteousness and judgment. When we go our own way and continue to actively sin and when we reject God's standards and replace them with the world's standards we alienate God. When we make excuses for our sins instead of confessing and repenting and we acknowledge God with our mouths but reject Him by our actions and attitudes, God will become displeased and angry. He can no longer show us compassion. We then become objects of His judgment and wrath! In essence, when we live this way, we are trampling the blood of Jesus under our feet. Everything will not be OK for those who continue in this vein. We cannot enjoy the benefits of salvation which Christ's blood supplies without also taking on the responsibility of holy living which the blood also affords. If we continue to backslide and reject God by our actions we will surely reap what we sow.

THE ESSENCE OF BEING A CHRISTIAN

Jeremiah 24:7 "I will give them a heart to know Me, that I am the Lord. They will be My people, and I will be their God, for they will return to Me with all their heart."

As followers of Jesus Christ and servants of God we should do our best to live holy lives and walk faithfully every day. Our desire should be to please Him and to dwell in the center of His will. When we fall short or get distracted by our own will or the flesh we need to flee back to our heavenly Father, returning to Him with all of our hearts. Day by day we pray, fellowship, feast on His word, praise and worship Him and make God more and more the dominant theme of our daily life until that moment when we open our eyes and behold our Savior face to face. We are actually cultivating an authentic relationship with the King of Kings! And although the actual working out of our living for Christ is filled with challenges, twists and turns, and daily surprises, having a relationship with God pretty well sums up the essence of what being a Christian is all about. Adding to the wonder and joy of being His disciples is the fact that He gives us not only the strength, wisdom and grace to accomplish this task moment by moment, but also puts within our hearts the desire to know Him and serve Him. He indeed is worthy of eternal praise!

GOD'S ULTIMATE GOAL

Jeremiah 32:41 "I will rejoice in doing them good and will assuredly plant them in this land with all my heart and soul."

We are all aware that God wants us to love Him with all of our heart, soul, strength and mind. It is His will and command. His desire is that we be completely devoted to Him and that we strive daily to live in obedience and conformity to His will. But do we also realize that God is equally devoted to us? His desire is to bring us joy, contentment and victory. He wants to bless us and 'rejoices in doing us good'! And He does it with all of His heart and soul. We need to remember, though, that God's ways are much higher than our ways. We may be tempted to see in this verse a promise for earthly wealth, comfort and blessing. And even though every good thing we enjoy comes from our Father, God views His work and blessing in our lives through the eyes of eternity. His purpose is not to make us happy and comfortable in this life on earth. He has prepared a better place for us in eternity and has done everything to assure our safe arrival. But until that day, God's will for us centers on using us to bring others whom He also loves into His eternal presence. His ultimate goal is to plant all of us in the land of His eternal kingdom.

BEING PATIENT

Jeremiah 42:7 "Ten days later the word of the Lord came to Jeremiah,"

The leftover leaders in Israel were in a tight spot. There had been a revolt against the Babylonian rule, people had been murdered and now answers were needed from God as to what direction to take. Yet it was ten days before God got back to Jeremiah with the answer; ten long, fearful, anxious days. In today's world of instant gratification and 'got to have it now' impatience, the grace and discipline of waiting on the Lord has been lost. So many times we allow our circumstances to force us into making decisions for ourselves. We mistakenly think that if we don't do something, then everything will get all fouled up. On top of it all we use our situation to fabricate a false sense of God's leadership. We trust in our own ability and reason instead of trusting in God's assurance that He will give us guidance and direction. Saul was another impatient leader. He could not wait for Samuel but, instead, allowed his circumstances to lead him into disobedience. God knows what He is doing and also the best time to do it! We would do well to rediscover what it means to wait patiently for the Lord.

MAKING GOD SMILE

Lamentations 3:33 "For He does not willingly bring affliction or grief to the children of men."

This is an interesting verse to find in the middle of a book lamenting the punishment and destruction being administered by the judgment of God. It is also a very revealing verse. God is not some celestial eavesdropper waiting to send anguish and discipline for our willful disobedience at the drop of a hat. God's judgment on the Israelites followed years of continual rebellion and earnest pleadings and promptings from God for His people to repent and obey His commandments. The fact that the world today is full of wickedness and sin, yet God continues to withhold the full measure of His wrath and judgment, is testimony to His great grace and mercy. It is in the very nature of God to nurture, love, bless and care for those He has created. And though our sins will bring about His judgment and correction, His desire is to bring us good. Nothing speaks more to this fact that the passion of our Lord. It is an encouraging truth that God is much more willing to be a loving and caring Father than a stern and punishing judge. Living in obedience, holiness and love brings a smile to God's face and joy to His heart!

SPIRITUAL DRYNESS

Ezekiel 3:7 "But the house of Israel is not willing to listen to you because they are not willing to listen to me, for the whole house of Israel is hardened and obstinate."

Ezekiel's call was to prophesy to his own people, to be a missionary and a pastor to his own nation and to call God's chosen back to repentance. There was only one problem- they were unwilling to listen to Ezekiel, and God, because of their hardened and obstinate hearts. It is still true in a significant way today. There are many in the church that have either lost their focus or have become part of the church through false pretenses. The religion they practice is centered on their own agenda and desires instead of God's will. They have obtained positions of influence and have become the political power brokers in the church. They know the language of the redeemed and are well versed in doctrine. But the lack of spiritual fruit, selfless love and humble compassion belies the true condition of their heart. Their only reality of God today consists of the vapid memories of what they experienced years ago. The dryness of their present walk with God has created a spiritually shriveled shell of self-centered religious hypocrisy. Such is the fate of those who cease to daily listen, obey and desire to keep God first in their lives.

HOPE IN A WEARY WORLD

Ezekiel 7:8 "I am about to pour out My wrath on you and spend My anger against you; I will judge you according to your conduct and repay you for all your detestable practices."

There is no doubt that wickedness is increasing and abounding in these days. Not just the obvious evils of murder, rape, lust, adultery and the like, but also the more subtle evils of hearts and minds turning away from the knowledge and influence of a holy God and turning toward the wanton and indiscriminate satisfaction of selfish and fleshly desires. We have witnessed the slide from wholehearted devotion to half-hearted acknowledgement and ending with self-centered gratification. We are witnessing a wholesale abandonment of the morals, ethics and societal integrity founded on belief in God and the responsibility we have to live according to a higher standard. This has been replaced by a blatant humanistic mentality which embraces a philosophy of 'if it feels good' and 'what's in it for me?' and that has denigrated God to a spiritual something who's sole purpose is to aid and abet us in accomplishing our will and fulfilling our every whim and desire. Yet in the midst of this spiritual fiasco God is still on the throne and in control! And for those who have not sullied their walk with God He promises His sustaining presence and sure deliverance!

THE FOUNDATION OF SPIRITUAL GUIDANCE

Ezekiel 13:3 "This is what the Sovereign Lord says: Woe to the foolish prophets who follow their own spirit and have seen nothing."

There is a dangerous trend in the church today that places personal convictions, private revelation and self-centered worship above all else. The attitude is that one's walk with God is personal and private and is no one else's business. These people are primarily directed by feelings, emotions and 'spiritual encounters' which are usually devoid of scriptural authority or any accountability to the body of Christ. When divine guidance becomes centered in the realm of our feelings and emotions we become susceptible to erroneous and even dangerous decisions and actions. Emotions cannot be trusted by themselves. Most people do not have a consistent track record of Spiritual leadings. They rather exhibit a jerky see-saw of emotional triumph and tragedy. Depending on inner spiritual direction and clearly hearing the Spirit's guidance and voice requires spiritual maturity developed through prayer, the study of God's word and affirmation by the fellowship of believers. Much of what passes for God speaking to people today is based in emotional sentiment and has no foundation in the Bible. Be assured that God's inward voice will never lead us where His word does not confirm.

WHAT PLEASES GOD

Ezekiel 18:23 "Do I take any pleasure in the death of the wicked?" declares the Lord. "Rather, am I not pleased when they turn from their ways and live?"

There are those who reject the idea of a God who is anxious to condemn evil doers and who can't wait for someone to sin so He can punish them. They are right. But neither should we accept the idea that God will look the other way at sin and allow the unredeemed sinner into His presence. God has provided a way that all of the world can be saved from their sin through Jesus Christ. It is when we turn from our own ways and embrace the new life afforded to us by God through Jesus Christ that we will be able to truly live in a way pleasing to Him.

SEEING SIN FOR WHAT IT IS

Ezekiel 36:17 "Son of man, when the people of Israel were living in their own land, they defiled it by their conduct and their actions. Their conduct was like a woman's monthly uncleanness in My sight."

God loathes sin. He hates disobedience. The vulgar descriptiveness of this verse should make that clear. A part of our relaxed attitude toward sin lies in the fact that we do not truly realize the awesome holiness of God. We make excuses and wink at our own shortcomings. We justify our fleshly attitudes and then shrug off the seriousness of our spiritual malaise by claiming God's grace and mercy while we continue to fall short. There is no true remorse or desire to live holier lives. God can more than provide the cleansing and the power to live holier lives and to grow and mature us in our walk with Him. But we must still have the desire and will to want victory over all sin and to live Godly lives. If we would truly love God with all of our heart, soul, strength and mind as Christ commands we should realize how much our laxness and our lazy tolerance for sin disgusts our Heavenly Father. Then we would immediately come to Him in humble and sincere repentance and avail ourselves of all the resources that God is so willing to abundantly supply to enable us to live lives that are holy, righteous and pleasing to Him.

GOD GLORIFYING GOD

Ezekiel 36:22 "Therefore say to the house of Israel, 'This is what the Sovereign Lord says: It is not for your sake, O house of Israel, that I am going to do these things, but for the sake of My Holy name...'"

What things was God going to do? If we read a little further in this 36th chapter of Ezekiel we discover those things- blessings both physical and spiritual- including the promise of a new heart and a new spirit. Throughout history it has always been God taking the initiative. Creation, the call of Abraham and Moses, the choice of David as king, the work of the prophets, sending His only Son and the day of Pentecost are all the result of God reaching out to His children for the sake of His holy name. All that we are and have is a direct result, not of our puny efforts and works, but of His wonderful grace, mercy and love. God's greatest glory comes not in the awesome majesty of His brilliance and light or in the manifestations of His great power and might. His greatest glory comes through His love- love perfectly displayed in His redemptive work through Jesus Christ. The fact that a lost and sinful humanity can be drawn back, convicted, forgiven, healed, have their heart changed from stone to flesh and be restored to a vibrant and healthy relationship with a Holy God is God's greatest achievement in bringing Himself glory.

HUMBLE RESOLVE

Daniel 1:8 "But Daniel resolved not to defile himself with the royal food and wine, and he asked the chief official for permission not to defile himself this way."

If anyone had good reason to compromise it was Daniel. Here he was a captive in a foreign land who had probably seen many of his family and friends slain. To top it off he was still in his teens. And now he was being offered the finest food and drink in the kingdom. Yet Daniel was still resolved not to defile himself. And his resolve was not a self-righteous, defiant, in-your-face rebellion. He remained submissive to his captors and asked permission not to partake of the kings table. Daniel's resolve had a firm foundation. He obviously had a strong relationship and commitment to God, even at his young age. His request to the chief official was more than likely bathed in prayer. His lifestyle up to this point had already gained him favor in this official's eyes. And Daniel's compulsion to stay pure was based on a sincere desire to please God. In the church today there is a lot of clamor about our rights as Christians and we are quick to bristle with righteous indignation when our freedoms are threatened. But we need to make sure our resolves are founded on prayer, Godly character and our spiritual integrity, coupled with a true concern for the needs of others and a sincere dedication to the will of God.

CLEMENS RUSSELL

FAITHFUL WHERE YOU'RE AT

Daniel 6:5 "We will never find any basis for charges against this man Daniel unless it has something to do with the law of his God."

Many have spoken about the impossibility of keeping all of the Mosaic rules, laws and regulations. Yet when we think of Daniel we always picture a righteous and holy man of God. Even Daniel's enemies recognized not only his impeccable dispensing of his political duties, but also his unswerving devotion to God. They ended up creating a scenario where Daniel's consistent and unwavering commitment to God would bring him into conflict with the king. And as most of us know, Daniel's rock-steady faith triumphed. But it is fascinating to note that Daniel could not perfectly keep the law in his situation. He was unable to offer the prescribed sacrifices for atonement and sin. Ceremonial cleansing was impossible without the blood of goats and lambs. The best that Daniel could hope for was to watch his diet, live according to the moral code and pray faithfully three times a day while facing toward Jerusalem. The point is that Daniel was faithful where he was at and with what he had. This needs to be true of us as well. We need to stay loyal in the basics of holy living and prayer. We must remain faithful, not in the realms and areas of another's life or in the hope of different circumstances, but in the places and positions in which God has placed each of us today.

BACKSLIDDEN?

Hosea 5:4 "Their deeds do not permit them to return to their God. A spirit of prostitution is in their heart: they do not acknowledge the Lord."

Notice the three traits of a backslidden person. Their deeds are sinful, their heart is divided and they are no longer concerned about what God may think. It is impossible for a person to return to God while they remain in this condition. Only true repentance can bring someone back to God. To live this kind of life and believe that you still have a walk with God is a mockery and a dangerous self-deception. But a healthy relationship with God carries the opposite traits. Their deeds are holy, their hearts are faithful and whole toward God, and they pursue God and His will on a moment by moment basis. Now is a good time to do this simple 3 point check on the health of your relationship with God. Are you living right? Are you feeling right? Are you thinking right?

ALWAYS ROOM FOR IMPROVEMENT

Hosea 10:12 "Sow for yourselves righteousness, reap the fruit of unfailing love, and break up your unplowed ground; for it is time to seek the Lord until He comes and showers righteousness on you."

Seldom do we see the immediate results of righteousness. Much of the good that we do may never even be rewarded in this world. But we can be certain that God will reward those who are obedient and consistently do the right things. We need to be faithful in sowing righteousness. We must continually return good for evil and live as citizens of the kingdom of heaven. The fruit that we reap, unfailing love, affects not only our relationship with others but also God's relationship with us! When we commit ourselves to righteousness and strive to live in obedience to our Lord it will impact how we feel towards others. We discover that our capacity for compassion will increase and God's ability to work in our lives and partner with us in accomplishing His plans also improves. Yet to remain where we are and as we are is unhealthy. There are always areas in our lives, 'unplowed ground', where we can grow, improve and yield to the lordship of Christ. Whatever your circumstance or situation it is time to seek the Lord. Seek Him until He comes. And He will come to give you all you need to serve Him faithfully and wholeheartedly.

TRUE REVIVAL

Joel 2:12-13 "Even now, declares the Lord, return to Me with all your heart, with fasting and weeping and mourning. Rend your heart and not your garments. Return to the Lord your God, for He is gracious and compassionate, slow to anger and abounding in love and He relents from sending calamity."

Return from what? Return from being driven away from God because of your disobedience. It is amazing how many people are living in sin yet have somehow deceived themselves into believing that their heart is right with God. Sin not only separates us from God, it forces God to have to drive us away. He will never compromise His holiness. It is not our religious posturing or our self-justification that keeps us right before God. It is only the blood of the Lamb. The great news is that, if you have allowed sin to once again enter your life and are living in disobedience outside of His will, you can still return to God. But you must look for Him with all your heart and soul. Of course that means you desire to turn away from your sin with all your heart and soul as well. Remember that you cannot serve two masters. True repentance not only involves feeling sorrow for your sinful way of life- 'fasting and weeping and mourning'- but it also shows willingness and desire to seek God and return to Him with all your heart and soul! When this occurs you will personally discover the meaning of true revival.

MORE THAN AN OBLIGATION

Amos 8:5 "...saying, 'When will the New Moon be over that we may sell grain, and the Sabbath be ended that we may market wheat?' skimping the measure, boosting the price and cheating with dishonest scales."

There is a phenomenon in the church today where people will do their duty of attending church. They give and do whatever their particular denomination determines is proper in order to stay in good standing with God on one day- or even one hour- of the week. But for the other six days they will indulge in whatever fulfills their own desires and ambitions- only to come again to make 'payment' on their spiritual fire insurance. But this way of life is nothing new. The Israelites had succumbed to this lifestyle centuries ago. They couldn't wait for their obligation to God to be over so they could get back to their own selfish and wicked lifestyles. When our service to God becomes an obligation and our own devotion to Him a drudgery and burden we are on dangerous ground. When our yearnings shift from living our lives with Christ at the center to being consumed with our own self-centered needs and when loving God with all of our heart, soul, strength and mind is just another verse instead of the heartbeat of our existence then we need to return to Him with true sorrow and repentance. When the Israelites lived this way they did not escape God's judgment. Neither will we!

THE FRUIT OF DISOBEDIENCE

Jonah 1:15 "Then they took Jonah and threw him overboard, and the raging sea grew calm."

There is no doubt that our actions create consequences, not just for us, but for those around us as well. Someone may decide to drink and drive and as a result destroy their life and the lives of others. A married man may choose to make one adulterous indiscretion and cause immeasurable heartache, not just to his own family, but to others in his circle of influence as well. Jonah, in his attempt to run from God, put the lives of the entire ship's crew at risk. He also extended the wickedness of the Ninevites where he was supposed to be preaching repentance. We may see our 'one small mistake' as innocent or insignificant. But the truth is that we will never know the repercussions our willful failure may cause. Our call from God to live lives of holiness and obedience is not just for show or to parade perfection. It is so that we may reflect the image of Christ and the glory of God. It is so we may always be ready to be used of Him and to be a light to a fallen world. It is so we may be brokers of peace and hope in the midst of turmoil and darkness. Even though Jonah eventually repented and did what God commanded, much loss and tribulation could have been avoided if he had obeyed from the start. When we sow disobedience we will always reap a harvest of heartache and failure whether we see it or not.

ESCAPING THE BELLY OF THE FISH

Jonah 2:1 "From inside the fish Jonah prayed to the Lord his God."

Most of us have gotten off track at one time or another. Perhaps stress or frustration took their toll and we stumbled. Or maybe, like Jonah, the Lord commanded us to do something we were unwilling to do and so we refused. Some may have yielded to temptation and were drawn back into sin. Whatever the reason, we found ourselves out of God's will and our fellowship was broken as we stubbornly continued in our rebellion. Yet God still loves us and His desire is to forgive, cleanse and restore us to Himself. Unfortunately that will not occur until we are willing to repent and turn to Him. For Jonah it took the belly of a great fish to wake him up. For the prodigal son it was when he was slopping the hogs and desiring to fill his belly with pig slop that he came to his senses. When they turned toward God, He was waiting to bring forgiveness, deliverance and restoration. It is hard to understand why we wait so long and subject ourselves to a fish's belly or pig slop before we are willing to return to God. It is a testimony to the power of pride and the depth of self will when we exchange God's glory and love for the scum of this world. And it is also a testimony to God's great love and faithfulness that He is willing to forgive, cleanse and restore us to Himself time and time again!

PICKING UP WHERE WE LEFT OFF

Jonah 3:1-2 "Then the word of the Lord came to Jonah a second time; 'Go to the great city Nineveh and proclaim to it the message I give you.'"

When Jonah disobeyed God he went through much adversity-the storm, the belly of the fish, being vomited out onto land and, most assuredly, the overwhelming guilt and anxiety caused by his disobedience. Avoidable trials and tribulations come to all who backslide and disobey God. And many times the point at which disobedience begins involves God touching an area of our lives that we are unwilling to surrender to Him or perhaps a situation where we refuse to submit to the lordship of Christ. The result is a pitiful and useless shadow of pseudo-spiritual existence that is a mockery of what a vibrant and growing relationship with God is supposed to be. Fortunately God never gives up on us. He will chasten and chide us until we either close ourselves off to Him for good or we come to our senses and return to the lover of our souls. The last hurdle we must cross is that very point, just like Jonah's call to Nineveh, which began our path down the road to disobedience in the first place. When we return to God we don't have to start from the beginning. But we do need to pick up where we left off- hopefully a lot more humble and wise and more steadfast and determined in our submission and commitment to the Lord.

THE SUBTLE LURE OF THE FLESH

Micah 2:11 "If a liar and deceiver comes and says, 'I will prophesy for you plenty of wine and beer.' he would be just the prophet for this people."

This person would be popular in today's society. But most are not acquainted with any Christian prophets who prophesy plenty of wine and beer. But we have heard many who teach that you can be in the world and of the world as well. The problem for the Israelites, as well as for us today, begins when what we want becomes more important than what God wants. When we allow our walk with God to become stale and unproductive then the flesh will begin to exert pressure and start clamoring to be satisfied- with wine and beer or whatever else will turn our focus away from God and onto ourselves. And everywhere there seems to be modern day prophets exhorting us that material prosperity, good health and emotional security are ours by right. When our emphasis in prayer and praise is upon obtaining from God material and physical blessings, and they become the primary sign to us that our hearts are right and that we are in the center of His will, then we have subtly succumbed to the lure and temptation of the flesh. We must remember that our peace, contentment and good cheer does not come because of success and ease in this life but because, like Jesus, we have overcome the world!

THE DISCIPLINE OF LISTENING

Habakkuk 2:1 "I will stand at my watch and station myself on the ramparts: I will look to see what He will say to me, and what answer I am going to give to this complaint."

Prayer is a wonderful privilege that most Christians practice on a regular basis. The awesome wonder of being able to come into the presence of a holy God whenever we desire through the blood of Jesus is truly one of this life's great miracles. But a miracle of even greater majesty is one that few Christians take the time to acknowledge- God answers us! Most of prayer consists of praise and petition. Yet an equally important facet of prayer is listening for God's response. We need to seek answers from God to our prayers in order to truly benefit from the power of prayer. Imagine going to the doctor with a list of symptoms and ills, laying them all out before him with sincere, passionate concern, then getting up and leaving without waiting for the doctor's response. That is how many of us operate in our prayer life. We need to begin to practice the equally important aspect of listening in our prayer lives. God will speak to us- through His word, His Spirit, His people and through His world!

KEEPING THE JOY

Habakkuk 3:18 "Yet I will rejoice in the Lord, I will be joyful in God my Savior."

The prophet had just given a list of calamities that would devastate his life- no figs, grapes, olive oil, crops, sheep or cattle. These things were the mainstays of existence for the people of that time. Yet even without them, not only does Habakkuk pledge continued loyalty to God, but he says it will be joyful loyalty! When trials and tribulations assail Christians today it seems that joy is one of the first things we abandon. We grouse and grumble and become ornery and cantankerous and blame our ungodly behavior on 'I'm having a bad day.". Yet Habakkuk knew that if he kept his focus on God and not his circumstances that he would be able to rise above his situation. With all the worldly voices clamoring for our loyalty and attention we would do well to take a lesson from little known Habakkuk. Let's not be so tied to this life that when we suffer loss and things 'go south' we don't lose our joy in God. For those committed to Christ everything is guaranteed to be all right no matter how bleak things may appear. Our hope is not in the grapes and crops but in our promise of one day seeing our Savior face to face.

THE GREATEST MIRACLE

Zechariah 5:9 "I looked again- and there before me was a flying scroll!"

When was the last time you saw a flying scroll? Or witnessed a burning bush? Or watched an ax head float? Or heard about a blind person's sight restored? The truth is that for millions of Christians their daily walk is devoid of supernatural manifestations. They go to work, enjoy their families, eat, sleep, play and worship without ever seeing great mystical visions or unexplainable phenomenon. This is called living by faith. Sadly there are many Christians who pursue supernatural experiences as a way to bolster their faith. Their spirituality is rooted in their next 'divine' encounter instead of the bedrock of faith in Christ. The acid test of faith is evidenced by those who are living a holy life in the crucible of a mundane world. The emotional bursts of supernatural spiritual encounters may be refreshing and pleasant but they become an unstable foundation upon which to build our faith. If you've never seen a 'burning bush', don't fret. All miracles pale in significance to the miracle of salvation. That God can take a lost and sinful person, forgive them, make everything new and give them citizenship in His kingdom is the greatest miracle of all!

THE OTHER SIDE OF THE TRACKS

Matthew 2:23 "...and He went and lived in a town called Nazareth. So was fulfilled what was said through the prophets; 'He will be called a Nazarene'".

Funny thing is, none of the prophets we know make this claim. What they do say is that Jesus would be despised and ridiculed- just like someone from Nazareth. You see, Nazareth was considered the 'other side of the tracks'. Think of the part of your community that is the least desirable and has the lowest property values. If Jesus had come today, that's where He would have been from. It's a small wonder that respectable people didn't follow Him. Yet in God's eyes the 'other side of the tracks' is not a place, but a position. His perfect holiness is on one side and our sinful condition is on the other. What a wonderful thought that God came to our side of the tracks to redeem and restore us to Himself! Let's be grateful that God, through His Son Jesus, delivered us from our sinful Nazareth to live forever with Him in a New Jerusalem!

REPENTANCE

Matthew 3:8 "Produce fruit in keeping with repentance."

There are three main aspects to repentance. First is the Godly sorrow which leads to repentance. We must truly be sorry for our sins, not just upset about sin's negative consequences. We should also have within our heart a desire and hunger for God. Conviction comes from God and reveals to us the scope of our wickedness and rebellion. We realize the magnitude of our lost condition and our hearts are pierced with our own remorseful and humble anguish. Second is the word 'repentance' itself. To repent means to change your mind. It is realizing we are sinners, being sorry for our sins, and desiring to not sin any longer. Repentance removes us from the realm of a self-centered life into a God centered life. It is when we decide to follow Jesus instead of the ways of this world. Finally there is the fruit that is produced by true repentance. Our prime directive no longer comes from within ourselves but emanates from the throne of God. His word comes alive to us as we strive to live our lives for His glory. The fruit of repentance, the natural outcome of someone truly sorry and desiring to change, is a righteous life. And all of this is accomplished only through God's grace and mercy and by the power of the Holy Spirit.

COUNTING THE COST

Matthew 4:19-20 "'Come follow me,' Jesus said, 'And I will make you fishers of men.'" At once they left their nets and followed Him."

Many have a misconception about this passage. The idea is that Peter and Andrew were minding their own business and simply doing their daily job when Jesus calls them out of the blue to follow Him. They drop everything, without a second thought, and become His disciples. The reality is that Peter and Andrew were already disciples of John the Baptist and had previously had contact with Jesus. (John 1:35-42) Scripture teaches that it is necessary to count the cost before choosing to follow Jesus. And there is most definitely a cost involved. Salvation is indeed a free gift from God that can never be earned or deserved. But in order to take hold of this gift we must let go of the ownership and control of our lives. Many are more than willing to accept Jesus as Savior and receive deliverance from the guilt and punishment of sin. Who would not want eternal life? But Jesus also wants to be our Lord and Master. We cannot partake of the one without submitting to the other. Leaving everything to follow Jesus means surrendering our will and what we want to God's will and what He wants. The cost of following Jesus is our all!

USED OF GOD

Matthew 5:11 "Blessed are you when people insult you, persecute you and falsely say all kinds of evil against you because of Me."

There are those who feel obligated to loudly condemn sin and shout from the rooftops their disgust at the ways of the world. They see everyone they meet as an opportunity to decry sin and thrust the Bible down their victim's throat. Then they bask in the inevitable persecution that follows. Others meekly walk through life not saying a word because 'a person's life is witness enough'. They try to live a good and moral life but the world has no clue as to why. They view these silent Christians as just good people. The truth is found in the middle of these two extremes. We should always be ready and willing to share our faith and hope with others- remembering that the gospel is 'good news'. The focus for our hatred of sin should not be what people do but what sin does to people. We must also live our lives so that others can see Christ in us. Our effectiveness as witnesses does not come from being able to out-shout our opponents or from living good, holy, but silent Christians lives. We are being used of God when people see Christ in us and we boldly share the gospel with them in a loving and compassionate way. Then their response, positive or negative, becomes a result of God's Spirit working through us.

EXCEEDING RIGHTEOUSNESS

Matthew 5:20 "For I tell you that unless your righteousness surpasses that of the Pharisees and the teachers of the Law, you will certainly not enter the Kingdom of Heaven."

This must have been a very difficult teaching for the people to receive. In their eyes the Pharisees and the teachers of the Law were the ones who had the money, time and knowledge needed to understand and keep all of the Law. It is similar to the attitude of many today who view their pastors as holier and closer to God that themselves because 'that's their job'. But God looks on the heart. The righteousness He looks for is one that springs from a heart purified by faith in Christ and 100% devoted to doing His will. The flaw in the Pharisees righteousness was the sin of self-righteousness. True righteousness realizes its emptiness apart from God, seeks to glorify God, and dwells in the simplicity of faith and total commitment. When someone loves God with all their heart, soul, strength and mind they strive to live holy and Christ-like lives. This holy living is in response to His grace and mercy and not to feed their own egos or attempt to gain His favor. Our righteousness exceeds that of the religious elite when its motivation springs from a heart purified by faith, a heart full of love and dedication to God and a heart that seeks to please God above all else.

THE GIFT THAT COUNTS

Matthew 6:3 "But when you give to the needy, do not let your left hand know what your right hand is doing"

It is very easy to slip into the error that someone is a great Christian because they give great gifts and offerings. Many of today's church buildings are adorned with placards and plaques recognizing different people for their generous contributions. Yet there is probably nowhere to be found an inscription honoring someone who gave a couple dollars unless it's the generic-'and everyone else who gave'. In a world that recognizes wealth as fame, power and prestige it is hard for us to keep focused on the truth that God honors the heart, motivation and sacrifice behind the gift and not the gift itself. There are too many people who give out of an obligation or who see their gift as a method of insuring God's blessings. They even give to make a show and gain attention and influence for themselves. Jesus was serious about not letting you left hand know what your right hand is doing. Proper giving that truly honors God has as its prerequisite a heart that is already surrendered to the Lord, a spirit of compassion and obedience, and an attitude of willingness and joy in being able to serve Him by returning to God what He had originally given to us in the first place.

GOOD CITIZENS OF THE KINGDOM

Matthew 6:33 "But seek first His kingdom and His righteousness, and all these things will be given to you as well."

This is a very popular verse that encourages us to put God first and not to be overly concerned with our physical needs. But what does it really mean to give God the preeminence in our lives? In three short phrases our Lord sums up and simplifies what our lives on this planet are all about. First we are to seek His kingdom. God's kingdom is not a physical structure or a man-made organization. His kingdom is made up of those who have surrendered their lives to the lordship of Christ and are truly born again. It is those who have sincerely, and with Godly heartfelt sorrow, repented of their sins and have been reconciled to their Heavenly Father. And it is those who, through prayer, desire and work are striving to see God's kingdom come into the lives of all who are still lost. Second, we are also to seek His righteousness. This righteousness begins in our hearts and attitudes and then becomes manifest in our actions- actions that reflect His holiness and that set us apart as citizens of His kingdom. Third, when we are living with our priorities in order we can be confident that God will provide for all of our necessities- food, drink and clothing. The people of this world extend and expend themselves to obtain the things that appeal to the flesh. The people of the Kingdom of God work for His will to be done and trust Him to provide their earthly needs, not so they can be self-indulgent, but so they can be more effective citizens in His realm.

WHEN WE SHOULD JUDGE

Matthew 7:1 "Do not judge, or you will be judged."

This is a typically misunderstood and misquoted verse. Many see this verse as a blanket command never to judge when in actuality it is a verse condemning hypocrisy. Jesus Himself judges the Pharisees, calling them white-washed tombs. Paul says that judgment begins in the house of God among believers. Even in this passage Jesus admonishes us to remove the plank from our own eye so we can see clearly to remove the speck from our brother's eye. The essence of this passage can be found in the old saying about the pot calling the kettle black. What is condemned in scripture is the hypocrisy of someone eager to point out everyone else's sin when there is hidden, unconfessed or even blatant sin and in their own life. It is similar to the prominent evangelist who condemned sexual sin in a fellow preacher while he was himself guilty of sexual misconduct. When we find forgiveness from God and are committed to living holy lives we have an obligation to speak out against the wickedness of this world. But it should not be with self-righteous disdain. It should come from the humility and compassion of one who, through God's grace, found forgiveness and deliverance and desires others to find it as well.

FACING STORMS

Matthew 8:24 "Without warning, a furious storm came up on the lake, so that the waves swept over the boat. But Jesus was sleeping."

The truth is that sometimes in our stormy moments it seems like Jesus is sleeping. We feel as if we are struggling alone. We cry out but our condition stays the same or even worsens. Yet Jesus is there! He knows and understands and is ready to help. Faith is to believe and trust when feelings and circumstances say the opposite. And just maybe the storm we are so terrified of is of minor significance to our Lord. We do have a tendency to get carried away with worry and stress over things for which God has already given us promises- like food, clothes and shelter. But, big and real or small and insignificant, whatever storm we are facing, we need to cry out to God. He will always hear and answer. And maybe, if we are willing to listen, He will try to teach us something along the way.

OPEN TO CHANGE

Matthew 8:34 "Then the whole town went out to meet Jesus. And when they saw Him, they pleaded with Him to leave their region."

What could have been a great revival ended up being a rejection of the Lord. Perhaps it was fear of the unknown. Two demon possessed men, who were probably icons and legends in the region, are healed. Maybe it was the loss of their livelihood. (It was a questionable livelihood at that as pigs were unclean animals.) Or it could have simply been resistance to change and having to move out of their comfort zone. Whatever the reason, the whole town missed a great opportunity. So Jesus left. Never, as far as we know, to return. We need to always keep our hearts and minds open to Jesus and to whatever work He desires to do. Without a doubt it means change. And sometimes that change is of the drastic variety. But we can rest assured that it will always be for the best!

WHERE HOLINESS BEGINS

Matthew 9:4 "Knowing their thoughts, Jesus said, 'Why do you entertain evil thoughts in your hearts?'"

It is sobering to truly realize that Jesus knows our thoughts. More accurately, what is condemned by our Lord are the inward, evil reasonings. We all battle evil thoughts every day- whether they are rooted in anger, lust, envy, bitterness, hatred or any other undesirable soil. That is part of the continuing challenge of living a spiritual life while still imprisoned in a fleshly body. The thoughts, like birds flying over our heads, cannot be prevented. It is when we take those thoughts and begin to entertain them, like allowing the birds to perch on our shoulders, that we cross the line into sin and disobedience. God knows everything we think about. All the deepest ponderings of our most secret desires are to Him an open book. God's will for us is to keep our thought life pure. That is where true holiness begins. And God provides the strength and wisdom to make it possible. We tend to be lax when it comes to purity in our thought life because we can usually keep it effectively hidden from others. There also seem to be no immediate negative consequences for our less than holy reasonings. Yet that is exactly where most of our unholy actions begin. Purity of heart and holiness in our thought life is the foundation for living a holy life!

LOVING THE CROWDS

Matthew 9:36 "When He saw the crowd, He had compassion on them, because they were harassed and helpless, like sheep without a shepherd."

They were people who, for whatever reason, had come to Jesus to see His power and to hear Him speak. They were searching and yet unfulfilled. They were curious, bored, and inquisitive- they were harassed and helpless. They needed God in their lives in the worst way and Jesus knew it. That is why He had compassion on them. Look at the crowds today. They pack sporting events, concerts, political rallies, theme parks and shopping malls. They are all looking for something to give them satisfaction, meaning and contentment. Yet without Christ their search is a never ending quest of futility. In the midst of all the wickedness in this world, which even of itself is a search for fulfillment and satisfaction, there is still a great hunger for God. He created the crowds. He loves the crowds. He died for the crowds. And He still has compassion on the crowds. So it is our responsibility as Christ's ambassadors to bring the crowds to Him. We need to see what Jesus saw when He viewed the masses. We need to see sheep that are helpless and harassed and in need of a Shepherd. Our hearts must be filled with the compassion of Christ so that we can be the fragrance of hope and life to this despairing and dying world.

THE LIGHT CAN HURT

Matthew 10:25 "It is enough for the student to be like his teacher, and the servant like his master. If the head of the house has been called Beelzebub, how much more the members of his household."

We are called to be like Jesus. Not the sterile representation that the world proposes. They like to emphasize His love, forgiveness, acceptance and tolerance while ignoring His call to be holy, His confrontation of sin and His claim to exclusiveness. The world has a Jesus that fits nicely into their pocket- safe and comfortable but unworthy of any true allegiance or loyalty. When we choose to become followers of Jesus all other commitments and loyalties become secondary. The Jesus we believe in and follow should cause the world to hate us. The truth is that men love darkness rather than light and when the true light of Jesus disrupts their darkened existence they lash out against the light and try to extinguish it. This light of Christ is not a heavenly phenomenon that suddenly shines down from above. We are the light of Christ in the world. When we live victorious, holy lives by the power of the Holy Spirit we expose the world for what it really is. As a result we receive their scorn and anger because we reveal by our transformed existence the emptiness and futility of their own wicked lives.

STORING UP IN OUR HEARTS

Matthew 12:35 "The good man brings good things out of the good stored up in him, and the evil man brings evil things out of the evil stored up in him."

Most people today see those who are exceedingly good- many call them saints- and those who are exceedingly evil. Then there seems to be a wide range in between where they hope that they fall on the upper end of the scale. Jesus simplifies it for us by only casting two categories- good and evil. We can view the teaching of 'the good stored up in him' two ways. One is when we have Christ as our Savior and He is reigning in our hearts. Then our light will shine and the good things we bring out have as their source the Holy Spirit. But if we set up ourselves in our hearts as supreme then the outflow of our hearts will reflect our selfishness, weaknesses and the inherent evil of our lives. The other view is that the things we store up in our lives as a result of our habits, entertainments, recreations, devotions, thoughts and meditations determine the quality of what we say and do. The truth is that both views are valid. The only hope we have of doing and being good is to have our hearts changed by the power of Christ. But then we must continually guard our hearts by monitoring the quality of our daily walk so that what we store up in our hearts honors the One who resides within.

WE NEED A SAVIOR

Matthew 12:36 "But I tell you that men will have to give account on the day of judgment for every careless word they have spoken."

There are probably very few people who are not made at least a little uneasy by this statement of our Lord. For those who hope that the good they do will outweigh the bad this verse tips the scales strongly against them. Yet there is consistency in the teaching of Jesus about the severity of blasphemy which involves both the mouth speaking out of the overflow of the heart and the tree being recognized by its fruit. This verse shows us quite clearly that we cannot make ourselves acceptable to God or walk in holiness and purity of heart by our own efforts and strength. We need help! We need grace and mercy. We need a Savior! What is impossible with man is possible with God. Part of the miracle of redemption is that God removes from us our heart of stone and gives us a heart of flesh. In other words, He removes our stubborn, sinful, self-centered nature and replaces it with a nature that truly loves God. He creates in us a clean heart and we are born again. We become new creatures in Christ and we are transformed! This is not accomplished by our redoubled efforts but by the power of God through the Holy Spirit. And when it does happen we know it without a doubt!

CHRISTIAN SCAM ARTISTS

Matthew 15:11 "What goes into a man's mouth does not make him 'unclean', but what comes out of his mouth, that is what makes him 'unclean'."

No one likes a scam artist. They present themselves as something they are not. But when push comes to shove they are usually exposed for what they really are. They seem to know what they are talking about but they only know just enough to pull the wool over your eyes, deceive you, then take the money and run. They can talk the talk but can't walk the walk. This is what Jesus is talking about. We like to have rules and regulations because we need to live within boundaries. And there are behaviors that Christians need to avoid and also to practice. But when the basis of our Christian life digresses from who we are to what we do we risk the danger of becoming Christian scam artists. The life we live in public must mirror what we do in private behind closed doors. If our motivation for righteousness is not rooted in our hearts we end up running a spiritual scam. We try to present ourselves to others as Christians while harboring envy, jealousy, bitterness, lust and the other sins. But eventually we will be revealed for who we really are. True holy living can only be inspired by a holy heart.

A NEW HEART

Matthew 15:18 "But the things that come out of the mouth come from the heart, and these make a man unclean."

So many today are caught up in the effort to make themselves clean. They vow to quit doing this or start doing that. They go to counseling or join a support group to curb destructive behavior. The cults and religions that seem to be growing the fastest are those that appeal to spiritual pride and teach that you can earn Gods favor and eternal life by the good things you do. Yet it seems that the harder humanity tries to clean itself up the dirtier it becomes. The problem lies in the fact that wickedness and sin are not rooted in the will or in society or in our environment. Wickedness is rooted in the heart which is the Bible says is 'desperately wicked'. We work furiously to clean the outside of the cup but are powerless to deal with the filth and corruption on the inside of the cup. Only through the regenerative power of God can we find true cleansing. The need is not for a change in our actions but for a new heart. This is one reason why we need Jesus Christ. He is the only one who can thrust through the façade of our own self-righteousness and change our heart. He is the only one who can clean the inside of the cup so that we can live holy and pure lives through the power of His Spirit within us. Without this miracle of renewal all of our righteousness is filthy rags.

CONVENIENT OR COMMITMENT?

Matthew 16:1 "The Pharisees and Sadducees came to Jesus and tested Him by asking Him to show them a sign from heaven."

This seems to be a curious request. Jesus has continually been doing miracles but the Jewish leaders ask Him for a sign- and this is not the first time! If they had been following Jesus faithfully they would have seen plenty of signs. But these men were coming to Jesus at their convenience. They were not looking to believe in Jesus. They were looking for reasons to reject Him and to continue living their own way. People do the same thing today. They live their lives their own way with God tagged on as a convenience instead of a commitment. When they are confronted with the shallowness and hypocrisy of their faith they throw out a challenge that if God will do such-and-so then they will believe in Him and surrender to His lordship. Instead of humbling themselves to God and repenting they use their own selfish desires and ambitions as a litmus test for whether they are going to allow God into their life. The arrogance of such an attitude is sadly laughable. When we submit to God on His terms- humility, sorrow, repentance and devotion- He will be able to work the greatest miracle of all in our lives; redemption and regeneration!

'WHO DO YOU SAY I AM?"

Matthew 16:15q "'But what about you?' He asked, 'Who do you say I am?'"

There are a lot of opinions about who Jesus Christ is. Even in the church the beliefs about Jesus are varied. Many would like to believe that He was just a great man or a wonderful prophet. Then they don't have to come to terms with His teachings or His claims of lordship on their lives. They can then feel free to accept or reject whatever does or does not fit into their agenda. But when Jesus confirmed Peter's confession that He was the Christ, the Son of God, it took who and what He is to a whole new level. If Jesus was simply an extraordinary man then men could admire Him, follow His teachings and even enshrine Him. But the truth about Jesus demands much more from us. He demands our allegiance, our devotion, our love, our obedience and our worship. We must come to no uncertain terms with the claims Jesus made about Himself and the claims He lays upon us. He alone is the only way to God, and forgiveness and restoration are found only through Him. Our answer to the question when Jesus asked, 'Who do you say I am?' will determine whether He is just a great man to be emulated or if He is indeed the Son of God and Savior of all mankind. It will determine whether He should be simply admired or if He is indeed worthy of our total commitment, dedication, devotion and worship.

KEEP LOOKING UP

Matthew 17:8 "When they looked up, they saw no one except Jesus."

There are plenty of distractions in this life that can take our eyes off Jesus. It could take the form of our circumstances that would pull us under, much like the wind and waves that caused Peter to take his eyes off Jesus and begin to sink into the water. For some it is the lure of wealth and the preoccupation with money, much like Judas who continually looked into the purse and took his eyes off his Master and Lord. In this verse it was Moses and Elijah that diverted the disciple's focus, much like our church involvement and our efforts to live holy and righteous lives. These can shift our gaze from Christ to the lesser good and our inadequate deeds. It is a good discipline as we live our day to day lives to look up on a regular basis and see only Jesus. It is so easy to get distracted by the many lights, bells and whistles of life in this world. These things can divert or obstruct our view of Jesus. They are not necessarily wrong in and of themselves, and many times even good and beneficial. But it is a wise habit to consistently and continually look up to see only Jesus. This helps us to maintain the right perspective and keep the things of this world in their proper place.

GUARDING THE TONGUE

Matthew 17:24 "After Jesus and His disciples arrived in Capernaum, the collectors of the two-drachma tax came to Peter and asked, 'Doesn't your teacher pay the temple tax?' 'Yes, He does,' he replied.

For most of us living the Christian life is done in the framework of living in an earthly condition. Very few of us spend the majority of our time praying, studying the Bible, meditating and being continuously involved in Christian service. Our walk with God is fleshed out in the reality of a life that may include a family, a 40 to 60 hour work week, struggles with bills, breakdowns and daily burdens- all of the nitty gritty that constitutes living. So it is inevitable that we will at times be caught off our guard and, just like Peter, blurt out something that we are unsure of or that may not even be true. Fortunately God loves us even in our weakness. He will confront us with our indiscretion and give us the opportunity to make things right. He may either allow us to follow through on our rash statements or give us the grace and courage to repent, admit our mistake, seek forgiveness from those we have spoken to, and make restitution. Learning to hold our tongue, as challenging a task as that is, can still be easier than cleaning up the debris of unbridled words. God is more than able to give us this victory even in our most earthly condition!

EASILY FORGIVING OTHERS

Matthew 18:35 "This is how my Heavenly Father will treat each of you unless you forgive your brother from your heart."

Do you remember when you first asked God, from your heart, to forgive you of your sins and you were born again? The freedom and joy you felt were indescribable! We are all wise enough to know that as we walk in the light we are constantly in need of continual forgiveness. Our initial forgiveness was based on God's grace and mercy and required faith and true repentance on our part. And the continual, daily cleansing and forgiveness we need is also based on grace and mercy. But it also requires that we walk in the light and forgive one another from our hearts. Jesus stated it bluntly when He said, 'But if you do not forgive men their sins, your Father will not forgive your sins." The importance of unity and love among the body of Christ is of vital importance to God. Some may think that it is impossible to forgive certain people because of all the evil and pain they have caused. Yet, compared to the heartache and hurt we have caused God because of our own sin and rebellion, what others have done to us doesn't even begin to come close. We are forgiven a debt in the billions while God only requires us to forgive a debt of a few cents. By remembering the things that God daily forgives us of each time someone needs our forgiveness, any difficulty we may face in forgiving others from our hearts will be quickly removed.

CLEMENS RUSSELL

SIMPLE, CHILDLIKE FAITH

Matthew 19:13 "Then little children were brought to Jesus for Him to place His hands on them and pray for them. But the disciples rebuked those who brought them."

Sometimes when we become involved in what we consider the 'weightier matters' of Christianity we lose focus on what is truly important. Jesus had been teaching and discussing with the religious leaders. As His disciples relished in His wisdom and the attention they were receiving, the entrance of some insignificant children probably disrupted their spotlight and disturbed them to the point that they 'rebuked those who brought them'. Fortunately the Lord intervened and brought everything back into the correct perspective. The kingdom belongs to the children- those whose childlike faith results in complete love, trust, faith and obedience. Just because we have a tendency to complicate Christianity and replace the simplicity of redemption with deep theology and scholarly ponderings does not change the truth that even a child can understand the basics of the gospel. Those who have a deeper knowledge of scripture and who are able to study in the original languages and those who have been gifted with keen intellects and insights must guard against losing track of the fact that the gospel is meant to be embraced and comprehended by the simplest of us all- a little child. There are multitudes of Christians worldwide that cannot even read but whose child-like faith puts many of the most educated and knowledgeable of us to shame.

THE FALLACY OF SALVATION BY WORKS

Matthew 19:16 "Now a man came up to Jesus and asked, 'Teacher, what good thing must I do to get eternal life?'"

This verse summarizes how those in the world, who confess a belief in the divine but reject the Lordship and divinity of Jesus Christ, see the path to salvation. The theory is that if you are able to pile up more good deeds than bad by the time you leave this world then the heavenly scales will tip in your favor and you will be safe. So the quest for eternal life becomes a celestial gambit in the hopes that you have enough chips to cash in at the end of the game in order to gain entrance at the pearly gates. But there are at least three glaring problems with this brand of theology. First, there is no way to remove the stains that the 'bad things' leave. Even in our worldly relationships there is a need for sorrow, confession and repentance when we wrong another person. If we are unable to buy another person's forgiveness by good works then what makes us think that we can buy a holy God's forgiveness? Which brings us to the second point- God is holy and no unforgiven sinner will be allowed into His presence, period. The absolutely exclusive means for the purging of sin is the shed blood of Jesus Christ. And thirdly, salvation by works as a way to obtain eternal life is selfish and rooted in the ego. It is only when our desire for our own eternal life is usurped by our desire for reconciliation with God that we will discover the humility necessary to truly repent and surrender to Christ.

FILLING THE LACK

Matthew 19:20 "'All these I have kept', the young man said, 'What do I still lack?'"

There are those who say that as long as you live a good life and do the best you can that things will be all right in the end. But the truth is that everyone suffers from lack. That is why there are a lot of unhappy people in church. They get salvation and then mistakenly begin to trust in the things they do in order to keep God's favor. Their life becomes bondage to rules, regulations and taboos that rob them of their joy and freedom in Christ. Holy living becomes a warped end in itself that perversely strokes the ego as they parade how much better and more righteous they are than others- all the while languishing in the hidden reality that they suffer from great lack and emptiness. So then they deepen the cycle by trying even harder until they collapse in a heap of exhausted frustration and defeat. Jesus' solution is simple. Let go of self and grab hold of Him. Make His will paramount. Give up the pseudo-riches of your own self-serving and self-righteous ways and follow Him in love, simplicity and truth. When we admit to our selfish ambitions and surrender everything to God our lack will disappear and we will find the true contentment and satisfaction our hearts are starving for.

HOW TO HAVE TREASURE IN HEAVEN

Matthew 19:21 "Jesus answered, 'If you want to be perfect, go, sell your possessions and give to the poor, and you will have treasure in Heaven. Then come, follow me.'"

Usually we do well in our service to others. We will give to charities, help the less fortunate and keep ourselves from really 'bad' sins. And this helps many to fall into the delusion that they are becoming good enough to gain God's favor and make it to heaven. Yet God is not interested in our cursory and feeble righteousness. His desire for us is that we put Him first in our lives. For the gentleman in this story wealth was the most important thing in his life- a thing he was unwilling to give up for God. It could have been a career, a relationship, a family, a position or a possession. Whatever stands in the way and interferes with putting God first in our lives is the very thing God will put His finger on. He commands for us to surrender that thing and then follow Him. When our dreams and aspirations are anchored in the things of this world our hearts will always be divided. Putting our hope in God and placing Him continually first in our lives makes us perfect, content, fulfilled and at peace. This is because our desire and motivation becomes pure and our foundation is on the rock of Christ and not on the sinking sand of this world.

CLEMENS RUSSELL

TO SERVE OR BE SERVED?

Matthew 20:26 "Not so with you. Instead, whoever wants to become great among you must be your servant."

It is interesting how through the ages the disciples and other church leaders have been put on pedestals. Even today we give titles and special privileges to the clergy and other spiritual leaders. From the reserved parking space in the local church to the admiration and devotion given to televangelists, it seems like many servants of God are caught up in being served instead of serving. This is just another example of the deceitful damages of the flesh. It is not the type of sin or the severity of the action that condemns us. It is the desire to serve our own self-interests and to fulfill our own personal needs. It is when we seek our ease and comfort at the expense of others that we are lead into the error of self-serving pride and which causes us to focus on ourselves at the expense of others. While the disciples seemed to continually squabble over which of them would be the greatest, Jesus was perfectly modeling the 'came to serve, not to be served' philosophy. We need to periodically evaluate whether the tenor of our lives is one of self service or one of honest and humble service to Christ and to others.

PROPER ATTIRE

Matthew 22:12 "'Friend,' he asked, 'How did you get in here without any wedding clothes?' The man was speechless."

The gospel is universal in its appeal and crosses all the lines of culture, social standing and race. All who call on the name of the Lord will be saved. While all other religions and cults depend on the person adopting the culture of the group and the outward appearances they promote, Christianity transcends culture and allows the believers to truly adopt the culture of the kingdom of God. Though the worldwide church is vastly different from a cultural and ethnic standpoint, we are all unified in heart and in our devotion to, and love for, our Savior Jesus Christ. At the marriage supper of the Lamb there will be a unified diversity that this world cannot imagine and will never know. Our differences will all melt away as we are cast into a new mold of a white-robed throng praising and glorifying God for all eternity. God cares not for our earthly heritage or condition. But His one pre-requisite must be met- that we are clothed properly. We must put off the old man and, through the redeeming, cleansing and sanctifying blood of Christ, put on the new man. This man must be made in the image of our Savior. Pure white garments are the only acceptable attire for the great wedding feast and for citizens of the kingdom of God!

THE ESSENCE OF LOVE

Matthew 22:40 "All the law and the prophets hang on these two commandments."

Loving God with your all and loving all others as yourself. Jesus boils down all the do's and don'ts and all the rules and regulations, into this simple formula. Yet still we fudge and fumble. One of the reasons is that we don't have a clear idea of love. It is easy to say we love God. But in this area actions do speak louder than words. The love Jesus is referring to is a love that puts God and others ahead of us. This love is centered in our will and, although it can create emotion, its fulfillment is not dependent on how we feel. The root of this love is found in loyalty, dedication, faithfulness and sacrifice. Simply put, it is putting the will of God and the needs of others ahead of our own wants and desires-i.e. ahead of ourselves. The acronym JOY- Jesus first, others second, yourself third- is a fairly accurate summary of what Jesus is teaching. There is miraculous power to be discovered for all who choose to live this way. Even though it seems to be a contradiction to the way the world claims we need to live, putting God and others ahead of our own selves is the only path to true peace, joy and contentment.

THERE IS JUDGMENT

Matthew 23:25 "Woe to you, teachers of the law and Pharisees, you hypocrites! You clean the outside of the cup and dish, but inside they are full of greed and self-indulgence."

So Jesus does judge. There seems to be this mistaken notion that Jesus never condemned people or confronted sin. But that is just not true. Jesus set the highest standard of living by His teachings and His life. God does hate wickedness. And one type of wickedness He detests in particular is the hypocrisy of presenting on the outside what contradicts the condition of the heart. In two words, greed and self-indulgence, Jesus sums up the root of hypocrisy. When we present to the public a life in control and dedicated to God, when we practice praise and worship with actions of devotion and honor, when we speak forth wisdom and knowledge of the scriptures and their application to life- while all the time our hearts are entangled with the secret sins of lust, unforgiveness, bitterness, self-pity, despair and selfishness- we become the recipients of the same judgment and condemnation Jesus gave the Pharisees. We must continually make sure that our outward actions are truly motivated by the inward condition of our purified hearts.

LIVING INSIDE OUT

Matthew 23:26 "Blind Pharisee! First clean the inside of the cup and dish, and then the outside also will be clean."

So much for Jesus being just a meek and gentle person! There were some things that got Jesus fired up. Mistreating children and dishonoring the Father were two. Hypocrisy was another. Hypocrisy is more than just saying one thing and doing another. It is centered in the heart. When we live outward lives of relative goodness yet harbor unforgiveness, jealousy, envy, hatred or spiritual pride in our hearts it not only grieves God. It also angers Him. Not only is it out of the fullness of the heart that the mouth speaks but it is also our actions 'behind closed doors' that reveals the true nature of our hearts. We present to the church an image of righteousness while in our homes we lash out in anger and verbally abuse those closest to us. We project to the world a picture of godliness while we privately indulge in lust, gossip, slander and moral compromise. We call ourselves Christians yet do not enthrone Christ in our hearts but continue to pursue our own will and agenda. It is then that we fall under the same condemnation as the Pharisees and teachers of the law. We need to make certain that the inside of the cup and dish is continually clean so that our outward lives reflect the inward image of Christ our Lord.

THE ESSENCE OF HYPOCRISY

Matthew 23:23 "You snakes! You brood of vipers! How will you escape being condemned to hell?"

With these stern words Jesus sets off an explosion in the midst of the complacency of smugness and self-righteousness. Probably the most prevalent sin in the church today is hypocrisy. People present themselves as believers but the belief they have is not backed up by a lifestyle of holiness. Outside the church there is little to distinguish them from the world. It seems that much of Christianity today has become a matter of personal preferences and private convictions and is no longer rooted in the authority of God's word. There is a good chance that if Jesus were to visit some of our churches today this same harsh judgment would ring out. This is not because we don't do good deeds but because many Christians today have shifted the focus of their faith from God to themselves. Their Christian life is lived with the prime motivation being 'what's in it for me?" instead of living for God's glory. Everything is about success and comfort in this life and the anticipation of that mansion in heaven. The fact that Christ died to reconcile us to God and reestablish our relationship with Him is either given only lip service or ignored altogether. This self-centered aberration of Christianity is the true essence of hypocrisy.

AS LOVE GROWS COLD

Matthew 24:12-13 "Because of the increase of wickedness, the love of most will grow cold, but he who stands firm to the end will be saved."

We have all seen those who were once an active part of the church but have turned away from God and fallen back into the snare of this world. We are inundated with divorce and betrayal in the church as affairs abound and families are destroyed. The church is in the midst of a moral crisis as well as we wrestle with homosexuality, cohabitation, abortion, euthanasia and the dilution of our Christian faith. And many in the church are battling for the acceptance and validity of other religions. It is true that love, (not the emotional irregularities of our feelings but the devotion, commitment and loyalty to God, Christ, the Bible and one another), is growing dangerously cold. Jesus has this message for us- stand firm. The Authorized Version uses the word 'endure' but to many today that implies just bowing our heads, hunching our shoulders and trudging along in discouragement. Standing firm is much more than that. It involves letting our light shine brightly and being faithfully obedient. Our light shines brightest when we return good for evil and remain loyal to Christ. We must live courageously and allow our love for others and for God to continually increase and abound. In the midst of this increasingly evil world that seems to be invading even the church we must always remember that God is still in complete control. After all- He is the one who said it would happen!

BEING READY EVEN WHEN YOU'RE ASLEEP

Matthew 25:5 "The bridegroom was a long time in coming, and they all became drowsy and fell asleep."

There is no doubt that Jesus is coming again. All the signs point to the truth that we are living in the end times. How then should we be living and what can we do to remain ready? First and foremost we need to be His servants. We need to be born again. Second, we need to be living in daily obedience to His will and in anticipation of His return. The difference in the ten virgins of this parable was the extra oil. Note that they all became drowsy and fell asleep. We all have earthly lives to live that require us to have jobs, pay bills, maintain households, raise children and all the other tasks of daily living. What we need to be careful of is that our earthly lives do not become the central focus of our hopes, dreams and aspirations. We need to stay in tune with the Lord and with His purpose for us. We need to have the 'extra oil' so that we do not burn ourselves out with the cares and worries of this life. We need to be about the King's business in the midst of our day to day tasks. We need to be living in the center of His will so that when He returns, even if we are 'asleep', we will be ready. We will not have time to take care of unfinished business or get our lives back in order. To be ready for Christ means that we need to be right with Him moment by moment no matter what our situation.

USE <u>YOUR</u> TALENT

Matthew 25:18 "But the man who had received the one talent went off, dug a hole in the ground and hid his masters money."

Whether he was jealous of the other two servants who got more or lacked confidence in his own abilities, we just don't know. We do know that this 'wicked, lazy servant' was afraid of his master. And his crime was not stealing or squandering his talent. His crime was that he did not use his talent. And when he was confronted all he could do was make excuses. Many people today are sitting on their talent. They are jealous of those who have more or afraid of failure. They are just going through the motions of being their master's servant. God has entrusted us with these talents, whether one or ten, to be used for His kingdom. We need to make sure that we are using His talent to the best of our ability. It is interesting that the servant who received five wasn't jealous of the ten talent servant. He simply went to work and did the best he could. Accept the talents entrusted to you, whether one or ten, get to work, and do the best you can with what God has given you for your Master's glory!

STEADFAST LOYALTY

Matthew 26:10 "Then He returned to His disciples and found them sleeping. 'Could you men not keep watch with Me for one hour?' He asked Peter."

It's significant that, although all the disciples had been sleeping, Jesus directs His admonition to Peter. If you read a few verses earlier you find Peter vowing to follow Jesus to His death and to never fall away. It is a part of human nature to boast of great loyalty and faithfulness yet not follow through. It is easy to proclaim about what our hearts desire to accomplish while we are outside of the crucible of the actual test. Yet Jesus only led them to the garden to keep watch with Him while He prayed. This was not the actual test of Peter's loyalty... or was it? 'I'll follow You to Your death, Lord, but a weary, hour long prayer meeting?'... God's desire is not for us to boast of great things in a moment of emotional fervor. He wants us to walk with Him moment by moment in obedience to whatever He wills. Although times of elation are encouraging and can stir the soul, true commitment and dedication are found in our faithfulness and steadfastness in the common episodes of everyday living.

OVERCOMING DOUBT

Matthew 28:17 "When they saw Him, they worshipped Him; but some doubted."

We don't know if more than just the remaining eleven disciples were here. But whoever was here, some still doubted. After all of His teaching and miracles some still doubted. After showing them time and again His love, faithfulness and care some still doubted. After His suffering and death some still doubted. Even after He rose from the dead and stood before them some still doubted. Why is it that we can be cruising along in our walk with God and then become so quickly derailed when troubles come? They don't even have to be major trials. Maybe it is something as simple as a car breaking down or the washing machine quitting or someone saying something annoying or disagreeable to us. Whatever the situation might be, in crash the doubts, worries, fears and frustration, and we are once again floundering in our faith. But if we pay attention, not to the disciples who doubted, but to what the rest of them did, we can discover a key to overcoming our weaknesses. The other disciples worshipped. This implies their recognition of the lordship of Jesus. By worshipping Christ they were acknowledging His kingship, deity and authority. When we truly worship doubt cannot co-exist because we have settled the issue of whom and what Christ is to us.

THE NECESSITY OF OBEDIENCE

Matthew 28:20 "…and teaching them to obey everything I have commanded you. And surely I am with you always to the very end of the age."

Most of us are familiar with the first part of the great commission- to make disciples of all nations. But the message of salvation does not stand alone. Making disciples must start with salvation for no one can be a Christian without first confessing their sins, sincerely repenting, and having their heart cleansed by the blood of Jesus through the power of the Holy Spirit. This must be more than just a mental acknowledgement of Jesus. All who are truly saved have experienced something supernatural and unexplainable. This is the wonder of being forgiven and cleansed from our guilt and sin and the assurance of the undeniable fact that we are without a doubt born again and spiritually alive in Christ. But unless the message of salvation is linked to the life of obedience the new believer will not develop the roots necessary to flourish and bear fruit. They will either wither quickly like the seed planted in shallow ground. Or they will digress into a life of self-centered, empty and futile works devoid of the motivation of a heart full of love for God and others. That love is the true backbone and inspiration for victoriously obedient living.

HIS PERMEATING INFLUENCE

Mark 1:35 "Very early in the morning, while it was still dark, Jesus got up, left the house and went off to a solitary place, where He prayed."

Some would say that Jesus was a morning person. So they have devotions in the morning while the day is still fresh. Others are night owls who take their spiritual nourishment when their minds are most awake. Then there are those who try to squeeze their time with God in whenever they can. The important thing is that you have a daily time alone with God. But it is even more important that our daily lives reflect a consistent devotion to God. We cannot compartmentalize our lives by saying that this time belongs to God, this time to our jobs, this time to our families, this time to me. While the focus of our lives does change we must remember that ALL we do should spring from our devotion to God. He should be the permeating influence for every aspect of our lives. Our personal devotions may be morning, noon or night but our devotion to God should dominate every area of our lives. Each moment and aspect of our lives should be lived as time spent with God. After all, He is always with us at our jobs and with our families, during our rest and recreation, and even in our most private moments.

THE DANGER OF 'GOOD FEELINGS'

Mark 1:43 "Jesus sent him away at once with a strong warning."

Jesus had great compassion on the leper in this story and brought about a wonderful healing miracle. Now here come the mundane tasks of obedience. We may be tempted to make excuses for the cleansed leper. After all, he was healed and was thrilled and emotionally high after this amazing event. How could he not help but spread the news about his miracle? But this man's rash and emotional act of disobedience cost Jesus the ability to enter the towns and villages. He was forced to change His tactics. So many times we become emotionally charged and storm ahead of God. We should be listening to His still, small voice and immersing ourselves in His word. But instead of allowing His Spirit to guide us into His plan we try to act on the strength and wisdom of our own upbeat feelings. Like Peter, we believe we can follow the Lord anywhere and accomplish anything- not realizing we may be only one step away from failure and disaster. Be assured that God will never guide us outside the truth of Scripture. He will not have us do anything that would compromise His word or our love for Him and for others no matter how good or right it may feel. Obedience and not feeling is the acid test of our love for Him.

NEVER BY WORKS

Mark 2:17 "On hearing this, Jesus said to them, 'It is not the healthy who need a doctor, but the sick. I have not come to call the righteous, but sinners'"

It is a commonly accepted truth that the first step in dealing with a problem is to admit that there is a problem. Jesus knew this truth centuries ago. He was willing to minister to anyone but He could only minister to those who were honest enough to acknowledge their need! 'All have sinned' the Bible tells us, but because of their acts of righteousness the Pharisees believed that they were holy and above reproach. Yet we know that their hearts were full of self-righteousness, greed, pride, arrogance and disdain for those who could not measure up to their inflated and warped standard of holiness. The vast majority of people who benefited from Jesus' life on earth were those who recognized their own need and realized that they could never measure up to the standards that the religious leaders set. Jesus made God accessible to the masses by making faith the measure by which one could find forgiveness and restoration. This same battle still rages today. Multitudes are trusting in their own righteous acts to gain acceptance with God. They judge themselves by the good they do while ignoring the need of their hearts. It is only when we recognize our sins, admit our need, confess it to Jesus and receive His healing and forgiveness that we will find and keep peace with God.

WHY WE'RE STILL HERE

Mark 4:5 "He looked around at them in anger and, deeply distressed at their stubborn hearts, said to the man, 'Stretch out your hand.' He stretched it out and his hand was completely restored."

This is no minor show of irritation by the Lord. He was angry! He was deeply distressed! Why? Because of their stubborn hearts. They refused to budge from their traditions and comfort zones. Their pretense of self-righteousness and holiness were more important than the needs of the hurting and hungry who were all around them. When we become so engrossed in our own relationship with God and our own comfort and ease that others begin to become a nuisance and irritation to our lives, then Jesus has cause to be angry and deeply distressed at our own stubborn and selfish hearts. We remain on this earth after we are saved for one purpose- to be used by God to touch others with His saving, healing, strengthening and restoring power. Our personal relationship with God should focus on drawing closer to Him, striving to be like Jesus, and keeping our hearts and minds holy and pure. Then we will always be ready to be used by Him whenever and wherever He desires. That's why we're still here!

LEARNING TO GROW

Mark 4:24 "Consider carefully what you hear. He continued. With the measure you use it will be measured to you- and even more."

A Christian must always be growing. Growth is evidence of life and health! As we pray, read and study God's word, listen to sermons and participate in small groups, we should continually 'consider carefully what you hear'. Our attitude should reflect the conviction that we always have a need to grow and to learn more. Those who see themselves as having reached a greater spiritual level have only revealed by their spiritual pride how much further they need to go. God's desire for us is to never cease expecting Him to show us new and different ways that we can grow and continue to bear fruit year after year. We must also take the second step- receive what God has revealed to us and put it into practice. It's not enough to know more. Our increased knowledge must result in a vibrant, energetic and ever-expanding relationship with God and with others. We should be able to testify to the growth we have experienced in the recent past- not limited to our salvation but also to the life God continues to build on that foundation. As we use what God continues to give us we will discover that God will continue to give us 'even more'.

WATCH WHAT YOU TEND

Mark 5:17 "Then the people began to plead with Jesus to leave their region."

Why would the people want Jesus to leave? He had just performed a great deliverance. Surely there were others in their region that needed the Lord's healing touch. Perhaps these people did not want to be disturbed and moved out of their comfort zone. 'Yes, there was a demon possessed man, but he stayed in the tombs and was seldom a bother.' And don't forget the pigs. Although an unclean animal for the Jews they were still a profitable commodity for all the Romans and Greeks who populated that area. 'It is such a minor compromise for a good source of revenue.' Perhaps that reveals the true nature of their rejection of Christ. As we go through this life we are faced with continual challenges to compromise our convictions- to feed the pigs. Most of the time it involves small things such as a minor lie, a tax return indiscretion, an angry outburst or a jealous reaction But these compromises quickly add up and before long we are hosting a legion of demons or tending a large herd pigs! We become trapped in a lifestyle of discouragement, subtle disobedience and defeat. Worst of all, when Jesus comes and offers deliverance, we refuse to see the magnitude of our situation. We end up sending Him away instead of receiving forgiveness and the renewed life He offers.

TOUCHING HIM

Mark 5:31 "You see the people crowding against you," His disciples answered, 'and yet you can ask, who touched Me?'"

Much of what is considered Christianity today is simply people crowding around Jesus, "I have to go to church." or "I have to pray." or "I have to do this thing or that task." We all have an inclination toward God and a desire for the spiritual. And the Christianity that touches and feeds only the emotions but is scant on depth and substance is popular and convenient in today's world. We see the need in our lives but exhaust everything to try and fix it ourselves. Then we come to the realization that we are worse off than before. When we finally come to Jesus, broken and emptied of our pitiful selves, we reach out to touch Him. Only then do we fully believe He is the only one who can help. Now Jesus is truly able to meet our need. It is encouraging to know that in all the press of today's clamoring, egocentric Christianity Jesus can still see and feel us sincerely reaching out with our need. We must simply realize that any efforts we put forth to clean up our lives or seek spiritual renewal apart from the miraculous power of Christ are in vain. These are the times that we need to curb our own efforts, quit struggling, and just reach out to Him.

RAISING OUR EXPECTATIONS

Mark 6:3 "Isn't this the carpenter's son? Isn't this Mary's son and the brother of James, Joseph, Judas and Simon? Aren't his sisters here with us? And they took offense at Him."

This is a sad episode in the ministry of our Lord. Here He is in His home town among people He knew well and He could do almost nothing because of their familiarity and pride. Their expectations were based on what they thought they knew instead of what God could do through His Son. So the hometown folks missed out on something wonderful and miraculous by refusing to move out of their comfort zone. It still happens today. We develop a relationship with the Lord and over time our expectations become mundane and predictable. The impact of the supernatural is either the memory of what God did for us long ago or the vapors of the miraculous that we hear God has done for others. Our belief that God desires to do something fresh and new for us and that He wants to disrupt our lives with the miraculous has all but dried up. The expectations that there are daily wonders and blessings accessible to us have all been stunted by our deceptive lack of faith and the slow fading of our desire to increase and abound in our relationship with Christ. His mercies are indeed new every morning. When was the last time they were truly new for you?

WE CAN DO ALL THINGS

Mark 6:38 "How many loaves do you have?" He asked. "Go and see." When they found out they said, "Five- and two fish."

Jesus had challenged His disciples with a tremendous task- to feed a huge crowd of hungry men, women and children. All they could come up with were five small loaves and two small fish. But they offered them to Jesus and a great miracle occurred. Our Lord continues to challenge us today with tremendous tasks. He calls on us to return good for evil, to love our enemies, to turn the other cheek, to forgive wholly and unconditionally, to rejoice in tribulation, to be content in whatever our circumstances, to do good to all men and to live holy and upright lives. Through our own efforts, by our own strength, and with our meager resources these are impossible commands and insurmountable challenges. But when we take the five small loaves of our commitment and devotion to Christ and the two small fish of our desire to be obedient to His will and offer them to Him then the miracles will occur. We discover that we can indeed do all things through Christ who strengthens us. This is so much so that, just as the disciples filled twelve baskets with leftovers, we will discover that God's ability to empower us is limitless and above all we can ask or imagine!

HYPOCRISY DEFINED

Mark 7:6 "He replied, 'Isaiah was right when he prophesied about you hypocrites; as it is written: 'These people honor me with their lips but their hearts are far from me.'"

Here Jesus gives us a simple and clear definition of hypocrisy. Honoring God with just our lips involves not only speaking about Him but also keeping those trivial, man-made traditions we find easy and comfortable and that ease our conscience. Meanwhile our hearts are filled with jealousy, anger, lust, greed and a host of other evils that plague our souls. Our heart needs to be centered on God and reflect devotion and commitment to Him. When we desire His will above our own and when obedience becomes a joy and pleasure instead of a burden that we must endure in order to keep away God's displeasure hypocrisy will not be able to gain a foothold. The fruit of the Spirit must sprout effortlessly and abundantly from our hearts. Then we will know that our holy living comes from the power of His Spirit and not from our own feeble efforts. The church today is rank with those who claim to have a walk with God while still tolerating sexual immorality, evil thoughts, selfishness, pride, arrogance, anger, unforgiveness and a host of other evils. This reveals the true nature of their hearts and the fact that their faith is not built on the solid rock of Christ, but rather on the sinking sand of their own selfish efforts, desires and will.

THE DANGER OF TRADITIONS

Mark 7:8 "You have let go of the commands of God and are holding on to the traditions of men."

All of us have traditions and doctrine in our lives that we follow. They may reflect the particular beliefs of our church or even the things we do in our personal lives such as daily devotions or holiday rituals. In and of themselves, there is usually nothing wrong with them. They can help bring order and stability to our lives and offer us tangible ways to express our faith in Christ. It is when our traditions become an end in themselves that we fall into the trap of legalism and self-righteousness. Too many have replaced a sincere love for God and for others with a list of dos and don'ts as the primary motivation for their Christian walk. They have digressed from a free life of faith to an existence of bondage to works. This eventually leads to bitterness, discouragement, frustration and defeat. When we begin to look at what we do as the proof of our Christianity instead of who we are through the merits and mercy of Christ, we open the door to pride, arrogance and self-reliance. The inspiration for our acts of righteousness should always be our love for God and for one another. We also need to remember that the power, desire and ability to live righteously ultimately comes from our Lord as well.

CONTINUED SPIRITUAL GROWTH

Mark 8:16 "They discussed this with one another and said, 'It is because we have no bread.'"

They have been walking with Jesus for some time now. They have witnessed His miracles and listened continuously to His wonderful teachings. Yet when Jesus attempted to give them a spiritual message they could only interpret it through fleshly eyes. Not only did they fail to understand it initially but, even after discussing Jesus' statement, they still came to the wrong conclusion. So our Lord reminds them of what He had already done and, upon further reflection, the disciples finally come to an understanding of what Jesus is teaching. What is our track record like with the Lord? If we have been living half-heartedly, bouncing back and forth from the carnal to the spiritual, then we will always be challenged when God attempts to teach us or to stimulate growth in our lives. We will be so focused on ourselves that we may miss a wonderful opportunity to mature in our walk with Him. Be cautious when seeking other's opinions as well. If we are lax, self-centered, and somewhat casual in our walk with God then chances are that those we have been associating with may share those same weaknesses. They will only end up clouding God's teaching and His will even further. View what God is doing through spiritual eyes, seek council from godly people, and determine to respond whole heartedly and move forward in your relationship with Him.

SEEING JESUS ONLY

Mark 9:8 "Suddenly when they looked around, they no longer saw anyone with them except Jesus."

Even in the church there can be positive distractions. Meetings to go to, boards to serve on, and programs to implement- the list goes on and on. At the transfiguration Peter wanted to build shelters for Moses, Elijah and Jesus; honoring the law and the prophets as well as the Lord. Yet in Jesus was one greater that the law and the prophets. God Himself instructs the disciples to listen to Jesus who was the fulfillment of the law and prophets. Jesus was bringing a new way of life- one motivated from who we are inside and not what we do outside. He was introducing both new wine and new wine skins! As we serve the Lord in our devotional life, our church involvement and our daily walk we need to remember to concentrate on what is truly important- not what we do but who Jesus is. Let's take the time to allow the Lord to touch us so we can no longer see anyone or anything except Jesus.

MADE FOR THE VALLEYS

Mark 9:14 "When they came to the other disciples they saw a large crowd around them and the teachers of the law arguing with them."

Mountain top experiences are great. They refresh our spirits and restore our hearts. They also give us a glimpse of the joy and wonder that eternity has in store for us. But we also know that we must return to the valley and continue the work God has called us to do. The valley has its crowds that need to be comforted and helped. The valley has arguing, strife, tribulation and conflict. The valley is where hearts are broken, tears are shed and the battles are raging. And, as long as God allows us to remain on this earth, it is in the valley where He wants us and where He needs us to labor and dwell. If we will commit ourselves to His service and allow ourselves to be expended in the valleys, then we can be comforted and encouraged that God will be with us. In the valley He restores our soul. We will find our greatest joy and fulfillment in the valley and realize that the valley is the place where we will best discover His grace, mercy and peace. To do the will of God should be our greatest desire. Without a doubt God's will leads us down into the valleys where He can best use us to bring hope, salvation and restoration to a lost and dying world.

THE NEED TO SEE JESUS

Mark 9:15 "As soon as all the people saw Jesus, they were overwhelmed with wonder and ran to meet Him."

The reaction of the crowd to Jesus can be explained in several ways. First, they had already either heard or seen His miracles. His reputation at this point in His ministry was very strong. Second, they had been witnessing the feeble attempts of His disciples to cast out a demon and the resulting controversy. The scene was probably one of chaos, curiosity and frustration. The question was, 'Where is Jesus?' Third, when they did see Jesus, they undoubtedly had great expectations about what would happen. Finally things would be made right. Only Jesus could straighten out this messy situation. And, of course, He did.

There are obviously some parallels in this story to our own lives. Like the people, we have heard about, and experienced, the miracle working power of Jesus. And, even though we have a resume of His grace and power in our lives, like the people we still stumble during times of crisis, doubt and frustration when we also ask, "Where is Jesus?" And, like the people, we need to see Jesus in a way that overwhelms us with wonder and causes us to run to Him. We need Jesus to speak to us in such a way that no matter how discouraged we may feel, or how daunting our situation, we know that He will make it right!

PUTTING CHRIST ON THE THRONE

Mark 10:21 "Jesus looked at him and loved him. 'One thing you lack,' He said, 'Go and sell everything you have and give to the poor, and you will have treasure in Heaven. Then come, follow Me.'"

There are a few interesting points in this verse. First, it tells us that 'Jesus...loved him'. We know that Jesus loves everyone. So why does Mark make a specific statement that Jesus loved this man? One reason could be that the rich young ruler seemed ready to go beyond the religiosity of works. He had kept the commandments since he was a boy but he obviously wanted more. Many today are also imprisoned by their bondage to works. Their faith has degenerated from a relationship to a job. They believe that it is what they do that keeps them in good standing with God. When Jesus realized this man desired more than the emptiness of his legalistic life He challenged him to forsake all and follow Him. Second, Jesus struck to the heart and put His finger on the one thing the young man had enthroned in his life above God- his riches. When we tire of our works-based facade of Christianity and seek more reality and substance in our walk with God we must be prepared to give up whatever Jesus exposes in our life that we have put ahead of Him. We must surrender everything that would keep us from truly putting Him first.

RENEWING OUR ASTONISHMENT AND FEAR

Mark 10:32 "They were on their way up to Jerusalem, with Jesus leading the way, and the disciples were astonished, while those who followed were afraid."

Nowadays many people speak of Jesus as if He were only a man- just like themselves. We can understand somewhat the fact that God became flesh and dwelt among us. And because He did this incredible act Jesus can relate to us on our own level. But it is important to realize that Jesus was not a man pursuing the divine but that He was the divine pursuing man. Look at the reactions of those who followed Jesus. His miracles and teaching inspired astonishment and fear. In our Christian walk there is a definite danger that we can become too familiar with our Lord and too complacent about the miracles and teachings He desires to impart to us. Our prayers and expectations have become rote and mundane. We somehow lost the astonishment and fear that is a vital part of our relationship with Christ. Perhaps it is because we have been following Him too far behind. Maybe we have allowed the distractions of this world to get between us and Him and obscure our view. If we wish to once again feel His blessed presence, to experience anew His miracles, and to hear His guiding voice, then we need to close the gap and draw near to Him. He is waiting to draw near to us as well.

WHEN QUESTIONING GOD

Mark 11:33 "So they answered Jesus, 'We don't know.' Jesus said, 'Neither will I tell you by what authority I am doing these things.'"

God does not mind our questions. It's the motivation behind our questions that concerns Him. Jesus was asked many questions and the reasoning behind these inquiries ranged from ignorance through self-justification then to outright animosity. Even today people ask unreasonable questions of God in order to pursue their own agenda of sin and self-centeredness. "If You are real, God, then…" or "I'll believe in You or serve You if You will…" And, when God doesn't respond in their prescribed or preconceived way, they feel justified to continue in their rebellion and disobedience. Jesus becomes our teacher when we truly become His disciples. This means we are willing to commit our lives to Him and follow Him with all of our hearts. It is amazing what God is ready and willing to teach the person who has yielded their life completely to Christ. When our greatest ambitions are to glorify God, do His will, and build His kingdom He becomes much more willing to share with us His heart.

KNOWING THE SCRIPTURES

Mark 12:24 "Jesus replied, 'Are you not in error because you do not know the Scriptures or the power of God?'"

There is a lot of confusing theology in the world today. It seems that new cults and variants of Christianity continually sprout up while people run to and fro trying to figure out what, if anything, to believe. Jesus, in His response to the Sadducees concerning marriage, gives us a simple formula for having a sound theology. First, it must be based on knowledge of the scriptures. While most of the Christian deviations claim a biblical base, upon closer inspection they are exposed for the narrow and self-focused religions that they are. Scripture must be taken as a whole. The best commentary on the Bible is the Bible itself. True Christianity is not founded on a few select verses of scripture but on the whole tenor and scope of God's word. The second part of the formula is to know the true power of God. We must realize that God can do anything. His power is unlimited. Just because we can't figure it out does not mean that it isn't true. Part of recognizing the power of God is realizing that we cannot even begin to know His greatness. Another part of knowing His power is discovered in the experience of salvation. Only through the eyes of faith of one who has been born again can an honest and clear understanding of the whole scriptures begin.

THE TRUE VALUE OF THE GIFT

Mark 12:44 "They all gave out of their wealth; but she, out of her poverty, put in everything- all she had to live on."

This is a wonderful example of how man looks on the outward appearance but God looks on the heart. By gauging our gifts on the sacrifice involved Jesus put us all on a level playing field. He allows the poorest Christians' gifts to have the same impact on God's kingdom as those who have been more materially blessed. But in this day of expansive ministries and expensive building endeavors we tend to focus on the $10,000.00 donation from the wealthy business person and ignore the $10.00 donation from the single parent with four children. While in theory we acknowledge the truth of Jesus' observation, in practice we honor the wealthy donors with stained glass windows and wing dedications while delegating the lesser givers to a generic 'thank you to all who gave'. We seldom realize that the rich giver is driving home to their beautiful house with well-stocked pantries while the poor giver is wondering how they will buy gas or feed their four children for the rest of the week. We will even overlook moral or ethical inconsistencies in certain people so we don't risk offending the affluent and losing that all important tithe. Church organizations are businesses that require a continual inflow of capital to operate. But we must be careful that we don't emphasize the material value of the gift and neglect the personal sacrifice that the givers made. In God's eyes this is the true indicator of the greatness and value of the gift.

OVERCOMING OUR ENVIRONMENT

Mark 13:12-13 "Brother will betray brother to death, and a father his children. Children will rebel against their parents and have them put to death. All men will hate you because of Me, but he who stands firm to the end will be saved."

There is no doubt that wickedness is increasing every day. Not only are acts of wickedness on a sharp rise, but the foundations of morality, family and truth, which have been vital in keeping evil in check, are crumbling at an alarming rate as well. We have all felt the discouragement of trying to live holy lives in this septic environment. And many of us have been troubled by the senseless evil of our era. Therein lays one of the more subtle dangers of self-centered living. As this world continues to batter those who belong to God our tendency is to recoil and retreat into looking out for number one. Loving God becomes a mental assent and ceases to produce a life of praise, worship, adoration, service and faithfulness. Love for others degenerates to a self-serving idea devoid of sacrifice and risk. This idea seeks to first protect ourselves and our families from harm or hurt. We must not allow the abounding wickedness in this world to rob us of our desire and motivation to faithfully love God and others. Maintaining God's perspective while we wade through the muck and mire of this world will substantially help us to stand firm.

OUR GETHSEMANE

Mark 14:39 "Once more He went away and prayed the same thing."

There is no doubt Jesus struggled as He prayed in Gethsemane. Words like 'sorrowful', 'troubled', 'deeply distressed' and 'anguish' fill the gospel accounts. He even sweats drops of blood. On top of all that His disciples fell asleep after He had specifically asked them to keep watch. So in His greatest hour of need Jesus struggled alone. But what exactly was this battle being raged over? Certainly Jesus did not wish to die a cruel death at the hands of the Romans. He wanted this cup to pass from Him. But the more serious conflict was the battle over the will. This is the battle each of us must also fight. Jesus had reached the point where there would be no going back. It is interesting to note that after Gethsemane there no longer seemed to be any question or doubt in Jesus' mind and actions about fulfilling His mission. The real test had been passed and there is an almost serene submission by our Lord to the horrors of His arrest, trial and execution. Remember that Jesus did not simply pray 'not My will, but Yours'. He agonized and persevered as He went back two more times praying 'the same thing'. Self-will dies hard and it is a lonely and anguishing battle. But when we have our own 'Gethsemane' we will come back on the other side prepared to faithfully follow our Lord no matter what might lie ahead.

PEER PRESSURE

Mark 15:15 "Wanting to satisfy the crowd Pilate released Barabbas to them. He had Jesus flogged, and handed Him over to be crucified."

Peer pressure is a powerful force. It caused Pilate to go against his better judgment and have Jesus crucified. It pressured Herod into beheading John the Baptist. It caused Peter to deny his Lord three times. And there is no doubt that in this day many have fallen because of the pressure of the crowd and have compromised their walk with God. Sometimes it's hard to stand alone- as Elijah found out in I Kings 19. Yet it can be done, as proved by men like Daniel, Joseph, Steven and Jesus Himself. We are social creatures and there is sometimes a lot of pressure to 'satisfy the crowd'. But we can overcome peer pressure by making sure we know what we believe. Knowing without a doubt what God's will is and being totally committed to Him can help give us the courage and strength we need to resist the temptation to give in to peer pressure. What also helps is to make sure we are hanging with the right crowd. Mingling too closely with the people of this world can quickly lead us into compromising situations. We need to walk with God daily. We also need to make every effort to walk among His people- people who share our convictions and lifestyle.

WHAT WILL YOU DO WITH ANOTHER CHANCE?

Mark 16:7 "But go, tell His disciples and Peter, He is going ahead of you into Galilee. There you will see Him, just as He told you."

It has been three days since Peter denied his Lord. The last time Peter saw Jesus was after his third denial when Luke tells us that Jesus looked straight at Peter. We probably can't even imagine what that look was like. Peter, in his utter shame, broke down and wept. Now Jesus, at least in Peter's mind, is dead. Peter's hope is gone and he is surely still in misery. Yet in this message from God's angel comes a word of hope- tell His disciples AND PETER! In Peter's darkest hour and on the heels of his greatest failure Jesus singles him out to offer him another chance. God's love for us is never dependent on whether we fail or succeed. No matter what we may do He stands ready to forgive and restore. It's up to us to decide where our tears and remorse will lead us. They can lead us to true sorrow and repentance, like Peter. Or they can cause us to give up and spiritually hang ourselves like Judas. That choice belongs to us!

CLAIMING THE PROMISE OF HOLINESS

Luke 1:74-75 "to rescue us from the hand of our enemies, and to enable us to serve Him without fear in holiness and righteousness before Him all our days."

For all who are Christians Jesus came to rescue us from our enemies of sin and death. He saves us and enables us to serve Him without fear because our salvation is no longer based on what we must do but rather on what God has done for us. Grace, mercy and forgiveness are freely and abundantly offered to all who ask. But, sadly, many Christians don't follow through on the remainder of Christ's purpose for coming to this world. He also came to enable us to serve Him in holiness and righteousness before Him all our days. The truth is that we not only have victory over the guilt and punishment of sin but we also have victory over the power of sin in our lives. Holiness is not immaculate perfection but it is the ability to live daily without willfully sinning against God. Most who struggle with willful sin are not battling the devil so much as they are battling their own will and desires. Victory over the lure and power of willful disobedience comes when we, as believers, totally surrender our will to God. God's promise is for the ability to live holy and righteous lives all of our days. Complete and absolute surrender is the key to claiming that promise.

THE PEACE GOD CAME TO GIVE

Luke 2:14 "Glory to God in the highest, and on earth peace to men, on whom His favor rests."

Most of the little sayings found on church signs and in church bulletins are usually cute but can also be somewhat shallow or trite. But one recently making its rounds has a tremendous truth. 'Peace is not the absence of war; it is the presence of God.' On a night like any other God came to earth. We are all familiar with the circumstances surrounding Jesus' birth. But when the angels can no longer repress their excitement and they burst into praise they rightfully give glory to God. This is truly a magnificent thing God is doing. Then, the angels proclaim 'peace on earth'. Today the world has latched on to this proclamation in a purely physical sense. They desire and work for the abolition of violence and war. But the true essence of peace that God promises is the inner peace that comes from a life forgiven and cleansed from sin and restored to sweet communion with God. This is the true reason for the baby in the manger. Jesus is the evidence that God's favor rests on us- for God so loved the world that He gave....

AVOIDING THOSE 'OPPORTUNE' TIMES

Luke 4:13 "When the devil had finished all this tempting, he left Him until an opportune time."

When we speak of the temptation of Jesus we think of this episode after His 40 days of fasting in the wilderness. But Jesus was tempted much more than just at that time. There were many opportune times during Jesus' ministry where the devil, lurking about for just the right moment, tempted our Lord. Today satan is looking for opportune times to tempt us as well. And although he is always lurking about, there are two situations where we can be especially vulnerable. One is when we are experiencing trying circumstances. Our tendency is to become centered on our plight in this world and allow self-pity to set in. The other is when we have experienced a great milestone or spiritual victory in our lives. There is a very real opportunity for spiritual pride and arrogance to creep in. In both cases the danger lies in our focus shifting from God to ourselves. When our primary desire shifts to our own wants and needs instead of Gods plan and will we provide an opportune time for the devil to tempt us and disrupt our lives. The crux of satan's temptation of our Lord was in trying to get Jesus to put His own needs and desires above God. The same is still true today as our adversary seeks to take our eyes off of our Heavenly Father and put them on our own fleshly wants.

TRUSTING GOD

Luke 5:5 "Simon answered, 'Master, we've worked hard all night and haven't caught anything. But because You say so, I will let down the nets.'"

Part of the nature of Christianity is that it flies in the face of the wisdom and convention of this world. As we live for God we are called upon to do some things that just don't seem to make sense. And, like Simon Peter, we sometimes look at the logic and facts of our situation and wonder what God is trying to do. An important point to remember is that, although Simon had his questions, doubts and reasonings as to why letting down the nets would be futile, he obeyed the Lord. God has never said we should not have questions, doubts and reasonings. It is challenging to step out of the world we must live in every day and trust in an approach that seems to be contrary to what makes earthly sense. God does not require that we fully comprehend His ways. He does require obedience. Too many times we sit around trying to figure out how our obedience will work in our particular circumstances when what we need to do is simply trust and obey and leave the results to God.

POWER FOR HOLY LIVING

Luke 5:13 "Jesus reached out His hand and touched the man. 'I am willing.' He said. 'Be clean.' And immediately the leprosy left him."

One of the many mysteries of God which has not been fully understood is in the area of miraculous healing. There is no doubt that God does heal physically. But much of the who, why and how of it are still unclear. There are a few things, though, that are clear. First, God heals when it is His will. And many times it is not His will to bring physical healing. Death is proof enough of that. Secondly, when God heals, or does any other miraculous deed, it is always for His glory. Too many times we ask God for things for our own benefit with little regard as to what would be best for His kingdom. The truth is that even suffering and death are a part of God's plan and will. What happened to Jesus is the best example of that. But multitudes of Christians have also suffered sickness, disease and martyrdom and thereby have brought tremendous glory to God and have advanced the cause of His kingdom and work. Although we are blessed and encouraged when we are able to experience the supernatural power of God, we find that we best tap into His power when we live in continual victory over sin and dwell in the center of His will. That power is freely bestowed by God. Holy lives bring our Lord the greatest glory.

BLESSED TO BE PERSECUTED

Luke 6:22 "Blessed are you when men hate you, when they exclude you and insult you and reject your name as evil, because of the Son of Man.

No one wants to be hated- especially by all men. Yet in this day it seems that there is a strong and increasing opposition to those who believe that Jesus is the only way to the Father and that all other ways are dead ends. The majority of people are preaching tolerance and acceptance as the new gospel and are casting aside the authority of the Bible. Those who commit lewd acts and live to fulfill the lust of the flesh are recognized as the new icons of our land while we who faithfully follow Christ and live holy lives in obedience to His word are treated as enemies of society. Meanwhile a sad and quiet compromise seems to be sweeping the church and paralyzing the proclamation of the true gospel. It's amazing that 2000 years ago Jesus saw it coming. And it is also amazing that in the midst of this persecution that we are called 'blessed'. Everyone experiences troubles, whether Christian or not. But when we suffer because of the Son of Man and when we are verbally mistreated because of our stand for Christ we receive His strength and grace. When we are treated as the 'refuse of the world' because we seek to live lives of integrity and holiness then we are blessed. We know that the light of Christ is shining through us. Only in Christ can we truly live lives worthy of the angst of this world.

BUT FOR HIS GRACE

Luke 6:36 "Be merciful, just as your Father is merciful."

Many Christians have entered into their faith at a very early age. Raised in a Christian home and guided by God's word since they can remember, they have not been involved in the more hideous sins of the world. Yes, all have sinned. But for many their sins seem relatively minor and insignificant compared to the truly wicked- murderers, child molesters, prostitutes, drug addicts, drunkards, armed robbers, rapists and the like. Therefore the temptation arises to view themselves as 'not that bad'. This mindset can interfere with our ability to extend mercy to others when we have not committed such heinous sins ourselves. But the truth is that without God's continued grace and mercy in our lives we would be equally as wicked. Those who think that they would never do those horribly wicked things need to remember that, not only does God's grace and mercy forgive and cleanse us from all sin; it also keeps us from sin. We are able to resist the more evil practices and are spared from viler behavior because of God's constant grace and mercy, not because we deem ourselves somewhat better or holier than others. Apart from God, we would also be thieves, murderers, sexually immoral and commit any of a host of other 'bad' sins. 'But for the grace of God go I' should not be a slogan of the self-righteous but a constant reminder that it is only His grace that keeps us pure and gives us continual victory over sin. And we need to extend that same grace and mercy to this world's worst- which could have very well included us!

WHAT'S IN YOUR MEASURE?

Luke 6:38 "Give, and it will be given to you. A good measure, pressed down, shaken together and running over, will be poured into your lap. For with the measure you use, it will be measured to you."

This is a very popular verse for those who believe that the money you give will be returned to you in a much greater amount. But upon closer examination of the context of this verse we discover that it has very little to do with 'heavenly investment' and much to do with holy living toward our fellow man. What is to be given is not that financial seed faith with the promise of a much greater financial return but acts of Christian charity to all- in particular our enemies. We are to give them love, blessings, prayers, humility, and possessions. We are to be agents of love, forgiveness, generosity and mercy to those who are most likely to use us, berate us and cause us grief and harm. When we give of ourselves in this manner then we will see a greater and better return than we would ever experience by giving money in the hopes of receiving back more money. We will have a great heavenly reward. We will become more like Christ and we will have a much greater impact and witness to the world. We will enhance our spiritual walk while discovering an increased futility with, and aversion to, the things of this world. We will be 'sons of the Most High"! (vs. 33)

STORING UP IN OUR HEARTS

Luke 6:45 "The good man brings good things out of the good stored up in his heart, and the evil man brings evil things out of the evil stored up in his heart. For out of the overflow of his heart his mouth speaks."

What's in your heart? Actually this is an easy question to answer by asking "What flows out of your life?" If we are secretly harboring bitterness, unforgiveness, jealousy, hatred, lust, anger or any other 'hidable' sins they will eventually show themselves. They will probably stay hidden in church or around our fellow believers or in front of our boss. But they will more likely reveal themselves in our homes or around our fellow workers. Maybe they will be exposed in our car when someone cuts us off or in our private moments when we think no one is watching. If our efforts of holy living spring from the flesh and our desire to be viewed as being godly then righteousness begins to become a chore. We manufacture what is necessary to keep the appearance of the outside of the cup clean while the inside remains filthy. Then when we are caught off guard and are forced to respond on the spur of the moment, without having a chance to compose ourselves or get under control, our hearts are exposed for what they actually contain. We need to continually store up good in our hearts by keeping our thought life, our personal time, our inmost desires and our private activities holy to the Lord.

NEVER DESERVING

Luke 7:4-5 "When they came to Jesus, they pleaded earnestly with Him, 'This man deserves to have You do this, because he loves our nation and has built our synagogue.'"

It's interesting how perspectives flavor our theology. The Jewish elders believed the Centurion deserved to have Jesus come help him because of his good works. Yet, when Jesus drew near, the Centurion sent friends to tell Him not to come because he did not deserve to have Jesus under his roof. No one earns or deserves God's grace and mercy. Those who, in our eyes, seem to deserve it because of their 'saintly' lives have usually arrived at that point because they realize they will never deserve God's favor. They have simply yielded their lives completely to Christ. We continue in our spiritual mediocrity by believing we could never be as holy or good as so-and-so. What we need to do is believe that the same power that enables that person to live a holy life is available to us if we would also yield our hearts and lives completely to Christ. Instead, we dwell on the edge of true victory hoping we are good enough to at least make it to heaven. But not only is it by grace that we are saved. It is by grace that we are also able to live victorious, holy and sanctified lives. The same power that cleansed us from all sin is able to keep us from willful disobedience- from deliberately sinning against God!

ETERNITY'S INHABITANTS

Luke 7:16 "They were all filled with awe and praised God. 'A great prophet has appeared among us,' they said, 'God has come to help His people.'"

The people were right in their observations. Jesus was a great prophet and God had indeed come to help His people. But they were wrong in their expectations. Jesus was much more that a great prophet. He was the Son of God. And even though God had come to help His people, the help was of a nature that they were not expecting. They saw in Jesus the power and authority to free them from their Roman bondage. God gave Jesus the power and authority to free them from their bondage to sin. When Adam and Eve sinned God knew He would have to destroy this world now that it was polluted by sin. Then He would create a world pure and clean once again. He also knew what was necessary to create a new man to populate that world. This world will be destroyed along with all those who only seek satisfaction and fulfillment in the here and now and live their lives according to the flesh. But the new world is for those who, through Christ, have forsaken this world. It is for those who seek their fulfillment and satisfaction in God and who now live according to the Spirit.

LITTLE OR MUCH?

Luke 7:47 "Therefore, I tell you, her many sins have been forgiven-for she loved much. But he who has been forgiven little loves little."

It is noteworthy that Jesus bases the greatness of our love for Him on how much we have been forgiven. Lest we fall into the error of thinking that we have not sinned a lot and therefore do not need as much forgiveness as truly wicked people, let's remember that God always forgives much. Being forgiven little is strictly from our perspective. We base the 'much' or 'little' of our sins on the effect and results that those sins produce. Murder, adultery, homosexuality, stealing, drunkenness and such are in the 'much' category whereas gossip, envy, selfishness, covetousness, jealousy, unforgiveness and other seemingly less vile and objectionable sins we classify as 'little'. Yet God views all sin as equally wicked and damning. Earlier in this eleventh chapter of Luke a Centurion requested healing for his servant from Jesus. The Jewish elders he sent to Jesus proclaimed all the good the Centurion had done as reasons why he deserved to have Jesus come. But the Centurion himself, realizing his true condition, stated that he did not deserve to be in Christ's presence. When we realize we have all sinned 'much' and that our righteousness is as filthy rags we will begin to open the door to loving much.

MATURE AND PERSEVERE

Luke 8:15 "But the seed on good soil stands for those with a noble and good heart, who hear the word, retain it, and by persevering produce a crop."

It is interesting that in the parable of the sower the successful seed was not the seed that sprouted. It was the seed that produced fruit. Whether this seed is the fruit of the Spirit in Galatians 5 or the work of bringing others to Christ has long been a subject of debate. Very likely it is both! In order to be effective witnesses and to bring others to the Lord our lives must exhibit the characteristics of Galatians 5:22-23. Many have gladly received Christ only to fall by the wayside because of troubles, persecution or the cares of this world. It is the person who perseveres that produces a crop. Perhaps this is where the noble and good heart comes into play. There needs to be a commitment and submission on our part in order to retain the word, mature and persevere. And the one who is able to mature, persevere and produce a crop is not the one who gets a hold of God. They are the one who allows God to get a hold of them.

HAVING ENOUGH TO DO THE WORK

Luke 9:13 "He replied, 'You give them something to eat.'

It can, sometimes, be overwhelming to see the unfathomable needs of this world and realize we only have two hands and two feet. The disciples must have felt that way as they looked upon this vast crowd of hungry and weary people. Their initial response was to get rid of the problem by sending them away. But Jesus tells them that they need to solve the problem. Then here comes their excuses. We don't have enough of what it takes to do the work. The truth is that we never have enough. We need to take our meager and inadequate resources and, instead of exhausting ourselves trying to make them work, lay them at the feet of Jesus. Then, when we allow Him to transform our five loaves and two fish into a feast for thousands, He will give us everything we need to do all that He has commanded us to do. We can do all things through Christ, who not only strengthens us, but also provides us with all the resources we need to do the impossible. He will thoroughly equip us to be able to live holy lives and to accomplish everything He calls us to do by providing above and beyond what we need. Remember…there were plenty of leftovers!

CRUCIFIED WITH CHRIST

Luke 9:23 "Then He said to them all: 'If anyone would come after Me, he must deny himself and take up his cross daily and follow Me'"

The flesh is alive and well- your body is alive, right? And in our humanness lies all the potential for sinful cravings which constantly beckon to the carnal and selfish nature. If we are determined to follow Jesus we must deny ourselves. We must put to death our carnal nature. We must surrender our will once and for all to His will. Sanctification involves allowing the Holy Spirit to have all of us. But the flesh is still there. Temptation is still real. The battle continues to rage. So what has changed? We have! We now take up our cross daily upon which our will and desire to fulfill the lust of the flesh has been executed and we follow Jesus. Each morning we should pray as Jesus prayed-'Not my will but Yours'. We should remind ourselves that we are not our own- we are bought with a price. We are now crucified with Christ. It is no longer I that live, but Christ that lives in me. As long as we are in this body we will face temptations to fulfill the lusts of the flesh. But when we have surrendered our will to our Lord and have 'crucified the sinful nature with its' passions and desires' on a daily basis we will find the courage and strength to live holy lives. We will be empowered to faithfully follow our Savior.

LOYAL IN HEART AND ACTION

Luke 9:59 "He said to another man, 'Follow Me.' But the man replied, "Lord, first let me go and bury my father,"'

There is absolutely no good reason to postpone or refuse the call of Jesus to follow Him. God's call and claim on our lives is total and complete. All other loyalties, commitments and desires must fade into insignificance in the light of Jesus. The list of activities and items most Christians have given up to depict their loyalty to Christ is usually made up of things that cater to the cravings of the flesh. But when it comes to the desires of our hearts we have the tendency to make excuses or justify ourselves. So often we choose the good at the expense of the best. When our families, friends or personal needs interfere with our walk with God, the true nature of our commitment is revealed. Too many times our personal circumstances cause us to compromise our walk with God. It is not necessarily done by succumbing to sinful disobedience. This type of compromise happens by allowing unholy tempers such as stress, discouragement, anger, frustration and indifference to sully our witness and make our service in His kingdom ineffective. Part of being strong in the Lord and in His mighty power is remaining faithful in our hearts and our actions when the things closest to our lives bring us anxiety or grief.

MORE THAN ANIMALS

Luke 12:7 "Indeed, the very hairs of your head are all numbered. Don't be afraid; you are worth more than many sparrows."

There are those who would have us believe that men and animals are on the same plain, that they have equal value. In fact, the value placed on endangered animals is sometimes greater than the value placed on human life. But even though God does care for the animal world and commands us to respect it as well, the Bible places a much higher value on us. David says that we are fearfully and wonderfully made. The very hairs of our heads are numbered which is more of an issue for some than for others! We are worth more than many sparrows even though they also have value in God's sight. As today's society seeks to put humanity and the animal kingdom on the same level, we are witnessing a much greater increase of lust, murder, violence and lack of conscience. We are seeing the increased manifestation of man's animalistic nature that is rooted in the flesh. Without the acknowledgement of our value as God's handiwork, created in His image and redeemed by His ultimate sacrifice, we will become equal to animals. This equality is not just in value and worth, but in the total loss of integrity, morality and the instinctive awareness of right and wrong.

WATCH OUT!

Luke 12:15 "Then He said to them, 'Watch out! Be on your guard against all kinds of greed; a man's life does not consist in the abundance of his possessions.'"

Most Christians, especially in the United States, don't consider themselves wealthy in this world. So how can we be greedy? It seems that we are working hard just to pay the bills and survive week to week. And if you ask people what their greatest need in life is, the predominant answer revolves around more money. This is usually disguised as a desire to get out of debt or for a bigger, better house or a newer car or any number of other financially based needs. Just because we may not lust, crave or covet the things of this world does not mean we don't struggle with greed. We willingly sing about being satisfied with 'just a cottage below, a little silver and a little gold' when God wants us to be satisfied with Him alone. Many of the things of this world are not evil in and of themselves. But they can clutter our lives and create undo stress and anxiety. They consume our time and effort and cause us to become too focused on this world as the primary source of our contentment and joy. We can all take steps to simplify our lives and become more efficient in our walk with God. We need to be diligent and to be on our guard so that our possessions do not dominate our daily existence.

PART OF THE COST

Luke 14:26 "If anyone comes to Me and does not hate his father and mother, his wife and children, his brothers and sisters- yes, even his own life- he cannot be my disciple."

Wait a minute... aren't we supposed to love everybody? Honor your parents? Husbands, love your wives? Certainly! Then what is Jesus saying? This is a verse about counting the cost of following Jesus. For many in this world choosing to follow Christ may go against the wishes of their parents. The choice to serve the Lord can very easily cause estrangement between a married couple and within the family. You may end up being the only Christian and feel the pressure of them trying to bring you down. And when we choose to follow Jesus the lifestyle He calls us to is constantly in conflict with the carnal and self-centered life of the flesh which seeks satisfaction in the things of this world. This is the life in which our unsaved family members are still entrapped! Don't choose to follow me, Jesus says, unless you are willing to give up everything in this world that could threaten to come between you and Me, including those closest to you.

SPIRITUAL PRODIGALS

Luke 15:17 "When he came to his senses, he said, 'How many of my father's hired men have food to spare, and here I am starving to death!'"

All of us are familiar with someone who has walked away from their faith in God and become entangled once again in the sinful web of this world. But you can become a spiritual prodigal as well without ever visibly turning your back on God. All it takes is an act of willful disobedience such as 'Lord, I want to do this.' or 'Lord, I want to serve You my way.' to remove you from the center of His will and hamper His ability to use you His way. Then jealousy and envy begin to creep in as you see others with 'food to spare' while your walk with God has gone stale. Spiritually you feel like you are 'starving to death'. All the while you are filling your life with 'busyness' when the real issue is obedience or the lack thereof. Perhaps it is time to 'come to your senses' and realize that God's will for you is best. It is much better than what you have been pursuing. A person becomes a spiritual prodigal the same way as a physical prodigal. They insist on their own way. But they also return to God the same way. They return by running back to the Father with a humble and contrite heart. They are ready to say 'not my will, but Yours be done'.

USING EVEN YOU

Luke 17:10 "So you also, when you have done everything you were told to do, should say, 'We are unworthy servants; we have only done our duty.'"

When we think of those who we believe have truly sacrificed their lives for the Lord the list will usually include martyrs, missionaries and inner city ministers. These have sacrificed comfort, security, ease and even their very lives to spread the Gospel of Christ. We hold our missionary conventions and have special offerings to support these groups. We put them on our prayer lists and admire the selfless work that they do. We may even take a short missions trip or involve ourselves in a food center or an inner city work day. And these are all good. But for most of us our work for the Lord is done in the shadow of the working out of our daily lives such as our jobs, families and recreation. We will even delegate the responsibility of reaching the lost or ministering to the hurting to our pastors and special committees while we continue to labor in our routines. But the truth is that we are all called to work where God has placed us. We are to be salt and light to a lost and sin blinded world. We are challenged daily to be Christ's servants and ambassadors and to do everything we are told- all of our duty. There are people around you that God wants to reach by using you! And when we have done all and are standing before the Lord we will all say 'We are unworthy servants".

WATCH THAT SELF RIGHTEOUSNESS

Luke 18:9 "To some who were confident of their own righteousness and looked down on everybody else, Jesus told this parable."

There is a subtle danger for those who have been raised in the faith or have been believers for many years. We can become secure in our own righteousness and knowledge of the things of God. We pride ourselves on the belief that we are not that wicked or that we have never done anything really bad. Our spiritual life then digresses to a self-centered mentality that views our own goodness and lack of 'badness' as a badge of superiority. We need to be reminded that sins of the heart are every bit as wicked as sins of action. The lustful look is adultery. The hateful stare is murder. Standing in judgment and criticism of sin in other believer's lives 'That I would never do!' is an equally evil and judgmental behavior. As long as we dwell in this sinful body, on a corrupt planet and among fallen humanity, we will continue to need the touch of the Great Physician. The truth is that the inner, hidden sickness is more dangerous than the obvious infirmity because we can deny it and it can be easily hidden from public view. We must not let our self-righteousness muffle or deaden the call of Jesus. We are all sinners who are all saved by grace and are all continually in need of Jesus' healing and restorative touch.

NEEDS-I

Luke 18:39 "Those who led the way rebuked him and told him to be quiet, but he shouted all the more, 'Son of David, have mercy on me!'"

Nothing was going to keep this poor, blind beggar from Jesus. He wanted to see and no amount of rebuke would deter him. So in the midst of his despair, desperation and need, regardless of the opposition and obstacles he faced, he cries out to Jesus. Jesus hears and responds. And not only does He restore the man's sight but now he can see and no longer needs to beg. His unconfessed needs have been met as well. Notice that the blind man recognizes his need- he is blind! In the physical realm this would be easy for anyone to diagnose. But there is a tremendous amount of spiritual blindness in the world today that goes unrecognized and undiagnosed. People believe they are just fine. Lacking the humility to confess their need they would rather view themselves as being 'not as bad as others'. They believe they do more good things than bad or that their sins aren't all that terrible or any of a multitude of other self-justifications. The truth is that we will only see our needs when we confess our own 'blindness' and cry out to the Lord, undeterred by any obstacles, interferences or pride. When we are honest with ourselves we will find in Jesus Christ the peace, joy, love, contentment and hope that He promises to give to all who recognize their need, persevere, and call on Him in faith.

NEEDS-II

Luke 18:41 "What do you want Me to do for you? 'Lord, I want to see.' he replied."

It's an interesting question- 'What do you want Me to do for you?' Jesus knew as He stood in front of those lifeless eyes what was needed. It was quite obvious that this man needed deliverance from his blindness. Everybody knew. Yet the question was still asked- 'What do you want Me to do for you?' The answer to that question is equally intriguing. On the surface it seems the honest, logical answer. 'Lord, I want to see.' Yet behind the answer lie two critical points. First the man humbly recognized his need. He knew all about his blindness and confessed his need. Second he believed Jesus could help him. He risked the ire and opposition of the crowd, who ironically were probably Jesus' disciples, to cry out his need. And that cry of faith was rewarded by the Lord. His sight was restored. The spiritual implications are powerful in this story. Imagine if the Lord were to ask us that same question. What is our own immediate and obvious need? When we recognize what our real need is and confess it to God, believing God desires to heal us, God will act. The main obstacle to this simple formula for spiritual health is still recognizing our need. We would rather justify or ignore our blindness, pridefully continue to assert our own self-righteousness, and surround ourselves with blind guides. What we need to do is acknowledge our need, confess it to God, and allow Him to restore us to spiritual wholeness.

TO SEE JESUS

Luke 19:4 "So he ran ahead and climbed a sycamore fig tree to see Him, since Jesus was coming that way."

Zacchaeus wanted to see Jesus. Everybody does. There is an aura of mystery, and even intrigue, surrounding Him. Today people flock to see movie stars. They arrive in droves when apparitions appear- faces of Mary on a wall or a weeping statue. If Jesus were scheduled to appear somewhere today, how many would show up? There would probably be millions. The crowd that day was large. Zacchaeus had to run ahead and climb a tree just to see Jesus. Already scorned, imagine the ridicule he must have suffered as he maneuvered his short little body up that tree. But then Jesus saw him! It wasn't his stature or his position in the tree, but the desire in his heart for something more and something better. Out of the thousands in the crowd Jesus zeroed in on Zacchaeus because He knew Zacchaeus was ready. His desire for Jesus was not based on curiosity or self-centeredness but it was rooted in his own dissatisfaction and need. Jesus saw in Zacchaeus his sincere desire for something better- his desire for God.

BE CAREFUL

Luke 21:34 "Be careful, or your hearts will be weighed down with dissipation, drunkenness and the anxieties of life, and that day will close on you unexpectedly like a trap."

Most Christians don't have to worry about dissipation (over-indulgence in sensual pleasure) and drunkenness in their lives-although there are a surprising number who are fighting these battles. As God's children we do pretty well at overcoming outward sins, especially in front of others. Where most of our battles rage is in the much broader area of 'the anxieties of life'. The stresses of living holy lives in an increasingly wicked world can very quickly weigh down our hearts. And when we face stress from those closest to us- our family, friends and fellow Christians- the weight becomes particularly heavy. But notice Paul's admonition. He challenges us to 'be careful'. God wants us to maintain the proper perspective. Christ is returning. And the only thing we have true control over is our walk with Him. Circumstances may overwhelm us and people may deeply disappoint us. Sickness and discouragement may sap our strength and we might be tempted to focus only on ourselves. But God's desire and will for us is to continue to look to Him as we keep our hearts unencumbered by this world. Lift up your heads for your redemption draws near!

BREAKING THROUGH OUR FRAILTY

Luke 22:35 "When He rose from prayer and went back to the disciples, He found them asleep, exhausted from sorrow."

The Lord understands our weaknesses and the hardships we face. He is slow to anger and quick to forgive. He knows we dwell in a body of flesh and are subject to sickness, exhaustion and weariness. Yet there are times when He still desires us to overcome our weaknesses. He wants us to deny ourselves, break through our frailty and gain faithfulness and victory. He is indeed always there to strengthen and encourage us. But sometimes we must dig down deep and give all we have. We need to press through our human faults and instability and be faithful and true to Him despite how we may feel. This has nothing to do with 'salvation by works' or trying to earn God's favor. It has everything to do with maturity, commitment and loyalty. The depth and strength of our dedication to our Lord is tested and stretched during these times of tribulation. This is when our lives are sifted like wheat and our faith is tried. Sometimes we must face head-on the evil of this world and the struggles that result from living in a body tied to the flesh. Jesus overcame the world through obedience to the Father- an obedience that led Him to the cross. His will for us is that we faithfully live in that same obedience wherever it may lead us!

THE LOOK

Luke 22:54 "Then seizing Him, they led Him away and took Him into the house of the high priest. Peter followed at a distance."

Let's see now… in the last 24 hours Peter was arguing with the other disciples over who would be the greatest, Jesus told him that satan wanted to sift him as wheat, he was told he would deny his Lord three times, he fell asleep in the garden- twice- and was reprimanded, and he foolishly cut off the ear of the high priest's servant and was again reprimanded. Not what you would call a good day. And now we find Peter following Jesus from afar and on the verge of denying his Master. We have all had times when the circumstances of life, coupled with our own bull-headed and self- centered ideas, have created a gap between us and our Lord. And without even realizing it we end up following the Lord at a distance. That is a dangerous place to be. If you find yourself in that position don't linger any longer. Before you fail completely look to Jesus, run to close the gap, and stay right behind Him no matter where He leads. When Peter failed and denied his Lord three times the scriptures tell us that Jesus turned and looked straight at Peter. That was a look that no one would want to experience. Don't wait until He has to turn and look straight at you with that same look.

BEGINNING TO DRY

Luke 23:31 "For if men do these things when the tree is green, what will happen when it is dry?"

Let's be honest. In America today it is relatively easy to live a shallow Christian life without any real persecution. Most Christians in our country live a good lifestyle and are blessed with more than adequate material blessings. Yet sexual indiscretion, divorce, anger, selfishness, greed and many other sins are prevalent in the church today. It seems like many Christians are simply coasting along and biding their time while believing that God will deliver them before the great tribulation. But the tree is beginning to dry. The grey areas that allow Christians to put their faith on hold while catering to their earthly needs and desires continue to shrink. Many churches today are taking the path of compromise- turning a blind eye to God's standards of holiness and righteousness under the guise of 'Christian love'. This has resulted in many people believing that they are right with God while they continue living sinful lifestyles. And let someone be so bold as to challenge this mentality and they are labeled as judgmental, intolerant or uncompassionate. Remember, the narrow road is the path of righteousness and holiness. We must live our lives according to His word and by His never changing standards.

WHY GOD OPENS SCRIPTURE

Luke 24:32 "They asked each other, 'Were not our hearts burning within us while He talked with us on the road and opened the scriptures to us?'"

Many have read the Bible from a historical viewpoint to obtain information about the ancient world. Then there are those who study the Bible with a scholar's eye by examining the languages, theology and other literary elements. But when we approach God's word on the basis of faith, with a personal relationship with Jesus Christ, then scripture literally comes alive and provides nourishment for our souls. We can also experience a 'burning within us' as Jesus opens the scripture to us, inspires our minds, and enables us to understand His word. This is not the shallowness of claiming promises that will give us ease or that may imply the fulfillment of our earthly needs. Neither is it a mystical revelation that inflates our spiritual egos. God gives us a practical understanding of scripture that encourages our hearts and helps us to live holy and obedient lives. His word enables us to serve Him efficiently and wholeheartedly and makes us effective and positive witnesses to a lost world. God desires us to be Christ-like. So the primary reason He intervenes in our study of the Bible is to mold us more and more into the image of His Son.

UNDERSTANDING THE BIBLE

Luke 24:45 "Then He opened their minds so they could understand the scriptures."

There are a lot of brilliant scholars out there. Many men and women can study the Hebrew and Greek down to the last jot and tittle. And those of us who are of lesser intellect benefit from them through the commentaries and study materials available today. Yet with all their knowledge many biblical scholars are still on the wrong track. They attempt to understand the scriptures primarily on earthly and intellectual terms. Focusing on their own efforts and knowledge they become unable to comprehend the miraculous and divine which flows through all of scripture. Yet the simplest farmer or laborer who reads the Bible with a heart devoted to God and a mind open to the Holy Spirit's voice can discern great truths from scripture. The Bible is more than just a great book. It is God's truth to humanity- a living and pulsating source of guidance and comfort. And just as the author of a great novel is the only one who can explain all the nuances and intentions of his book, so the Holy Spirit is the only one who can give us a true understanding of God's Word.

THE NEED FOR HARVESTERS

John 4:35 "Do you not say, 'Four months more and then the harvest'? I tell you, open your eyes and look at the fields! They are ripe for harvest."

This reference to the harvest appears in three of the four gospels. In Matthew it precedes Jesus' sending out of the twelve apostles to minister, stating that the harvest is plentiful but the workers are few. In Luke Jesus appointed 72 and sent them ahead with the same admonition about the plentiful harvest and few workers. In this passage Jesus has just spoken to the Samaritan woman at the well while His disciples had gone to buy food. It seems that there are three distinct and separate instances where Jesus refers to a plentiful and ripe harvest. As we read the gospels we find other stories and teachings repeated by our Lord but in different settings, such as the five talents in Matthew and the minas in Luke. Three different references to the harvest would seem to indicate that this is an important fact. And it is equally important that we realize this today. The truth is that there are multitudes that need Christ and have yet to hear the true gospel. Many can be found right in our own communities! We need to pray for harvesters and then be ready to be used by God as harvesters ourselves. We are all workers in God's fields and should all be reaping souls for His eternal storehouse.

STAYING TRUE TO GOD'S WORD

John 5:47 "But since you do not believe what he wrote, how are you going to believe what I say?"

One of the challenges Jesus faced was to get the Jews to believe the teachings of Scripture concerning Himself. They ignored, over-analyzed or misinterpreted what was written concerning the Christ. We face a similar challenge today. Many Christians have traded the authority of the Bible for a theology based on societal practices and personal preferences. God is no longer supreme and morals are no longer absolute. The philosophies of tolerance and religious pluralism have also polluted the purity of Biblical Christianity. Jesus made it perfectly clear that He was the only way to the Father. The Bible makes it perfectly clear how those who have accepted Jesus should live and what true faith involves. Yet, sadly, the love of many has grown cold while others have even fallen away. These are sure signs of the end times but they are also heart breaking for God and for us. We must continue to stand firm in our acceptance of the authority of the Bible and of the exclusive supremacy of the atoning work of Jesus Christ.

UNLIMITED RESOURCES

John 6:9 "Here is a boy with five small barley loaves and two small fish, but how far will they go among so many?"

Sometimes, when we look at the tasks at hand, we become frustrated and anxious. Whether it is living a holy life in the midst of an unholy world or ministering to the needs of a hungry and hurting people or proclaiming the gospel to a hardened and sin infested humanity we can feel overwhelmed, especially when we realize the meagerness and insufficiency of our resources. How can our 'five small loaves and two small fish' make any difference? Obviously they can't...unless we are willing to lay them in the hands of Jesus. What little bit Andrew was able to get he gave- and he gave it all without trying to hang on to a little for himself. When we attempt to serve God on our terms, in our own strength, and by our own efforts, we fail not only Him but also ourselves and those we desire to help. Before Andrew brought the loaves and fish to the Lord, Jesus already had in mind what He was going to do. That is an encouraging thought! God is in control and He has a plan. He simply wants us to take all we are and have and lay them at His feet for Him to use for His glory instead of trying to accomplish His will by our own means and efforts. Laying our all on the altar does not guarantee our success. It guarantee's God's!

OVERCOMING DISCOURAGEMENT

John 7:5 "For even His own brothers did not believe in Him."

Do you think Jesus ever got discouraged? He had just gone through a period where many of His disciples turned back and no longer followed Him. And now we read that even His own brothers did not believe in Him. It is certain that Jesus did feel discouragement. He not only felt it in this situation, but also when He wept over Jerusalem, or found His disciples asleep in the garden. He could have felt it while watching the rich, young ruler walk away unfulfilled. Discouragement is not a sin. It is allowing discouragement to defeat us and keep us from pressing on and living in continued obedience that is the sin. Sometimes we must move forward and continue living in God's will even when our emotions would attempt to lead us in the opposite direction. There will be times in our walk with God that faith in Him and His word will be the only thing that carries us through the turmoil of sadness, discouragement and loneliness. Jesus was able to go to the cross, not because He felt like it, but because He knew God's will and could stay focused on His mission. Despite His emotions and circumstances Jesus remained steadfast and true. And the truth is that we can most certainly do likewise.

DISCERNING HIS VOICE

John 10:4 "When He has brought out all His own, He goes on ahead of them, and His sheep follow Him because they know His voice."

The Lord desires to lead His sheep. He knows the safe paths, the best pasture, and the freshest springs. He can keep us from harm. But in order to benefit from the Shepherd's wisdom and care we have to be part of His own flock. Being born again is the primary prerequisite for joining His flock. The Lord will only lead those who are His. But notice that it is not enough just to be 'in the pen'. When Jesus goes on ahead we must be willing to follow Him. For us who are Christians salvation is more than just an event. There is a walk to be walked and a life to be lived. We must willingly, wholeheartedly and unswervingly follow Him. The biggest obstacle we then face is discerning His voice amidst the clamor and hubbub of the world. In church or our private devotions the Lord's voice can be easier to hear. But in our daily lives of work, school, recreation and leisure His voice can become distorted or even lost. The key to steadfastly recognizing His voice and following Him is learning its sound in the quiet moments of our lives. Then, when we find ourselves amidst the distracting chatter of this world, His voice will rise above the din and lead us on the paths He desires for us to follow.

TRUE GREATNESS

John 10:41 "...and many people came to Him. They said, 'Though John never performed a miraculous sign, all that John said about this man was true.'"

It is of interest to note that John the Baptist never performed a miraculous sign. Moses, Elijah and Elisha all were workers of the supernatural. Joseph, Jacob and Daniel were divine dreamers. Isaiah and Ezekiel received heavenly visions. But John only preached repentance and baptized. He lived as a recluse with a very unusual diet. It was even said about him that he had a demon! Yet Jesus testified that there had not arisen anyone greater that John the Baptist. Our tendency is to rate a person's greatness by their accomplishments. In the church those accomplishments seem to include miracles or supernatural manifestations. It is important to remember, though, that God rates greatness on the basis of humility, obedience and faithfulness. These are traits that abounded in the life of John. It is entirely God's prerogative whom He enables to perform miracles, dream dreams or receive visions- or to simply preach and baptize. When we discount some forms of ministry as being less powerful or spiritual than others because they seem to lack a divine element we not only discredit God's wisdom but we also reveal our own dependence on the supernatural to bolster our weakling faith. We need to remain humble, obedient and faithful and become the least in the kingdom of Heaven. For according to Jesus, it is those who are even greater than John.

FAITHFUL FOLLOWERS

John 11:16 "Then Thomas (called Didymus) said to the rest of the disciples, 'Let us also go, that we may die with Him.'"

On the surface this seems like a noble and loyal statement. Thomas has made a commitment to follow Jesus to the end. But when we realize that the disciples had tried to dissuade Jesus from going to Judea for this very reason and that they continued to be confused about Jesus' mission then Thomas' statement becomes more of a halfhearted resignation to a path he did not really wish to travel. Thomas even draws a premature conclusion about what will transpire when they get there. In our attempts to follow the Lord we easily slip into the same type of errors. We desire to be faithful and loyal to Him. But at the same time we focus too much on the circumstances we might have to face. We worry about the hardships or obstacles we may have to overcome or mistakenly map out the course and draw wrong conclusions. These conclusions are not based on faith in Christ but on our own analysis of the situation and our mistaken assumptions about the inevitable results. Then, when we begrudgingly get up and drag ourselves to follow Jesus, we have already planted the seeds of defeat in the soil of our doubt, fear and discouragement. Could bad things happen? Of course! But the issue is not 'What will happen to me?' The issue is, 'Am I willing to joyfully trust and obey my Lord?'

CLEMENS RUSSELL

EMOTIONS

John 11:35 "Jesus wept"

For being the shortest verse in the Bible this passage has much to teach us about our Lord. It is easy, while serving the risen Christ, to lose sight of the fact that He was just like us both physically and emotionally. Some of the emotions Jesus exhibited included weeping, deep distress, anger, joy, sorrow, gladness, frustration, weariness and compassion. At times He was moved deeply, overwhelmed and troubled. Emotions do have their place in the Christian life. But we get into difficulty when our emotions are controlled by the flesh. That is when they get out of control and lead us into trouble. Jesus was always in perfect control of His emotions because they were focused on the needs and conditions of others and not on His own self. They were aroused by the effects of sin on humanity and stirred Him to positive action. The dark side of emotions is manifest when our selves become our focus at the expense of others. We move out of God's will when we react emotionally without regard for other people and to the detriment of our walk and witness. Emotions are a powerful and important aspect of our personality that can either inspire us to great good or cause us to hurt others, stumble and fall. The choice is ours as to which path we will follow when our emotions come into play.

HIS WAY

John 11:37 "But some of them said, 'Could not He who opened the eyes of the blind man have kept this man from dying?'"

How many times have we questioned God about why things happen the way they do? Has He ever failed us or let us down? No! Many times we have seen Him work miracles in seemingly impossible circumstances. Yet how soon we revert back to doubt, fear and questioning when the next challenging circumstance comes along. Just like these Jews, we say 'Why couldn't God do it this way or that?' Faith in God means we believe God is going to do things in the best way for His glory, plan and purpose and not for our immediate benefit. Yet, even then, God has a greater benefit for us. We find the greatest peace and fulfillment when He is able to use us for the furtherance of His eternal kingdom.

FLIES IN THE OINTMENT

John 11:46 "But some of them went to the Pharisees and told them what Jesus had done."

You would think that after seeing such a great miracle as the raising of Lazarus that everyone would believe. You would think that the whole crowd would be awed into submission and that they would humble themselves before God. Yet within this crowd were stooges for the Pharisees whose wickedness and pride blinded them to the amazing miracle that occurred right before their eyes. They had come, like the rest, to show sympathy to Mary and Martha. But their hearts were hardened. Instead of seizing the opportunity to put their faith in Christ they 'went to the Pharisees and told them what Jesus had done'. It is a part of human, or rather carnal, nature to look for the negative in every situation. We face this problem constantly in the church today from people who relish in their role as 'doom and gloom' prophets. They grumble and complain, constantly and look for the negative in everything. They sit back and wait for failure and even contribute to the lack of success. Their reason is that they are 'just being realistic' or feel a need to proclaim their version of the truth. But the real truth really is that they are self-centered. They lack true faith and they enjoy the warped power and attention they receive from being the fly in the ointment. Wise, compassionate and constructive criticism is necessary and good. But those who consistently negate and berate reveal their selfish ambitions and unholy attitude and always do more harm than good.

THE LOVE OF MONEY

John 12:6 "He did not say this because he cared about the poor but because he was a thief; as keeper of the money bag, he used to help himself to what was put into it."

There is probably no better example of the lure and deceitfulness of the love of money than Judas. Not only was he a thief but he eventually sold out our Lord for 30 pieces of silver. His life is the epitome of how 'the love of money is a root of all kinds of evil'. What makes this episode even more incredulous is that Judas was one of the twelve. He had been with Jesus since the beginning of His ministry. He had seen the miracles, listened to the Lord's teachings and enjoyed the fellowship. He had even performed miracles himself when he was sent out two by two with the twelve. Yet in the end his own greed and selfishness took over and his name has been forever made synonymous with being a traitor. Many have speculated as to the 'why' of Judas' treachery, from being destined to be the betrayer and having no choice to him simply allowing sin to rule over him. It is obvious that Judas was self-centered and never truly understood or bought into Jesus' true mission. His own aspirations of glory and riches were pinned on the hope of Jesus establishing an earthly kingdom. When he saw that these would not be realized he decided to cut his losses and salvage for himself what he could. As a disciple, Judas' primary devotion never grew beyond his own needs and desires.

NOT PART OF THIS WORLD

John 12:43 "for they loved praise from men more than praise from God."

Have you ever noticed that whenever a celebrity or someone well known mentions God or alludes to Christ that the church parades it forth as some great and wonderful event? Not only that, but if someone famous receives 'Christ as their Savior' it seems as if they suddenly have instant access to pulpits across the country. And because of their celebrity status many believers hang on to their every word as gospel truth. Although it is wonderful that they have been saved, their worldly fame has nothing to do with their level of spirituality and wisdom. They are still 'babes in Christ' and as such need to be rejoiced over. But we should not look to them as spiritually mature leaders. Even the apostle Paul, a rising and zealous star among the Pharisees, spent several years in preparation before taking any leadership roles after his conversion. For some reason many Christians find a great satisfaction when the world accepts and respects them. These are usually indicators that we have compromised the truth of the gospel and are becoming more conformed to this world. When we live in the light and testify to a pure gospel then those in the world will not be pleased or give us as positive of a reception. The truth is that they love darkness rather than light. We should not be seeking their approval as confirmation of our walk with God or validation for our faith. We should only be seeking the approval of Christ.

DAILY CLEANSING

John 13:8 "'No,' said Peter, 'You shall never wash my feet.' Jesus answered, 'Unless I wash you, you have no part with Me'"

The custom of foot washing in Biblical times was a demeaning job reserved for the lowliest servant. By washing His disciples feet Jesus gave us an example of the true scope of our humble service to one another. But there is also a lesson here about our need for continual cleansing from sin. We who have been washed by the blood of the Lamb have had our sins forgiven and our hearts cleansed. But as we live our lives for the Lord the filth of this world of which we are still a part will sometimes cling to our feet. We may find that we have allowed some sin or compromise to enter our lives and we need to allow the Lord to wash away this contamination. Yet to admit our shortcomings and strayings can be a difficult and humbling task. Our spiritual pride may rear its ugly head. Instead of yielding to the gentle hands of our cleansing Lord we bristle with self-righteousness and attempt to justify our actions or attitudes. This is especially challenging when the area our Lord seeks to cleanse is one we have tolerated or even secretly enjoyed for years. We need to realize that unless we allow our Lord free access to every area of our lives and willfully submit to His cleansing in His way and when He wants we have no part with Him.

THE CONSEQUENCES OF FAILURE

John 13:30 "As soon as Judas had taken the bread, he went out. And it was night."

Jesus, who knows men's hearts and thoughts, knew from the start that Judas didn't cut the mustard as a disciple. Judas' intentions from the beginning were focused on himself. And as Jesus' ministry developed he more than likely became disillusioned that things were not going his way. So Judas steals from the bag and opts out of the organization by betraying his Master for 30 silver coins. His downfall was slow and inevitable because his commitment was shallow and self-centered to begin with. Peter was another who failed when he denied his Master. Yet the differences between Peter and Judas are significant. Peter was totally committed to Christ whereas Judas was conveniently committed. When Peter fell he wept bitterly and truly repented. Judas threw a fit then ended his self-centered life with a selfish act instead of facing up to his failure. And eventually, through the agony and bitterness of sorrow and grief, Peter was restored to fellowship with his Lord. The depth of our commitment to Christ will always determine the consequences of our failures.

LOVE FOR ONE ANOTHER

John 13:35 "By this all men will know that you are My disciples, if you love one another."

It is not because we go to church or because we tithe. Neither is it because of what we don't do or what we do. We can shout it all over town and put declarations in the news media. But the world will only know we are Jesus' disciples if we love one another. It's the new command. And just saying we love one another is still not enough. We must love one another as Jesus loved us. He loved us sacrificially and unselfishly. Our love for one another must be sincere. This love need to exhibit patience and kindness. It must not be envious, boastful, proud or rude. It is neither self-seeking nor easily angered. And this love truly forgives- keeping no record of wrongs. This is the love that reveals to the world that we are truly Christ's disciples!

TRUST IN THE DRY SEASONS

John 14:1 "Do not let your hearts be troubled. Trust in God; trust also in Me."

Our Lord desires us to be at peace and to not be anxious or stressed out. He wants us to not let our hearts be troubled. In this passage there are two important points to consider. First, although scripture supports the truth that we should not be troubled by any of the circumstances in this world, Jesus is giving a specific encouragement to His disciples concerning His previous statements that He was going to leave. This is followed up by His promise that He was going to prepare a place for us. Even though we have the constant presence of Christ through the Holy Spirit and He has promised never to leave or forsake us, we have all felt times in our walk with God when His presence seemed distant. Of course, disobedience and sin are major reasons why our fellowship with God can be broken. Only true repentance can repair that rift. But for those times when we are walking in the light and living in obedience, yet His presence still seems far away and we are experiencing spiritual dryness, the second point comes ringing through. Trust in Him! His promises are true. He has not left us or forsaken us. For whatever reason, our Lord is allowing us to walk an obscured path where feelings and emotions fail us. It is then that we must grasp His promises and keep our faith in Him. By trusting in His care and in His word we can remain strong, courageous and true to Him and continue to serve Him with joy and gladness.

WHAT CHRIST COMMANDS

John 14:15 "If you love Me, you will obey what I command."

The commands of Jesus are not too complicated. He commands us to love God with all of our heart, soul, strength and mind. This is a thorough and absolute love for our Heavenly Father that places Him in the most important position in our lives. Jesus also commands us to love our neighbor as ourselves. This is the motivation that is embodied in our Lord's teaching to do to others what we would have them do to us. We must not allow self-love to hinder our ability to lay aside what pleases or eases us to help someone else. And then Jesus commands us to love one another as He loves us. This is directed to our fellow believers. Many Christians do fine reaching out to those in the world. But when it comes to loving those in the family of God they struggle and even fail. But not only does Jesus command us to love each other, He also sets the standard of that love. His own unselfish, unconditional and sacrificial love for us is that standard. Finally, notice that the ability to obey our Lord's commands is anchored in our love for Him. Any attempt to keep the commands of Christ without the prerequisite love for Christ will result in legalism, hypocrisy and failure. Love for Jesus should always, and only, be our motivation for obedience.

THE PEACE CHRIST OFFERS

John 14:27 "Peace I leave with you; My peace I give to you. I do not give to you as the world gives. Do not let your hearts be troubled and do not be afraid."

So many today are seeking peace in this world. As we live out our lives on a daily basis we all seek relief from difficult jobs, financial woes, family strife, physical problems and many other, sometimes overwhelming, challenges. We seem to reach our limit and cry out, 'Can't I get just a little break?' only to have the next wave of tribulations come crashing into us. The truth is that anytime we seek peace in this world we will be disappointed. Our Lord plainly states that in this world we will have trouble! Jesus desires for us to have peace. But that peace is found only in Him. It is a peace that comes from the knowledge that we have been redeemed out of this world and promised a better place. It is a peace that can withstand the storms of life because we have the assurance of a better eternal life. It is a peace that anchors the soul amidst all of life's rough seas. It is a peace that, because Jesus overcame the worst this world could muster, gives us the assurance that we can overcome as well. It is a peace grounded, not on the unpredictable uncertainties of the things of this world, but on the unconquerable certainties of the things of God. We can indeed take heart!

REMAINING IN HIM

John 15:5 "I am the vine; you are the branches. If a man remains in Me, and I in him, he will bear much fruit; apart from Me you can do nothing."

This verse makes two significant points. First is that we are called to remain in Christ. The previous verse states this as a command-'Remain in Me…' Once we are saved we do not become permanently adhered to Christ. Scriptures abound with references to walk with, live by, and remain in Christ. We choose each day whether our lives will be lived in His shadow or whether we will launch out on our own merits and strength. If we are to bear much fruit we must consciously choose to remain in Him. And that brings us to the second point- what does Jesus mean by fruit? Some equate this to the fruit of the Spirit in Galatians 5. As we remain in Christ we excel more and more in holy attitudes and actions. Others see this fruit as bringing people into the kingdom through our witness and sharing of the gospel. Actually both are intertwined and equally true. We do produce the fruit of righteousness when we stay connected to Christ and we do have the courage and wisdom to be effective witnesses because we are growing into the image of our Lord. But when we try to do it on our own we meet with frustration and failure. Apart from Him we can do nothing. And apart from Him holy living becomes a legalistic quagmire and our witness becomes shallow and hollow. Remaining in Him is the key to fruitful and victorious living.

LOVE FOR OTHERS- SIMPLY PUT

John 15:12 "My command is this; Love each other as I have loved you."

It's pretty simple. Jesus says that the evidence of love for Him is obedience to Him. He has commanded that we love God with our all and that we keep Him first. Not our jobs, our families, our hobbies or ourselves. God becomes the major focus of our lives rather than just an obligation on Sunday and a few minutes Monday through Saturday. God is the primary topic of our minds musings and our hearts desires. He is our all in all. Jesus has commanded that we also love one another. We must not just say we love one another or try to convince ourselves that we love others. That is only fulfilling in our minds our obligation to God. Jesus' standard of what our love should be for others is His own unselfish, sacrificial and unconditional love for us. Love for others is not based on friendship or feelings. It is based on compassion and care and rooted in obedience. That is why Jesus commanded love. Love for others finds its motivation in our love for God and in the realization that we were not particularly lovable when He sought us. The essence of our love for others is embodied in our hope for their salvation and our desire for them to also live holy and victorious lives. This is what we should hope and pray for, and to work unceasingly to see accomplished, in all whom we meet.

WILLFULLY LOVING

John 15:17 "This is My command: Love each other."

John's gospel has several instances where Jesus commands us to love each other. The importance of this teaching merits continual observations. It is an interesting fact that Jesus takes love out of the realm of our emotions and places it in the realm of our will. He doesn't say to wait for or work towards a feeling of love for each other. Let's face it. Some Christians are difficult to feel love toward. But we have no choice. We must love them. Sometimes that means treating them the opposite of how we feel towards them. God's continuing plan for us is to be led by the Spirit and surrender our will completely to Christ. Then our obedience will be grounded in Him and not in our emotions. By living in this manner we will be amazed at how soon our emotions will get in line with our obedience. They will not be leading the way and controlling us but will be responsive and submissive to the obedience of our wills.

STRENGTH TO STAY TRUE

John 16:1 "All this I have told you so that you will not go astray."

Two important observations need to be made about this verse. First is the 'all this' that Jesus has told His disciples. He has just spoken to them in chapter 15 about the need, like branches to the vine, to remain in Him. This is necessary in order to bear fruit and to remain in His love. He has told them that they must keep His commands. The primary command is to love one another. He has also warned them that as they faithfully follow in His steps, serving Him by being witnesses, that they will face the same persecution as Him. Jesus' call to His disciples is not a sugar coated pathway to ease and contentment in this life. It is a gut wrenching summons to a life of total dedication, commitment, and loyalty to Him. It is a life that flies in the face of the mechanizations and methods of this world. We must completely sell out to Christ. The second observation concerns the reason Jesus told His disciples these things- so they would not go astray. The word literally means 'trapped' or 'to trip up'. Jesus uses the same word in Matthew 13:20 to describe the person who allows tribulations and persecution to cause the sown seed to sprout but not take root. That person lasts only a short time before he falls away. Simply put, Jesus is telling us that the life of complete consecration is not easy. Fortunately we have the help of the Holy Spirit. He will guide, strengthen and comfort us as we live in this world. And be encouraged by our Lord's own words. 'But take heart! I have overcome the world!' (vs.33)

SPIRITUAL SURGURY

John 16:6 "Because I have said these things, you are filled with grief."

There will inevitably be times when what the Lord has for us will bring us grief. It may come in the form of loss. Perhaps He will put His finger on something in our lives that we hold dear and that He wants us to give to Him. He may change our circumstances or have us leave a comfortable environment to live in a less desirable location. We may be called upon to speak the truth in such a way that we could lose friends or alienate family. There is a cost to be paid when we choose to follow Jesus and a cross to be carried as we walk in His footsteps. We are to totally surrender our lives to Christ and commit ourselves completely to doing His will. Sometimes this may result in Him having to pry our fingers away from the things of this world that we hold dear. Fortunately He will never demand something of us that we cannot do or challenge us beyond what we are able to withstand. Even later, in this 16th chapter of John, Jesus withholds much more than He had to say to His disciples because they were not able to bear it. (vs. 12) Our Lord is molding us into His image and that requires that He removes those things that mar His reflection. We can do much to ease the pain and grief of His spiritual surgery if we joyfully accept His diagnosis, willingly surrender those areas He desires to remove, and submit to the wonderful anesthetic of faith that His way is best.

TAKE HEART

John 16:33 "I have told you these things so that in Me you may have peace. In this world you will have trouble. But take heart! I have overcome the world."

No one reading this can deny the fact that everyone has trouble in this world. Christians and non-Christians alike seem to be continually fighting battles. Sickness, death, heartache and loss are shared by all of humanity. And those who have committed their lives to Christ are faced with the additional trials of satanic opposition, temptation to compromise their walk with God, and persecution from a Godless and carnal society. Yet in the midst of it all we can still have peace. This is because we will not suffer the fate of this 'Godless and carnal society'. Those without Christ are hopelessly tied to the fate of this world. They exhaust their lives looking to the things of this world to satisfy their hearts and bring them peace, but to no avail. Their final end is death in a dying world. We, on the other hand, have put our hope in the One who has overcome the world. We can take heart because we have joined ourselves to the One who will make all things new. We have been miraculously delivered from the raging torrent of this world as it plummets mindlessly toward eternal destruction and have been established on the rock of Christ with the new hope of a glorious future!

THE FOCUS OF ETERNITY

John 17:3 "Now this is eternal life: that they may know You, the only true God, and Jesus Christ, whom You have sent."

When we think of eternal life our minds turn toward heaven and all of the blessings we will receive when we cross over into eternity. The Bible has many references to the unimaginable joy and victory awaiting us. Eternal life will be a place free of sorrow and pain and full of incredible goodness. But in our anticipation of heaven we need to be careful that God is not delegated to a pious afterthought. The trials and tribulations of this world rightfully increase our desire for eternity but the true focus of heaven is God and our Savior, Jesus Christ. The whole purpose of our Lord coming to this earth was to restore us to a right relationship with the Father. That relationship will be fully restored when we cast off this earthly body and are reunited with God forever. It is of great importance that we do not allow our Christianity to digress to a self-centered relationship that primarily sees God as a means to make our lives easier, to keep us from harm, and to give us what we want. The focus of eternal life is that we may know God and Christ. The miracle of redemption is that we can begin to know Him right now! We have the opportunity through prayer, the Bible, and the Holy Spirit to pursue a close and vibrant relationship with our Lord today as we anticipate our complete union with Him for all eternity.

CLEMENS RUSSELL

THE COURSE OF SANCTIFICATION

John 17:17 "Sanctify them by the truth; Your word is truth."

Sanctification has many facets. There is the sanctification that occurs at salvation when God forgives us of all our sins and makes us as white as snow. Our initial holiness is completely dependent on the blood of Christ. There is the daily sanctification of the Christian as they explore and grow in their new life in Christ. Then there is the entire sanctification of our hearts and lives when we completely surrender our will to God. Jesus is totally embraced as our Lord and Master and self- the carnal man- is put to death. At salvation we possess all of the Holy Spirit. At entire sanctification the Holy Spirit possesses all of us. This is brought about by the power of God through the blood of our Lord. Now we continue the sanctification process at a much faster and more consistent pace as we grow and learn daily what God desires of us. We are now free to serve Him wholeheartedly, unburdened by the constant struggle between our will and His. It is the truth of Christ the Living Word and the truth of the Bible that daily guides and directs us. This allows us to dwell in the center of His will. Spiritual victory is possible not because we will it but because we have surrendered our will to God. It is no longer we that live but it is Christ living in and through us as we surge toward our final transformational sanctification. This will happen when we lay down this earthly body and are raised up with a glorified body which is made complete in the image of Christ!

FULFILLING GOD'S PURPOSE

John 17:19 "For them I sanctify Myself, that they too may be truly sanctified."

Jesus Christ was perfect when He walked this earth. He was able to sanctify Himself because He was sinless. His sanctification was setting Himself apart for the ultimate sacrifice. Gethsemane became a battleground for Jesus as He agonized over Calvary. His subjection of His will to the Father's will was the fruit of his sanctification. When Jesus fulfilled His purpose, as He suffered and died on the cross, He paved the way for us to be truly sanctified. When many think of the cross they only think of salvation. It is most certainly true that redemption can come only through the cross and that without the shed blood of Christ there is no forgiveness of sin. But it is also most certainly true that the cross is the source of our sanctification and the power behind our ability to live holy lives. Jesus' suffering and death not only saves us from the curse and penalty of sin but also gives us power over the control sin has on our hearts. God saves and cleanses us for a purpose. He wants to fill us with Himself so that we can be used by Him to minister all of the benefits of Christ to His church and to a lost and dying world. When we surrender our will to God, as Jesus did in the garden, then God is able to fulfill His purpose in our lives just as He did in the life of Christ!

WHO IS YOUR KING?

John 19:15 "But they shouted, 'Take Him away! Take Him away! Crucify Him!' 'Shall I crucify your King?' Pilate asked. 'We have no king but Caesar.' the chief priests answered."

On the surface, when we look at this verse, we cringe at the vicious callousness of the chief priests. Not only did they demand Christ's death but they also pledged their true allegiance to Caesar, the king of this world. But this is neither the first, nor the last, time that God's kingship would be rejected for this world. So many people today, like the chief priests, acknowledge a belief in God. They may even recognize Jesus Christ and practice religious activities such as prayer and attending church on a regular basis. But, when the issue of Jesus' lordship arises they falter. When they are confronted with Christ's kingship and the total commitment, loyalty and surrender that it requires, then the true ruler of their lives becomes evident. And though they may not yell 'Crucify Him!' they nonetheless make that very statement by choosing to continue living their lives by the dictates and standards of this world and of their own selfish interests and desires. We cannot serve two masters. Either Jesus Christ or Caesar is our king and the way we live our lives gives the evidence to the king we have truly chosen.

WHICH JESUS DO YOU SEE?

John 20:14 "At this, she turned around and saw Jesus standing there, but she did not realize that it was Jesus."

Mary loved Him, served Him and anointed Him. Yet, after His resurrection, she did not recognize Him. Seems pretty amazing! But how many times have we been struggling in the throes of grief or tribulation and have failed to recognize the presence of Jesus. Maybe it's because He appears unexpectedly when we are not really looking for Him. We are looking for the earthly Jesus to feed us, comfort us and heal our earthly bodies. But He now appears as the resurrected Lord desiring to raise us above our earthly concerns. Our God will supply all of our needs so we should always look for Jesus when needs arise. But when He calls your name and you turn toward Him, envision the true reality of our resurrected Lord. He desires for you to rise above earthly cares and to experience the far greater spiritual realities of what it encompasses to have a personal relationship with God.

CLEMENS RUSSELL

TRUE RESTORATION

John 21:17 "The third time He said to him, 'Simon, son of John, do you love me?' Peter was hurt because Jesus asked him a third time, 'Do you love Me?'

First there were three denials. Now there are three opportunities for restoration. Yet Peter was hurt when Jesus asked the third time, 'Do you love Me?' Maybe the memory of that horrible night came flooding back. Perhaps Jesus gave him the same look that Peter received when he denied his Lord the third time. We don't really know. But restoration is a humbling and painful task. Pride and embarrassment keep many from having a healthy relationship with God. When we fail our tendency is to make excuses. When we fall short or make selfish and lazy decisions we blame our circumstances or point the finger toward someone else. We will even create scenarios where we are able to justify to ourselves the reason for our failure and softly stroke our tender egos. But to find true restoration takes the honesty to admit our sin and the courage to follow the right course of action. We must exhibit humility in accepting the Lord's correction and take responsibility by making proper restitution. Saying 'I'm sorry' is the first step. But sometimes the healing process can be very trying and painful. When we persevere we will find that true restoration is worth it all.

GODLY LEADERSHIP

Acts 8:21 "You have no part or share in this ministry, because your heart is not right before God."

Peter proclaimed a strong indictment against a popular man. Simon was considered a person of influence in that area and was a valuable convert as he followed Phillip everywhere. Simon believed and was baptized. Yet there was still something not quite right. Peter said that Simon was full of bitterness and still captive to sin. When leaders and celebrities in this world become believers we immediately, and mistakenly, thrust them into positions of leadership and influence in the church. We need to pause and realize that the nature of Christian leadership is the opposite of the worldly leadership and influence that these new believers are used to. Earthly leadership caters to the flesh while Godly leadership is focused on the Spirit and the kingdom of God. That is why Jesus spent three years training His own disciples and why Paul tells Timothy that the leaders in the church must not be recent converts. One of the basics for Christian leaders is to be mature and well-grounded in the faith. Then leadership will be exercised to please God for His glory and not to please the flesh and our own selfish needs.

NOT BY LAW OR GOOD WORKS

Acts 13:39 "Through Him everyone who believes is justified from everything you could not be justified from by the law of Moses."

This verse, in essence, spells out humanities problem. Try as we might, with all of our might, we can never make ourselves justified in the eyes of God. The Jews were given the law but were not able to keep it. In fact, the Mosaic Law was impossible to keep. For if a person broke one small part of the law he was considered a law breaker and was guilty of breaking the whole law. And to make matters worse, parts of the law were broken just by people living their daily lives and being exposed to the uncleanness of their environment. Today the emphasis has shifted from breaking God's commandments to doing enough good things in hopes that they will outweigh or cancel our sins. The mentality says that people are basically good and God understands that we are weak. So, as long as we don't do anything really bad and try not to intentionally hurt others, God will wink at our indiscretions and allow us into heaven. But no one is justified by either keeping the law or by doing enough good things to cancel out the bad. Put simply, we are made right in God's eyes when we confess our sinfulness and truly repent. We must wholeheartedly believe in, and surrender to, Jesus Christ. Faith in Jesus is foundational and fundamental to our justification and to establishing a right standing with God.

OUR DESIRES AND HIS WILL

Acts 18:21 "But as he left, he promised, 'I will come back if it is God's will.' Then he set sail from Ephesus."

We all have desires and preferences in our lives. There are things we want and enjoy doing and there are things that we don't really care about. Our hobbies and interests vary from person to person. These have nothing to do with right and wrong. In and of themselves they are relatively neutral. Paul's desire to return to Ephesus was personal. But he was wise enough to make certain that God's will maintained preeminence in his life. It is interesting to note how quick we are to couch our lesser interests and more difficult decisions in 'will of God' phraseology. We then make some supernatural manifestation a requirement for our obedience or submission. But if it is something that we desire or perceive as a positive in our lives we will pursue that path with no regard as to whether God's will is being accomplished. In our day to day living we can trust God to lead us and guide us moment by moment. But only if we are walking in the light and have His will as our hearts desire. He knows the desires of our hearts and He wants to work His will in our lives to match those desires- but not every time. Paul did return to Ephesus and spent two years there. It is not a matter of God meeting our every desire. It is a matter of our desires being transformed so that they are submissive to being dovetailed with His will.

FEAR AND HONOR

Acts 19:18 "Many of those who believed now came and openly confessed their evil deeds."

This display of true transformation was preceded by two significant things, fear and honor. After the 'seven sons of Sceva' affair we are told that the people were seized with fear. The sons of Sceva had tried to use the name of Jesus without having a real knowledge of that name. Their resulting humiliation gave rise to widespread fear that Jesus was not to be taken lightly. We are also told that the name of Jesus was held in high honor. There was real power and depth behind His name and the people were not about to disrespect the Lord any longer. The revival that followed was, therefore, real and powerful. The believers realized that they needed to make a complete and total break from sin and commit themselves wholly to Jesus Christ. Today we can easily fall into the same snare. While salvation is free, it is neither cheap nor trite. Sometimes we need a wake-up call to the true majesty and awesomeness of the name of Jesus and what that name represents. When fear and honor are once again a part of our mindset concerning His name we too will openly confess our own 'evil deeds'. Then we will experience complete cleansing, renewed commitment and a fresh revival in our hearts and in our churches.

DOING GOD'S PERFECT WILL

Acts 21:14 "When he would not be dissuaded, we gave up and said, 'The Lord's will be done'.

Just because we are experiencing difficult times or challenging circumstances does not mean that we are outside of God's will. Paul was compelled by the Spirit to go to Jerusalem even though the prophet Agabus foretold of Paul's arrest and Paul's closest companions tried to talk him out of going. Paul was determined to be obedient. Too many Christians today base their knowledge of God's will on their circumstances. If their direction brings about positive results then they are in God's will. But if their journey is beset by problems, trials or obstacles then they reason that they must have wandered away from His plan. Our Lord's will does not exist to pamper and please our own personal desires and to bring comfort to our earthly existence. God's will is to accomplish His work in this world by using us any way He sees fit. Our responsibility is to be there. We need to be willing to be used by the Lord whenever, wherever, and however He desires to use us regardless of the personal cost or consequences to ourselves. We are crucified with Christ and have presented ourselves as living sacrifices. When we have put to death the old man with its self-centered cravings we will be able to clearly discern and obey God's perfect will.

THE PROOF OF TRUE REPENTANCE

Acts 26:20 "First to those in Damascus, then to those in Jerusalem and in all of Judea, and to the Gentiles also, I preached that they should repent and turn to God and prove their repentance by their deeds"

There is a facet of repentance that, although clearly stated by Paul in this verse, is relatively ignored or forgotten by many today. That is the proof of repentance by deeds. In our efforts to preserve the importance of salvation by faith alone, apart from works, the necessary works that result from true repentance are often swept under the rug. Works are important, not to earn salvation or God's favor, but to give evidence of true repentance. They confirm the existence of genuine faith and exhibit the regenerative work of the Holy Spirit. These works are far removed from the do-gooder deeds manufactured in the flesh to try and ease our conscience or to make us look moral and respectable to our peers. The works that result from true repentance are supernatural in that they come from a new heart and attitude. They are empowered by the Holy Spirit and spring from a humble, eager and willing mind. They are extraordinarily opposite of the character, ability and carnal inclinations exhibited by the individual before they encountered Christ. They are not works produced by our efforts to be good but by the working of the Holy Spirit in the truly repentant person.

GETTING OUT OF THE THORNS

Romans 6:21 "What benefit did you reap at that time from the things you are now ashamed of? Those things result in death."

One of the struggles people have in living holy lives has to do with their recollections of their past life of sin. Instead of sorrow and shame, many look back on their former lives in an almost wistful way. There are some who even go so far as to miss the 'fun' they had as they indulged the flesh and now view their present Christian existence as a tolerable bore that must be endured in order to insure entrance into heaven. At the root of this frame of mind is self. Their salvation experience focused on the need to be saved and gain eternal life but has not matured to the greater purpose of having a restored relationship with a loving God and Savior. So the daily outworking of their Christian walk revolves around self and what's in it for them and is reflected in their words, actions and even their prayer life. Although the need for salvation and the desire for eternal life are honorable reasons to become a Christian we must realize that God's ultimate goal is to reestablish a loving and reciprocal relationship with His children. Our love for God must be sincere and from our hearts in order for us to move beyond mere selfish obedience. If we don't we will become like the seed cast among the thorns which, because of the cares of this world, bore no fruit.

MORE THAN CONQUERORS

Romans 6:23 "No, in all these things we are more than conquerors through Him who loved us."

As most of us know it is relatively easy to believe and joyfully serve God under positive circumstances. When things are going well for us we are able to enjoy our relationship with our Father because we are less distracted by our own human needs and by the desires of the flesh. These are indeed wonderful times for us. It is when we are assailed by 'trouble or hardship or persecution or famine or nakedness or danger or sword' (vs. 35) that we can be challenged in our trust and confidence in God. This trust and confidence will be shattered if we mistakenly believe that God will deliver us from all and every trying circumstance. God's promise is that we are more than conquerors 'in all these things'! What we have to conquer is not the particular trial or circumstance we are facing. Most of us have already faced many rough times and have had to stay the course in its entirety. What we are able to overcome are the doubts and fears that bombard us as to whether we are following the right path or whether God still loves us and cares for us. Be assured that as long as you are dwelling in the center of God's will, and desire His way above all else, His love will continue to encourage you. He is in control no matter how dark your path may seem. No path is too difficult as long as we are walking in step with our Savior.

THE WAY OF THE CROSS

Romans 11:32 "For God has bound all men over to disobedience so that He may have mercy on them all."

When God sent His Son to die on the cross, and then raised Him from the dead, He opened a pathway for all mankind to follow. There is only one road to heaven and that road leads to the foot of the cross. By providing this way to Himself, God nullified all other methods and attempts to come to Him. Jesus stated in no uncertain terms that He was the Way, the Truth and the Life and that no one could come to the Father except through Him. Even the Jewish sacrificial system was replaced by faith in Christ and the slaughter of bulls and lambs ceased after 70A.D. There are so many religions in this world and so many different and confusing attempts to reach God. It can overwhelm us to try and sort it all out. Whereas the essence of all other religions, sects and cults revolves around man's efforts to reach God, the way of the cross is God's perfect and exclusive effort to reach man. Those who reject the ramifications of the cross are in the camp of the disobedient. Those who accept God's mercy and forgiveness, provided by the cross, join the camp of the redeemed. They are now a part of the fellowship of believers and the family of the born again children of God. The path of all who sincerely and wholeheartedly seek God will always lead to the foot of the cross.

ACTIVE AGENTS

Romans 12:21 "Do not be overcome by evil, but overcome evil with good."

God wants us to not be overcome by evil. We live in a world marred by, and teeming with, evil of all sorts. It assails us on every front by tempting us, discouraging us, frustrating us and distracting us from God's higher calling in our lives. And being overcome by evil involves much more that being tempted to sin and indulge oneself in the wickedness of this world. Many Christians have removed themselves from doing bad things but they are still overcome by evil. They may not be gratifying the flesh but they have allowed the world to paralyze them and render them ineffective in being the salt and light that our Lord has commanded us to be. These believers have adopted a 'hunker down' mentality and have succumbed to just trying to survive in this fallen world and make it to heaven. But God has also commanded us to overcome evil. This is not done by hiding from it or ignoring it or just trying to survive it. This is accomplished by overcoming evil with good. We are to be active agents of God's love and mercy in this world. We are to love sincerely, be devoted to one another, be zealous, have fervor, be joyful and patient, and be faithful in prayer. The list from verses 9-20 of this chapter goes on and on. Our goal is not to defeat the evil in this world. Christ already accomplished that. Our goal is to show and to share God's gift of deliverance to those He brings across our daily path.

MOTIVATED TO BE HOLY

Romans 13:5 "Therefore, it is necessary to submit to the authorities, not only because of possible punishment, but also because of conscience."

Paul gives us two of the most widely held and practical reasonings for obeying the law. The first is the threat of possible punishment. Most of us have glanced at our speedometer and tapped our brakes at the sight of a police car. We concentrate on doing our best when we are being observed by our supervisor. The possibility of negative consequences is a great motivator in keeping us within the boundaries of properly defined behavior. Then there are those times when we 'do the right thing' because we feel motivated by something within. We allow that person to go ahead of us in traffic even though we have the right of way. We do our best in our jobs even though we are not being observed. We choose the right entertainments even when no one is watching. And when we reach the place where our prime motivation for doing the right thing is conscience and not fear of punishment then we are said to have character and maturity. Obviously this applies to our spiritual life as well. The fear of punishment and retribution can be an effective deterrent to sinful behavior. But it is when we willingly walk in obedience to God's word and strive to be like Christ that we truly begin to grow. When we live in holiness because of conscience and because of our desire to please God we will begin to develop character and maturity in our relationship with our Heavenly Father.

RESPONSIBLE FREEDOM I

Romans 14:15 "If your brother is distressed because of what you eat, you are no longer acting in love. Do not by your eating destroy your brother for whom Christ died."

Our freedom in Christ does have its limits. We have an obligation to exercise responsible freedom. This is a freedom tempered by obedience to God's will. It is a freedom channeled by the crucifixion of the flesh and submissive to the needs our Christian family. Love for others must always win over self-love. Many would argue that you can't please everyone. And they would be correct. We may offend someone, create a disagreement, or even cause a conflict because of the freedom we practice. Paul was in constant conflict with the Judaisers who insisted on the need to be circumcised. It is not necessary to submit to everyone's whim and fancy. But scripture is clear when freedom is abused. It is when our freedom causes genuine distress or grief in our brother. It is when our freedom causes our brother to sin. It is when 'our freedom' has its roots in our own selfish ambition and the desire to do it 'our way' without regard for the consequences. It is when freedom itself becomes a warped bondage to personal preferences and spiritual pride. It is when freedom considers our own desires and wants above the legitimate needs of our brothers and sisters in Christ. Then we have reduced freedom to an abnormal indulgence of our flesh. The spiritual and emotional well-being of our weaker brothers should always take precedence over our 'freedom'- even if it leads to a cross!

HE IS ALWAYS IN CONTROL

Romans 15:31-32 "Pray that I may be rescued from the unbelievers in Judea and that my service in Jerusalem may be acceptable to the saints there, so that by God's will I may come to you with joy and together with you be refreshed."

Paul had a pretty straightforward prayer request- one that was answered in a very different way. He wanted to be rescued from the unbelievers in Judea but it was accomplished through the power and might of Roman soldiers. He desired for his service to be acceptable to the saints in Jerusalem but his outreach to the Gentiles alienated the Jews further and created a major division in the church. He hoped to eventually go to Rome to minister to the church there but ended up going, not as a missionary, but as a prisoner of the Roman military. This must not have been very joyful or refreshing. Paul knew what he desired but had no idea how God would accomplish His will. Yet God's hand is evident throughout Paul's entire ordeal. Paul gains the favor of his Roman captors and the leaders in the early church. His nephew overhears a plot on Paul's life. Paul's citizenship curries additional protection and favor. On his journey to Rome he is continuously protected and sustained. And when he gets to Rome, although a prisoner, he rents a house and is able to preach unhindered for at least two years. Our greatest desire should be to dwell in the center of God's will while leaving the methods and means in His hands. When we dwell in the center of His will we can be fully confident that everything that happens is guided and allowed by Him.

GLORYING IN OUR OBSCURITY

Romans 6:14 "Greet Asyncritus, Phlegon, Hermes, Patrobus, Hermas and the brothers with them.

This is not the roll call of faith found in Hebrews. In fact, this is the only place in scripture where these names are found. Somehow and somewhere in Paul's ministry and travels he met these people and they were important enough for him to send his personal greetings. It could even be that Paul had only heard of them. After all, he had not even been to Rome yet when he wrote this. But regardless of his relationship with these people, Paul mentions them here by name. There is no doubt that the stories of scripture are filled with the work and influence of thousands of once named or unnamed Christians. What does the name 'Patrobus' bring to mind? Virtually nothing. Serving God and working faithfully in His kingdom is not about making a name for ourselves. It is about glorifying God and accomplishing His will. Most of us will never be listed in a faith 'Hall of Fame' or even be mentioned once in the recorded annals of Christian history. We are relegated to 'the brothers with them'. But God's love for us is every bit as strong and real as it is for the headliners of Christianity. And God's blessings and reward are not based on whether we make the 'top ten list' of the shakers and movers in the church today. They are based on our loyalty, dedication, and commitment regardless of whether we are noticed or not.

DOORMATS

I Corinthians 4:5 "Therefore judge nothing before the appointed time; wait till the Lord comes. He will bring to light what is hidden in darkness and will expose the motives of men's hearts. At that time each will receive his praise from God."

Have you ever been misunderstood? Or perhaps you have done something good or positive only to have your intentions questioned. Maybe you have wondered what the 'real' motives were or why someone was acting a certain way. The truth is that we have no way of judging hidden motives. There are people who do have a secret agenda or selfish ambitions and will impersonate goodwill or compassion to see their goals reached. We have all probably been there at some time or other ourselves. But when we begin to question the reason behind every act or action that we see then we fall into a dangerous trap. Most people will judge motives because they don't want to be taken advantage of or they don't want someone to get away with something. Some even have a self-righteous desire to see people 'get theirs'. Yet when we live our lives in the image of Christ we will undoubtedly get used. The humility and meekness we are to exhibit will be viewed by many to be fear and weakness. That doesn't matter! What matters is that we live our lives faithfully in the center of God's will and submit to the underserved abuse that is inevitable from those who would take advantage of our Christlikeness. Then we can look forward to when God will make everything right. There are times that being a doormat could be just another way of washing someone else's feet.

KEEPING THE BRIDE PURE

I Corinthians 5:11 "But now I am writing you that you must not associate with anyone who calls himself a brother but is sexually immoral or greedy, an idolater or a slanderer, a drunkard or a swindler. With such a man do not even eat."

In this age of grace, mercy and acceptance a verse like this seems to stand in stark contrast to a gospel of love and compassion. Are we not to accept everyone without judging them and open our arms to anyone who wants to be part of the church? The confusion lies in the erroneous thinking that has infiltrated today's Christianity. First, we are to love everyone in the world and not judge them. But this verse is referring to those who live sinful lives yet call themselves Christians. Although we are all sinners saved by grace, once we have been saved our lives should be lived above the power and destructive influence of sin. There is a difference between stepping in the mud and wallowing in the muck. Second, it is necessary to have accountability in the church. We are the body of Christ and as such we have a responsibility to keep that body healthy and pure. A little leaven can infiltrate the whole batch of bread. Third, we must remember that the church is not a building but a blood bought, Spirit filled fellowship. We may open our doors to all but we must confront those who falsely believe that they are born-again children of God while they continue to live a sinful lifestyle. The holiness of God and the well-being of His body demand this.

PURE SEX

I Corinthians 6:20 "You were bought at a price. Therefore honor God with your body."

Much has been discussed about how we are to honor God with our bodies. The fact that our bodies are God's temple has fortified people's arguments against smoking, drinking alcohol, overeating, drug abuse and other negative habits. And although these addictions are harmful and undesirable in a Christians life, this particular admonition to honor God with our bodies relates directly to sexual sins. It seems to be that laxness and acceptance has invaded the church today regarding this area of rebellion and wickedness. There are many in churches who indulge in fornication on a regular basis. Divorce and remarriage are rampant. The sanctity of marital vows and commitments are continually set aside in order to fulfill selfish desires and fleshly lusts. The number of unmarried couples who are masquerading as devoted Christians, even being allowed to become church members while continuing to live together, keeps escalating. And many churches are in the throes of heated debate and sharp division over the acceptance, as Christians, of those who actively participate in homosexual behaviors. The biblical truth is that we honor God with our bodies when we refrain from any sexual practice outside of the marriage covenant. God's will is for sex to be the ultimate union between a man and a woman who are married. Anything outside of that is sin. This is God's standard and will.

RESPONSIBLE FREEDOM II

I Corinthians 8:9 "Be careful, however, that the exercise of your freedom does not become a stumbling block to the weak."

The freedom that we have in Christ is incredible. No longer are we bound to observe rituals and rules to make us acceptable to God, such as what to eat or drink, what to wear, how to wash and a host of other regulations. The danger comes when we focus our freedom on serving ourselves instead of on God and we use our freedom as 'an occasion for the flesh'. In today's Christian vernacular we couch this self-centered focus in phrases such as 'I deserve it' or 'I'm not hurting anyone' or 'God doesn't want me to be a doormat'. Thus we justify actions and activities that dishonor God, offend our brothers in Christ and sully our witness to the world. Our freedom is not to do whatever we want regardless of the consequences. Our freedom is that we are able to serve God unencumbered by rules, regulations and rituals that we must follow to be able to come into His presence. The only law we must follow is the law of love- love for God and love for others. The fascinating thing is that when we faithfully live our lives in the fullness of His love we begin to naturally and effortlessly live holy lives. The petty things we so ardently clung to as our right or privilege are replaced by the simple desire to love God and others regardless of the cost to ourselves.

HEED TO THE WEAK

I Corinthians 8:13 "Therefore, if what I eat causes my brother to fall into sin, I will never eat meat again, so that I will not cause him to fall."

If we ceased doing everything that someone would find disagreeable we would cease doing everything. There are so many different opinions on what is right or wrong, acceptable or unacceptable, offensive or non-offensive. We are then left reeling and spinning if we try to please everyone. And what if doing something offends one person and not doing it offends another? At the same time there are those who charge full speed ahead without any regard at all for the convictions of others. They use their 'freedom in Christ' as an excuse to forge their own way at the expense of their brothers in Christ. Fortunately Paul offers us a middle ground. First, it is our weaker brothers who are our fellow Christians that we need to heed to, not those in the world. This is echoed in another passage where Paul says that the strong ought to bear with the weak and not to please themselves. To knowingly allow our freedom in Christ to push our weaker brother backwards is selfish and sinful. Second, just because someone expresses a different opinion does not mean we should automatically give in. It is when our continued actions would cause someone to compromise their own convictions that we need to set aside our desires and put their spiritual welfare ahead of our own physical pleasure or emotional wellbeing.

GUARDING AGAINST THE FALLS

I Corinthians 10:12 "So if you think you are standing firm, be careful that you don't fall!"

We have all been there before. Maybe it's after a great service in church or a special victory in our lives. God is wonderfully close and our emotions are running high and we feel invincible when suddenly- WHAM! We blow it big time and depression and discouragement set in. Many times it is at our highest moments that we become most susceptible to falling. It is at those times that we have the tendency to take our eyes off Jesus and relish in our own spiritual strength and accomplishments. Then the proverbial truth that 'pride goes before destruction, a haughty spirit before a fall' comes home to roost. We need to keep Jesus as our 'all in all' and remember that without Him we would not only be lost but would be wallowing in the deepest depths of sin. We must keep our lives hid in Christ so that it is no longer I that live, but Christ that lives in me. We will do well to open our eyes to the truth- that at our highest point and in our greatest victory the Holy Spirit is still propping us up on every side and is the exclusive reason we are standing firm. When we look at, not how high we are, but at how much higher we need to be then we maintain the humility necessary to protest ourselves from those self-induced falls.

SEEKING GOOD

I Corinthians 10:24 "Nobody should seek his own good, but the good of others."

What exactly does Paul mean here? Is he saying that we should not seek or desire anything good for ourselves? Absolutely not! It is fine for us to want to enjoy physical and emotional well-being...as long as we remain within the center of God's will. After all, one of the strongest motivations for committing our lives to Christ is the promise of eternity. This verse needs to be taken in the context of the entire chapter. Paul is teaching us that, although it is permissible to seek our own good, we should put the needs of others ahead of ourselves. It is when our seeking becomes selfish and our pursuit of our comfort or needs becomes an offense or stumbling stone to others that we have crossed the line between legitimately pursuing our good and selfishly demanding our own will at the expense of others. Paul clarifies his teaching later in verse 33 when he states, "For I am not seeking my own good, but the good of many, so that they may be saved." We must remind ourselves that we remain in this world to be used of God to encourage and strengthen one another and to be witnesses to this fallen world of Christ's life changing salvation. Our focus should always be the salvation and restoration of others, not the ease and satisfaction of our own earthly lives.

BEING AN EXAMPLE

I Corinthians 11:1 "Follow my example as I follow the example of Christ."

The idea of being examples to others of what being a Christian is all about has been replaced today by a self-centered and privatized spirituality. Instead of living our lives in a way that would challenge other Christians and be a light to the lost, many have settled for a bare-bones faith that balks at scrutiny, resists accountability and leaves room for secret sins and unholy attitudes. Very few are bold enough and have the confidence to present their lives as a model of what being a Christian entails. This type of witness is not rooted in pride-'look how wonderful I sing, preach, teach', or in self-righteousness- 'look how holy I am because I do this and I don't do thus and so'. The validity of our example is anchored in the way that we follow the example of Christ. When we continually look to Him and strive to let the Lord's light shine through us, and when our lives have consistency so that our family sees the same Jesus that our co-workers and church family sees, then we are becoming that example. We must realize that it is only when we are completely yielded to God that we can be this bold of a witness. Then God can use us as a light on a hill to draw others to Himself and to be a source of strength and encouragement to our fellow believers.

A HEALTHY BODY

I Corinthians 12:14 "Now the body is not made up of one part but of many."

Have you ever noticed how often we take our bodies for granted? Most of us use our eyes, ears, hands, feet, mouths and noses every day. And unless there is something wrong, we rarely have a second thought about their functioning. They just continue working together in harmony to accomplish our will and to fulfill our needs. But let one part of our bodies get injured or lose its ability to operate and suddenly the whole physical engine gets out of sync. Many of us have seen this happen in our churches as well. It is of interest to note that, although the church is worldwide in its scope, Paul was addressing his teachings on the body to a particular fellowship- the Corinthians. There are definitely times when the universal church can come together to aid in some great disaster. And missionary work could not happen on as great a scale if it were not for many local churches cooperating together. But there is also a divine calling for each individual church to function as a body in fulfilling God's plan for their own community. This is accomplished by evangelistic endeavors, discipleship, compassionate ministry and Christian fellowship. This is most effectively done when each individual is committed to walking in the light and using the gifts God has given them to build up the body of Christ and further His kingdom.

CHRISTIAN MATURITY

I Corinthians 13:11 "When I was a child, I talked like a child, I thought like a child, I reasoned like a child. When I became a man, I put childish ways behind me."

What is maturity? For some it is becoming serious in their actions and demeanor. They are no longer interested in the 'toys' of life. Their smiles are wistful and they carry an air of smug superiority. For others maturity involves getting a job, paying their bills, raising their families and trying to continually stay on top of the challenges of daily living. Their smiles are rare and they carry an air of constant frustration, continual activity and consistent stress. Although we should be serious about certain things and fulfill our responsibilities to our jobs and families, this is not the maturity Paul is referring to here. Paul is speaking toward a spiritual maturity- a maturity that finds its culmination in perfect love as opposed to imperfect self-centeredness. Paul had just admonished the Corinthians in the previous verses for many incidents of selfish behaviors. These behaviors had infected their fellowship, distorted the exercise of their spiritual gifts and even corrupted their walk with God. The 'most excellent way' is the way of love. This love motivates us to truly unselfish actions and inspires us to holy attitudes. Paul's maturity would call us out of the childish instability of selfish motives and desires and into a mature and steadfast life of love.

HAVE YOU BELIEVED IN VAIN?

I Corinthians 15:2 "By this gospel you are saved, if you hold firmly to the word I preached to you. Otherwise you have believed in vain."

Paul pulls no punches in this verse. We must hold firmly to the true gospel and not allow ourselves to be deceived by false doctrines and teachings or dissuaded by smooth arguments as to why the Bible is no longer valid or relevant. We must not become discouraged in our walk with God to the extent that we fall back into a lifestyle of sin. To hold firmly does not imply salvation by works. That is God's free gift of grace. To hold firmly does mean that we live lives of faithfulness, holiness and Christ-likeness. That is a living and active faith and evidence of true salvation. Our walk with God is full of hills, valleys, bumps and turns. That is why we must be steadfast and hold firmly to the gospel by staying strong in the Lord. The church is littered with those who have begun the race but did not count the cost. They had no root or they allowed the cares and desires of this world to cause them to falter and fall. Our salvation is never earned, bought or deserved. But it still comes with the price of total rejection of sin, sincere faith and repentance, and complete surrender to the Lordship of Jesus Christ. When we are not committed enough to endure to the end then Paul states that we have believed in vain.

OUR COMPANY MATTERS

I Corinthians 15:33 "Do not be misled: "Bad company corrupts good character.'"

Paul's quote here is not a quote from Scripture but a quote from a worldly philosopher. God's truth is not an exclusively prized commodity only found among His people. It permeates the entire world and is readily evident to any who would seek truth and meaning in life. Most of the major religions of the world have a moral code that predominately mirrors the truth of scripture. In Romans Paul speaks of God's invisible qualities as being clearly seen. There is much of God's wisdom to be found in the world. His creation abounds with it. But when His wisdom is filtered through worldly and self-focused eyes then it can become corrupted. 'Although they claimed to be wise, they became fools.' (Romans 1:22) So even though Paul's quote does not appear in scripture until this point it now conveys spiritual truth. If we desire to maintain high morals and be people of good character then we must be careful of the company we keep. This not only refers to carnal and wicked people but also to those who may appear moral and religious but disseminate teachings that contradict God's word and undermine the doctrine of Christ. Paul is not telling us to be spiritual snobs or to exercise exclusiveness. He is telling us to use wisdom and sound judgment in choosing the people we would keep company with because they will definitely have an influence and impact on our character.

GOD'S WILL AND OUR PLANS

I Corinthians 16:6-7 "Perhaps I will stay with you a while, or even spend the winter, so that you can help me on my journey wherever I go. I do not want to see you now and make only a passing visit; I hope to spend some time with you, if the Lord permits."

There is a balance between God's will and our own plans and desires. There are those who would pray and seek divine guidance for every little detail of their lives. They are almost paralyzed with fear that they will somehow miss what God's perfect will is and He will descend upon them in judgment, ready to punish them for the least little shortfall. Then there are those who go charging through life. They make their plans without ever consulting the Lord or seeking His direction. God is usually tacked on at the end to ensure their success or as an attempt to gain divine approval for self-centered living. Paul, with words like 'perhaps' and 'hope', shows his desires and involvements with his planning while at the same time acknowledging God's ultimate control by stating 'if the Lord permits'. Having the Spirit gives us latitude in making plans as long as we are dedicated to Christ and are listening to, and obeying, His voice. This obedience remains steadfast even when He checks us, corrects our direction or tells us 'NO'. Proverbs 16:3 says, 'Commit to the Lord whatever you do and your plans will succeed.' This is not just asking for God's stamp of approval. This is submitting to His will and way in every area of our lives before we even begin to make our plans.

TRUE LOVE

I Corinthians 16:14 "Do everything in love,"

What a challenging and dangerous statement! Challenging because, with four words, Paul gives us a summary of what our motivation for any thought, word or action should be. He is probably giving the Corinthians a subtle reminder of his admonishment in chapter 13 about the importance of love. Regardless of our circumstances or condition, we should always have love as the preeminent reason and purpose behind everything we do. Love should be evident in our worship and work for God, in our witness and ministry to a lost world, and in our service and fellowship with our brothers and sisters in Christ. When we 'do everything in love' we are fulfilling the commandments of our Lord. We are also reflecting to all the essence of God. God is love! But this statement of Paul has a dangerous aspect as well. It is dangerous because the definition of love has been cheapened in today's world and has been delegated primarily to the emotions and defined by the feelings of the moment. Many erroneously believe that they are acting in love just because they feel it or because they have no intention of hurting someone. The primary focus of love becomes the self. It is whatever makes me happy or makes me feel good. Then our service to God and others becomes a means to that selfish end instead of the natural result of true, sincere and unselfish love.

FALLING SHORT OF THE GOAL

Galatians 3:3 "Are you so foolish? After beginning with the Spirit, are you now trying to attain your goal by human effort?"

It's an easy trap to fall into. We receive Christ by faith and are born again. Our lives are resurrected and our sins taken away. We now have a home with God for eternity. All of our previous futile efforts to make ourselves acceptable to God are obliterated by simply receiving His effort on the cross. But now we have fallen back into the prison of our own works. We once again try to make ourselves worthy of Him and become trapped in a quandary of do's and don'ts. Our holy living ceases to be predicated by our relationship with God and digresses to a self-centered motivation of wanting to be considered good. We are seeking to impress others instead of pleasing God. Our hearts have been robbed of the true incentive for living a righteous life. That incentive should be a sincere desire to please and serve the love of our lives- a holy God. Living an outward holy life devoid of the heartfelt passion to please God is the 'human effort' that will cause us to fall short of our goal.

BEING GOOD

Galatians 6:15 "Neither circumcision nor uncircumcision means anything; what counts is a new creation."

Basically it's not what you do. It's who you are that counts. There are many in this world today who are trying to be good. But they have an idea of what good truly is. Then what they think is good ends up becoming distorted as they try to live it out. That's why people can be up in arms about the mistreatment of animals but approve the slaughter of unborn infants. That's why people will be appalled at the sad state of our children and families while they themselves are living together and having kids outside of marriage. That's why folks rant and rave at the hypocrisy in church and will never darken the doors while tolerating that same hypocrisy on a daily basis at their jobs, with their families and friends, and even in their personal lives. When we attempt to be good on the outside without the transformation of our hearts, our efforts at righteousness are futile at best. Our hearts betray our true nature. The righteous life God desires and commands springs out of a heart that is continually renewed by the presence and power of the Holy Spirit. The holy life is not a result of our efforts to adhere to an arbitrary and subjective list of do's and don'ts. A holy life is accomplished by having a heart, mind and life totally renewed and devoted to God.

A WON WAR

Ephesians 6:13 "Therefore put on the full armor of God, so that when the day of evil comes, you may be able to stand your ground and after you have done everything, to stand."

God's will for us is to stand and to be strong in the Lord and in His mighty power. And, although God is the source of all that we need in order to stand, we must still dress ourselves in the full armor of God and do everything we can to live in obedience. He provides the armor but we must put it on and use it. Too many Christians meander about waiting for God to do everything when He has already done everything. He provides the protection we need and has commanded us to go preach the gospel and to let our light shine before men. We are to always be watchful and ready and there are dozens of other admonitions to engage the enemy. We have truth and righteousness, the gospel of peace, faith and salvation, the word of God and the power and guidance of the Holy Spirit through prayer. So what are we waiting for? We are called to fight battles in a war that has already been won!

A SPIRITUAL MID-LIFE CRISIS

Philippians 2:13 "for it is God who works in you to will and to act according to His good purpose."

As we grow and mature in our walk with God we sometimes lose sight of our motivation for holy living. Our personal devotions, church attendance, spiritual responsibilities and duties start to become routine and even mundane. We are in danger of experiencing a spiritual mid-life crisis. One reason for this predicament is that we can unknowingly become dependent on our own strength and experience. We forget the truth that all we are and do comes, not from our own efforts, but from God working in us. It is easy to let our spiritual source shift from God to ourselves. Our attitude begins to focus on our own spiritual strength and experience instead of on God as our only and ultimate source. It puts us in danger of replacing His continued grace, mercy and power with self-sufficiency and spiritual pride. Not only is it God who gives us the wisdom and ability to do His work but it is also God who puts within our hearts the desire and will to daily live for Him. It's simply a matter of keeping our focus on God and not allowing it to drift to ourselves and our own achievements no matter how holy and mature we think we've become.

FAITHFUL TODAY

Philippians 3:16 "Only let us live up to what we have already attained."

The Christian life is a life of continual growth. We should be constantly and consistently moving forward in our walk with God. One of the biggest hindrances to our growth is when we continually stumble over the same things. As God teaches us we need to put those teachings into practice. And we also need to be faithful in living up to those teachings in our daily lives. This is what we have already attained. God's desire and ability to abundantly bless us is dependent on what we are doing with what we already have and how we are using what He has already given us. Jesus taught that the person who is faithful in a few things would be made ruler over many things. We must faithfully walk in the light that God has already given us and live in daily victory over those sins which we have repented of and confessed. When our lives exhibit a steadfastness and consistency to those around us, and when we find joy and contentment where we are instead of where we think we want to be, then we will have discovered the essence of peace and will be in a position to truly be used by God for His glory and for the work of His kingdom.

KEEP YOUR MIND ON HIM

Philippians 3:19 "…their mind is on earthly things."

This indictment sums up the description of those who are enemies of the cross. These enemies may or may not be in the church. Regardless, they have focused on the things of this world instead of the things of God. Their flesh has taken precedence over their spirit. The world has become their pot of gold while the kingdom of God has been relegated to the back burner. Their 'destiny is destruction'. At first glance we might assume that these individuals would be horribly backslidden and wicked. But there are many today who, much like the Pharisees of old, know the right religious words to speak and the correct behaviors to showcase. Yet they are selfish within their hearts and their minds are 'on earthly things'. When someone lives in this shallow spiritual existence it is the trials and tribulations of life that exposes the useless chaff of their hypocrisy and double-mindedness. It is then that the true nature of their hearts is revealed in explosive anger, bitterness, hard-heartedness and continual disobedience. Sometimes it is difficult, as we dwell continually in this world and work to fulfill all the demands of our physical needs, to not allow our minds to drift toward earthly things. We need to remember what Isaiah said, "You will keep in perfect peace him whose mind is steadfast, because he trusts in you." Keep your mind on Him!

RIGHT WHERE YOU ARE TODAY

Colossians 3:23 "Whatever you do, work at it with all your heart, as working for the Lord, not for men."

Many of us work jobs that are far from ideal and leave us unfulfilled. We may even have bosses who are difficult, or even impossible, to please. Or perhaps our family situation is particularly challenging and we are dealing with an unsaved spouse, rebellious children or severe loneliness. Many desire a change in their circumstances. And even though they have cried out to God time and time again they still feel that they have somehow become trapped and see no light at the end of the tunnel. They feel enslaved by their situation and find it almost impossible to live up to admonitions such as this one that Paul gave to the Colossians. We should all 'work at it with all our heart, as working for the Lord', But it is of great interest to note that in this particular verse Paul was addressing slaves in particular! He was telling those who were in the most degrading and difficult strata of society to keep a holy and right attitude in the midst of their bondage. We must remember that if we truly love God and desire His will above all else then whatever situation we are in is part of His plan and will for our lives. We must make the most of this moment and live, not to just survive in hopes of a better tomorrow, but in a way that honors God right now and allows our light to shine forth brightly. Right where we are today is where God needs us now!

CLEMENS RUSSELL

A REAL ENEMY

I Thessalonians 2:18 "For we wanted to come to you- certainly I, Paul, did again and again- but satan stopped us."

Sometimes we lose sight of the fact that we are in a battle where satan is a real foe who desires, not only to thwart our efforts for the kingdom, but also to devour our souls. How? One way is by direct persecution from people in the world. Those who do not know Christ, whether they realize it or not, are pawns in the devil's war against the kingdom of God. They may be bold and aggressive in their attacks against Christians. Or they may be more subtle by couching their comments in religious phrases such as 'God loves everyone, He won't send anybody to hell.' or 'No one is perfect, we all sin but God understands. Just try to do more good than bad.' and even 'It doesn't matter what you believe as long as you are sincere.' Then those who faithfully follow God's word are labeled as intolerant, narrow minded or politically incorrect. Another way satan opposes us is by tempting our flesh with the things of this world. Whether it is the physical lusts in a society that sees drugs, alcohol and sex as the pinnacles of existence or the lure of wealth and possessions or the desire for popularity and fame, we are bombarded daily with temptations to compromise and fall short of our Lord's highest standards. For these reasons we need to be on our guard daily and constantly mindful of the fact that, in the midst of all these attacks, we can be more that conquerors!

A HEART FOR HOLINESS

I Thessalonians 3:13 "May He strengthen your hearts so that you will be blameless and holy in the presence of our God and Father when our Lord Jesus comes with all His holy ones."

There is no doubt that God desires for us to live blameless and holy lives. The challenge comes when we try to appropriate holiness on a daily basis. For many Christians holy living consists of a series of starts and stops. They continuously shift between drive, neutral, reverse and park. Fortunately the scriptures give us ample teachings on holy living. In this passage Paul reveals one of the most important keys to consistency. Holiness begins in our hearts. We must have an all-consuming desire to live pure lives. We must abhor sin and the wicked tendencies of the flesh. Our hearts must crave God and the pursuit of sanctified living. Yet for all that, we would still fall far short if it were not for God strengthening and encouraging our hearts. It is a wonderful testimony to His love for us that along with the clear command to be holy and perfect comes the strength and power to fulfill that command. It all begins when we surrender ourselves to Him, make Him the true desire of our hearts, and allow God to mold and fill our hearts with Himself.

ALWAYS THANKFUL

I Thessalonians 5:18 "...give thanks in all circumstances for this is God's will for you in Christ Jesus."

Are you a thankful person? In ALL circumstances? One of the challenges of living a Christian life is discerning God's will. 'Should I buy or rent? Chose college or a career? Stay or relocate? Keep this job or find another?' Yet here we see something that, without a doubt, is God's will for us. We must give thanks in all circumstances. When we are faithful in practicing what we know is God's will then His unseen will can become easier to discern and receive. Being thankful in all circumstances transforms the situations of our lives from being self-gratifying events to being God pleasing opportunities. Then the question of which direction to take becomes easier, not only to know, but also to accept. Notice that being thankful is God's will for us 'in Christ Jesus'. Another important aspect of following His will and being thankful in all circumstances is that we are faithfully serving Christ right now! Being in Christ Jesus means that we have forfeit our lives for His glory and purpose and that we are walking fully in the light of His path. When we are 'in Christ Jesus' we can be confident that life's uncontrolled events, no matter how disconcerting, are permitted and directed by our Father. He has allowed them in our lives for His glory and for our benefit.

HANG IN THERE

II Thessalonians 1:6 "God is just. He will pay back trouble to those who trouble you."

There seems to be a lot of injustice in this world today. We are all aware of the seeming success of wicked and evil people in this world. Those who live in the flesh and seek primarily to fulfill their own selfish desires are almost effortlessly able to do it. Hollywood, government, big business and even many churches are filled with those who live for themselves and appear to 'get away' with a multitude of indiscretions. Meanwhile, those of us who faithfully follow the Lord continue to struggle and fight to survive in this fallen world. Evil is abounding more and more as society continues to compromise God's standards while we just try to hang on and endure. Yet our day is coming…but not in this life. How long must we endure persecutions and tribulations? We must remain faithful until Christ returns. If we look for satisfaction, peace, and fairness in this world we will be sorely disappointed. Our hope for justice and retribution will come when we receive our eternal reward while those who live according to this world, both inside and outside of the church, will receive their just recompense and eternal punishment. It is coming. It will most certainly happen. Just continue to be patient, steadfast, persevering, courageous and strong. Don't become weary in doing good. And commit yourself daily to faithfully endure until the end.

WHOLLY SATISFIED

I Timothy 6:6 "But Godliness with contentment is great gain."

A lot of people put a lot of effort and expend a lot of energy into being successful in this world. We are all aware of the pitfalls of fame and fortune which can lead to a multitude of heartaches and sins. Yet there are many Christians who may outwardly deny the ways of this world but still have an inward hunger for prestige, success and popularity. We may be able to steer away from the more obvious evils. But these inward desires still remain and we may even begin preying on the church itself to satisfy these desires. The resulting envy, jealousy, competition and strife can severely wound the body of Christ while never satisfying these unholy cravings. Paul gives Timothy two key components to achieving true success. First is godliness which involves having the right attitude toward God. This results in not only being able to do the right things, but also in thinking the right way. Second is contentment which deals with being satisfied with the things we have and the life we live- the possessions and resources God has given us. The idea that living to please God will result in greater material blessings is unscriptural. Then the motivation for holy living becomes self-centered instead of Christ centered. It is a shallow lifestyle and reeks of the flesh. But it is those who are truly devoted to God and who are content with where God has placed them in this life that find satisfaction. Those who are striving to live righteously and desire His will above all else will find the real treasure of life which God has promised.

CORPORATE CHRISTIANITY

Hebrew 3:13 "But encourage one another daily, as long as it is called today, so that none of you may be hardened by sin's deceitfulness."

We were never meant to function alone as Christians. Our decision to repent of our sins and follow Christ is ours alone to make. But then we become part of a fellowship to which we are accountable and are impressed upon to serve. It is a grossly mistaken notion that we don't need the church. God has us on this earth to be a witness and a light to the lost. But we are also to be a strength and encouragement to others in the household of faith. Moses needed Aaron and Hur to hold his arms up as the Israelites defeated the Amalekites. Elijah needed to know that there were still 7,000 faithful in Israel and he also needed Elisha to help and support his work. Jesus desired for His disciples to watch with Him in Gethsemane. And Paul's letters abound with references to those who aided, helped and encouraged him. It is a warped version of Christianity that sees faith as solely a personal issue that minimizes or excludes the importance of the church. The need for the fellowship, influence and the admonition of other Christians is required in Scripture. This attitude of independence from the church is indicative of the deceitful hardening of sin. No one can profess love and devotion to God while removing themselves from accountability to, and responsibility for, other believers.

WHY OBEY?

Hebrews 4:6 & 11- "It still remains that some will enter that rest, and those who formerly had the gospel preached to them did not go in, because of their disobedience... Let us, therefore, make every effort to enter that rest, so that no one will fall by following their example of disobedience."

Our choices do make a difference. God's ability to work in our lives is based on our obedience. And when we are 'out of sorts' and choose to disobey then there are consequences. God is always ready, willing and able to forgive us. But what we sometimes neglect to consider are the impacts that our indiscretions create. The Israelites spent 40 years wandering in the wilderness. Moses could not enter the Promised Land because of an act of disobedience. David saw constant turmoil engulf his family because of sin. Just because forgiveness is so readily available does not give us license to take obedience lightly. God's will for every one of us involves using us for the furtherance of His kingdom, the building up and strengthening of His church and the accomplishment of His will. When we disobey we risk the possibility of disrupting, and maybe even ruining, our own lives. We also limit Gods ability to bless us and use us for the glory of His kingdom. God is, indeed, willing to forgive. But He is much more willing to give us the strength, courage and wisdom not to sin in the first place! Obedience is definitely the best way.

CHRISTIAN MATURITY

Hebrews 6:11 "We want each of you to show this same diligence to the very end, in order to make your home sure."

We live in a world of instant gratification and throw-away convenience. Do you want a new car or a new house? Sign on the line. Are you tired of your marriage? Get a divorce for only $295.00! How about getting that new furniture today? Plastic will take care of that. Get it now and pay later! Sadly, this mentality has crept into the church and invaded the spiritual realm as well. We have attempted to sanctify our worldly desires by buffering them with self-centered prayer. We have sought instant spiritual growth and maturity through books and seminars. We jump from one spiritual fad to the next to find new emotional highs or self-satisfying tidbits. The faith of many has truly become a mile wide and an inch deep. And when we become bored, dissatisfied or disillusioned we are quick to give in to the flesh. Some are even tempted to give up on their walk with God altogether. Words such as discipline, perseverance, diligence and self-sacrifice are given a hollow confirmation while we continue to pursue our own agenda and scamper after the next 'feel good' craze. Spiritual maturity is not purchased off the shelf of the neighborhood Christian book store. It is cultivated in the crucible of trials, tests and tribulations and ripens from a lifetime of faithfulness, obedience and commitment to the Lord.

WILLFULLY SINNING

Hebrews10:26 "If we deliberately keep on sinning after we have received the knowledge of the truth, no sacrifice for sins is left,"

It is a marvelous mystery that, although God loves us, desires for us to be with Him and has all the power to make us serve Him, He still gives us the choice whether we will acknowledge and return to Him after we backslide. There are so many today whose lifestyles do not permit them to give their hearts to the Lord. What is worse are those who say they are Christians or who claim to have been saved. Yet they continue in unholy relationships or allow themselves to keep doing the things that kept them from God in the first place. There is a major misconception that just because God loves us and is willing to forgive us time and time again that we can continue to sin. There is a world of difference between being overtaken by a fault and willfully disobeying God by committing the same sins over and over again. Our hearts need to be completely sold out to the Lord. If we are truly sorry for our sins as well as our sinful state, and if we sincerely repent and are willing to turn away from our wicked deeds, then God is more than able to forgive us, cleanse us and fill us with Himself. Those who claim a relationship with God while continuing to deliberately sin are entrapped by self- deception. No sacrifice for sins is left.

SPIRITUAL SPANKING

Hebrews 12:10 "Our fathers disciplined us for a little while as they thought best; but God disciplines us for our good that we may share in His holiness."

Discipline is a word that no one is truly comfortable with. It implies that we are doing something wrong, which is hard to admit. It is also seen as a form of punishment. Who likes to be punished? And sometimes punishment from our earthly fathers is subjective, undeserved and flows out of human weakness. But we need to consider that God's goal in disciplining us is His desire to keep us in continual victory over the flesh and to enable us to share in His holiness. As He molds us into the image of His Son we more easily submit to His firm and loving hands. Just as a child reflects the traits and qualities of their earthly parents so we should reflect the attributes of a holy God. We are Christians, which, by definition, implies that we are like Christ. When we accept Christ as our Savior there is much more involved than just being born again and having a home in heaven. God, through discipline, is molding us for citizenship in His kingdom. We will discover that when we completely surrender our will to Him and strive to live daily in obedience to His will that discipline will be replaced by discipling. God's work in our lives is then able to evolve from just being corrective to becoming teaching, guidance and spiritual growth.

FAITH AND WORKS

James 2:24 "You see that a person is justified by what he does and not by faith alone."

Can we work our way into heaven? Of course not! Salvation is a gift from God that can never be earned or deserved. There is none righteous. But when true faith in Christ is exercised, and someone becomes a follower of Jesus, there is a definite change in their actions and lifestyle. True saving faith will ALWAYS lead to a change in behavior and a desire to live for God. At the very beginning of salvation there is sorrow and repentance. There is also guilt and remorse for our sinful lifestyle and a sincere desire to turn from that lifestyle to a way of living that is pleasing to a holy God. Those who claim to be Christians yet continue to actively and willfully sin are deceiving themselves and mocking the power and purity of true salvation. Works before faith are self-centered and useless to save us or make us acceptable to God. Works after faith are the evidence of true salvation and the manifestation of God at work in our lives. These lives will continue to grow, mature, and flourish as long as we dwell in this world. We are being molded to reflect the image of our Lord- or at least should be. The way we think and act is the evidence that we are becoming more like Jesus every day!

REJOICE IN YOUR GIFT

James 3:16 "For where you have envy and selfish ambition, there you find disorder and every evil practice."

Envy and jealousy, which comes from selfish ambition, will cause strife and evil practices. When someone sees a person who is blessed in ways that they are not then that someone will usually begin to boast about themselves. This takes the focus off of God. This person, who tries to exalt themselves, will push forward their own agenda. They usually accomplish this by tearing down the one who has stirred up their jealousy in the first place. Then division in the body begins and the evil practices of gossip, slander, and back-biting start to set in. James bluntly states that this is of the devil. We, as God's children, need to rejoice in the gifts He has given others and unconditionally accept the gifts that He has bestowed upon us. We are working together for His glory and not our own. Remember…it's not about us, it's about Him!

AVOIDING SUFFERING

I Peter 3:17 "It is better, if it is God's will, to suffer for doing good than for doing evil."

Sometimes we get confused as to God's part in the trials we face. We question why God allows certain kinds of suffering or why He doesn't deliver us from a bad situation. Part of the answer lies in the reason or type of trial we are facing. When we suffer for doing good we can wholly trust in God to be with us and comfort our hearts- even if we do not get deliverance. Jesus said that we are blessed when we are persecuted for righteousness sake. But when we sin, and then suffer the consequences of our own disobedience, we are receiving what we deserve. Much of the suffering we see in this world that is on a grand scale is a result of evil. These evils include selfishness, greed, hate, jealousy and lust just to name a few. And much of the suffering we privately endure can be traced to sin in our own lives. This suffering may be a direct result of sin. You may have a ruined marriage because of adultery or broken relationships due to lying and deceit. It may also be a follow up result. When we sin and refuse to acknowledge, confess, cease and make restitution for our sin then our daily lives become distorted. We no longer have that close fellowship with, or guidance from, our Lord. By living in obedience and walking continuously in the light we remain anchored in the center of God's will and can spare ourselves much grief, sorrow and suffering.

UNTIRING AMBASSADORS

I Peter 4:19 "So then, those who suffer according to God's will should commit themselves to their faithful Creator and continue to do good."

Obviously everyone suffers. The aches and pains that humanity faces in this world are universal. Sickness and death, suffering and loss and the tragedies and heartbreaks of life are commonly shared by all mankind. That suffering can rarely be avoided. But the truth is that there is much suffering in this world that can be avoided by simply living holy lives. When we follow Gods commands and obey the laws of the land we have no need to worry about getting a speeding ticket or facing prison for murder. We won't get caught in a lie or found being unfaithful to our spouse. When we live Godly lives these particular areas of suffering can be avoided altogether. But the suffering that does occur when we live holy and Godly lives is unique to Christians. When we let our light shine in this ungodly world, exposing the truly wicked nature of fallen humanity, we are setting ourselves up to adverse scrutiny. We are also going to attract a lot of negative attention. There is no doubt that it is God's will for us to be compassionate witnesses to a lost world and moral sign posts in an immoral society. Then, when the persecution and suffering inevitably occurs, we must commit ourselves and our situation to God. We should continually strive to stay true to His will and keep on doing good. We must be untiring ambassadors for our Lord.

ASSURANCE

I John 4:13 "We know that we live in Him and He in us, because He has given us of His Spirit."

How do you know you live in Him? This is a question asked by many and answered in this verse. The confusion lies in how we know He has given us of His Spirit. Some would be broad in their thinking and say that God's Spirit is in and with all of us. Others believe the presence of the Spirit is evidenced by supernatural signs such as tongues or being 'slain in the Spirit'. But we find the most accurate answer couched in the context of this passage. The evidence of the Spirit is manifest by our ability to supernaturally love God and love one another. These are the two greatest commandments. Those controlled by the Spirit live a life of holiness and love that is impossible to obtain for those controlled by selfishness. It is the lifestyle that comes from being ruled by God's Spirit. It is a lifestyle reflected not just by our actions but also by pure thoughts and attitudes. This is what gives us the assurance that we are His children. Having His Spirit will always make a monumental change and impact in our lives by enabling us to love as Christ Himself loved.

BEING CHRISTIAN

I John 5:3 "This is love for God; to obey His commands. And His commands are not burdensome."

It is important to remember that what God desires of us is truly simple. We get caught up in the dos and don'ts of our Christian faith and sometimes lose sight of what is basic to our daily walk. Faith, grace, mercy, obedience, faithfulness and love are all vital elements of Christianity. But reverberating throughout the Bible is God's call for us to live out these important aspects of our belief with all of our heart and soul. If we are honest with ourselves we would admit the real problem. At the core of our spiritual battles is the conflict between our flesh, which is what we want, and our spirit, which is what God wants. This is the classic battle Paul shares with us in Romans chapter 7. Love and obedience become much easier when what we want becomes what God wants and we surrender our entire lives to Christ. God wants our whole heart, undivided by the desires of the flesh. Not until we sincerely say with Jesus "yet not as I will, but as You will', can we be able to grasp the true reality of what being a Christian entails. When God has our hearts He has us. Then obedience will become as simple and natural as breathing.

THE EXCLUSIVE SOURCE

I John 5:12 "He who has the Son has life; he who does not have the Son of God does not have life."

The truth in this verse is one of the biggest stumbling blocks to the world today. The predominant and acceptable belief is that many paths lead to God and all religions have elements of truth. So, as long as you sincerely believe whatever you believe in, you will be safe. This contradicts sharply with the teachings of Jesus that He is the only way to God. It also goes against the teaching of the early church that Christ is the only true path to God. Accusations of narrow mindedness and spiritual arrogance are levied against those of us who believe that Jesus is the one and only solution to mankind's estrangement from God. But these accusations do not diminish the absolute truth that, without the blood of the perfect sacrifice of the Lamb of God, there can be no forgiveness and cleansing from sin. When we allow the possibility that there are other ways to God besides Jesus Christ we deny the truth of the Bible. Our Lord then becomes just another good man in the quagmire of religious tolerance and spiritual mediocrity. We must see only Jesus as the way, the truth, and the life. He is the exclusive source of mankind's salvation and our only path for restoration to a relationship with God Almighty.

STANDING FIRM AND SECURE

Revelation 13:14 "Because of the signs he was given power to do on behalf of the first beast, he deceived the inhabitants of the earth."

There seems to be an increasing fascination today with the manifestation of the supernatural. People in the world are desperately seeking some tangible proof of another realm that is of a spiritual nature. Even in the church there are a significant number of Christians who thrive on ecstatic experiences and crave after the miraculous. Sometimes the foundation of their faith can even be based on these events. Unless they experience some type of emotional or unexplainable phenomenon, they become discouraged and introspective. This leaves them vulnerable to depression, moodiness and defeat. Only when our lives are founded on the truth of the Bible and the Rock of Christ will we be able to stand firm and secure in our faith. Positive emotional experiences are fine as long as they are not the lynch pin of our faith. Emotions cannot be trusted for they can be manufactured in the flesh. They can also be manipulated and counterfeited. This can quickly lead someone astray into a self-focused and self-centered corruption of true Biblical faith. A faith that is based on the truth of God's word and rooted in the facts of the doctrine of Christ will not be easily led astray by the instability of emotional experience or deceived by the unpredictable nature of 'supernatural' signs.

ONE METHOD OF READING THE BIBLE

One method that works well involves reading six different chapters a day- about 20 minutes. The Bible divides easily into six sections. These are the Pentateuch, History, Poetry, Prophets, Gospels and Early Church. By reading a chapter from each of these segments you can read through the Old Testament in about a year and twice through the New Testament. This method also gives you a great variety and helps to keep you from getting bogged down in some of the more challenging parts of the Bible. Simply use six bookmarks to keep track of where you are in each of the sections. This is the breakdown:

1. Genesis to Deuteronomy
2. Joshua to Esther
3. Job to Song of Solomon
4. Isaiah to Malachi
5. Matthew to John
6. Acts to Revelation

Printed in the United States
By Bookmasters

Printed in the United States
By Bookmasters